Yeats, it has been claimed, invented a country and called it Ireland. His plays, poetry and prose record his life-long commitment to establishing new forms of individual and collective identity. Marjorie Howes's study is the first sustained attempt to examine Yeats's invention of Irishness through the most recent theoretical work on literature, gender and nationalism in postcolonial cultures. She explores the complex, often contradictory ways Yeats's politics are refracted through his writing. Yeats had a complicated relation to British imperialism and the English literary tradition, an intense but troubled commitment to Irish nationalism, and a fascination with the Anglo-Irish as a declining ruling class. As a Free State senator, he participated in Ireland's postcolonial project of nation-building; he also confronted his own isolation as a Protestant intellectual in a deeply Catholic country. The various Irish nations he invented, she claims, are intensely powerful imaginative responses to a period of violent historical change. By placing Yeats's politics and poetics at the centre of debates on nationalism and gender currently occupying critics in postcolonial studies, Howes reveals the contemporary cultural codes governing representations of class and gender embedded in the poet's concepts of nationality. Ironically, in Yeats's works, the unity of the Irish nation is embodied in the relationship between the Irish peasantry and the Anglo-Irish aristocracy, and excludes the Catholic middle classes. Every public proclamation on national destiny involves an intensely private scrutiny of gender and sexuality. This accessible and thorough study will appeal to all interested in Irish studies, postcolonial theory, and the relationship between nationalism and sexuality.

D1166766

YEATS'S NATIONS

YEATS'S NATIONS
GENDER, CLASS, AND IRISHNESS

MARJORIE HOWES

Associate Professor of English, Rutgers University

CAMBRIDGE
UNIVERSITY PRESS

Published by the Press Syndicate of the University of Cambridge
The Pitt Building, Trumpington Street, Cambridge CB2 IRP
40 West 20th Street, New York, NY 10011 – 4211, USA
10 Stamford Road, Oakleigh, Melbourne 3166, Australia

© Cambridge University Press 1996

First published 1996
First paperback edition 1998

Printed in the United Kingdom at the University Press, Cambridge

A catalogue record for this book is available from the British Library

Library of Congress cataloguing in publication data
Howes, Marjorie Elizabeth.
Yeats's nations: gender, class, and Irishness / Marjorie Howes.
p.   cm.
Includes bibliographical references and index.
ISBN 0 521 56362 3 (hardback)
1. Yeats, W. B. (William Butler), 1865–1939 – Political and social views.
2. Politics and literature – Ireland – History – 20th century.
3. Politics and literature – Ireland – History – 19th century.
4. National characteristics, Irish, in literature.
5. Nationalism – Ireland – Historiography.
6. Social classes in literature.   7. Nationalism in literature.
8. Ireland – In literature.   9. Sex in literature.   I. Title.
PR5908.P6H69   1997
821'.8 – dc20   96–5392   CIP

ISBN 0 521 56362 3 hardback
ISBN 0 521 64527 1 paperback

Contents

Acknowledgments

I am very grateful for the personal support and intellectual inspiration I have received from various friends and colleagues. Sandra Gilbert and A. Walton Litz guided this project in its earliest form and helped me to see where it might go from there. I am deeply indebted to the generosity and critical insights of my colleagues who read and commented on the manuscript: Derek Attridge, Marcia Ian, Myra Jehlen, John McClure, and Bruce Robbins.

Special thanks to Elizabeth Cullingford for her encouragement and critical acumen, and for her meticulous and illuminating reading of the manuscript for Cambridge. Special thanks also to Seamus Deane, the other reader for the press, for his valuable comments. The friendship and expertise of Luke Gibbons, Siobhan Kilfeather, and Helen Sword vastly enriched this book and my experience in writing it. I am also indebted to the written work and conversation of Lyn Innes, David Lloyd, and Clair Wills.

I am very grateful to Ray Ryan at Cambridge University Press for guiding me through a sometimes daunting process with patience, humor and clarity.

A version of chapter 4 has been published in *Yeats's Political Identities*, ed. Jonathan Allison (Ann Arbor: University of Michigan Press, 1996), and I thank the Press for their permission to reprint.

My greatest debt is to Paul, and my greatest wish is that it will always keep increasing.

Abbreviations

AY   *The Autobiography of William Butler Yeats*, New York: Macmillan, 1965.

CT   *The Celtic Twilight*, London: Lawrence and Bullen, 1893.

KLI   *The Collected Letters of W. B. Yeats, Volume I, 1865–1895*, ed. John Kelly, Oxford: Clarendon Press, 1986.

EI   *Essays and Introductions*, New York: Macmillan, 1961.

EX   *Explorations*, New York: Macmillan, 1962.

L   *The Letters of W. B. Yeats*, ed. Alan Wade, New York: Macmillan, 1955.

LNI   *Letters to the New Island*, ed. George Bornstein and Hugh Witemeyer, New York: Macmillan, 1989.

Mem   *Memoirs*, transcribed and ed. Denis Donoghue, London: Macmillan, 1972.

SS   *The Senate Speeches of W. B. Yeats*, ed. Donald R. Pearce, Bloomington: Indiana University Press, 1960.

UPI   *Uncollected Prose, Vol. I*, collected and ed. John P. Frayne, London: Macmillan, 1970.

UPII   *Uncollected Prose, Vol. II*, collected and ed. John P. Frayne and Colton Johnson, New York: Macmillan, 1975.

VP   *The Variorum Edition of the Plays of W. B. Yeats*, ed. Russell K. Alspach, London: Macmillan, 1966.

VPI   *The Variorum Edition of the Poems of W. B. Yeats*, ed. Peter Allt and Russell K. Alspach, New York: Macmillan, 1957.

V   *A Vision*, New York: Macmillan, 1937.

VA   *A Critical Edition of Yeats's A Vision (1925)*, ed. George Mills Harper, London: Macmillan, 1978.

GY   *Always Your Friend: The Gonne-Yeats Letters 1893–1938*, ed. Anna MacBride White and A. Norman Jeffares, New York and London: Norton, 1992.

Introduction

> One can only reach out into the universe with a gloved hand, and that glove is one's nation, the only thing one knows even a little of.
>
> *LNI*, 174

> You cannot keep the idea of a nation alive where there are no national institutions to reverence, no national success to admire, without a model of it in the mind of the people. You can call it "Cathleen ni Houlihan" or the "Shan van Voght" in a mood of simple feeling, and love that image, but for the general purposes of life you must have a complex mass of images, something like an architect's model.
>
> *AY*, 334–5

Yeats's Nations sets out the changing ways Yeats imagined Irishness. I argue that each one depends upon specific configurations of gender and class. In order to focus on the interactions between Irishness and other categories, this book recasts the question of the poet's nationalism as the question of his diverse conceptions of nationality. The question of nationalism tends to produce reductive analyses that are largely confined to attacking or defending Yeats's politics or to revealing the presence or absence of nationalism. The question of nationality, in contrast, emphasizes the particular structures of his various conceptions of Irishness, their relation to social, political and cultural discourses, and their changes and continuities over time. This shift also enables re-evaluations of Yeats's representations of women and the role the occult plays in his thought and work.

My approach produces models of the nature and shape of Yeats's career that are at odds with much Yeats criticism. While I do point out Yeats's initial embrace and subsequent rejection of popular Irish

I

nationalism, for example, I am more interested in tracing what new deep structures emerged in his representations of nationality as a result. Yeats began his career believing that the individual and the nation were or should be homologous, and therefore harmonious; Irishness was a resource and support for individuals. Later he moved to formulations that complicated such propositions and emphasized conflict between individual and nation and the potential violence embodied in conceptions of Irishness. My analysis also goes against the grain of Yeats scholarship that imagines a progress from his early writings, which treat physical desire and women romantically, evasively, and through a haze of literary and occult conventions, to the later works' sexually explicit portrayal of unadorned lust and frank, assertive women. In contrast, I examine the ways in which the late Yeats's constructions of sexuality represent the partial subjuga-tion of desire and female personae to larger systems or purposes such as theology and eugenics. Finally, I suggest that Yeats's occult and metaphysical preoccupations were crucial components of his national and political concerns rather than a separate sphere in which he could either escape or represent those concerns.

I have chosen the term "nationality" rather than "nationalism" to designate the changing phenomena *Yeats's Nations* seeks to describe, partly because it is a term that Yeats himself used consistently, though not exclusively, and partly to indicate several of the principles that inform this book. One of these principles is illustrated in Benedict Anderson's generative and influential suggestion that we treat nationalism "as if it belonged with 'kinship' and 'religion,' rather than with 'liberalism' or 'fascism.' "[1] In other words, we should analyze nationalism not as a particular ideology, but as a virtually universal aspect of modern social organization that can be structured in varying ways with varying political implications and results. Nationality may involve nationalism as the desire for separa-tion and self-determination, or nationalism as the imperialist ag-grandizement of national territories, or neither. While the question of Irish nationality preoccupied him for most of his life, over time and according to his mood Yeats's style of wrestling with that question varied in form, content, and intensity. As the epigraphs suggest, for Yeats, Irish nationality was both a fixed origin and an elusive utopian end; it was a way of seeing or knowing, a mode of feeling, a set of institutions, and a mass of images – a national symbolic.[2] It provided the inspiring resources of tradition for the artist, and was also always in the process of being created through new cultural productions. Yeats's nations incorporated a wide range of issues: the lineaments of national character, the bases, scope and forms of national community, the individual's relation to that community, the production and functioning of national symbols and tropes, and the sources and expressions of national culture. When he formulated Irish nationality in his writings on the theatre, Yeats was preoccupied with collectivity and intersubjectivity. In contrast, his meditations on Anglo-Irish nationality rejected horizontal collectivity and imagined nationality as a solitary gesture of inter-generational solidarity with those who are similarly isolated.

Eve Sedgwick has proposed the term "habitation/nation system"[3] to indicate the enormous variations in the discursive construction of nationality, an idea that finds its corollary in Gayle Rubin's foundational substitution of "sex/gender system" for "patriarchy."[4] Both formulations rely on a notion of mediation between a natural and given raw material, biological sex or "the physical fact that each person inhabits, at a given time, a particular geographical space,"[5] and a set of discursive structures that shape and organize the raw material.[6] I prefer nationality for several reasons. First, I wish to avoid the connotations of "system," which suggests singularity and coherence. Rather than a single system grounded in a particular geographical space, this book examines a series of formulations with varying degrees of attachment to the idea and the material realities of place. Given the volume and rapidity of various exchanges across national borders and the importance of migration, exile and diaspora in national discourses, geographical space functions as a particular foundation for nationality to varying degrees. Nationality also suggests an appropriately Yeatsian dialectic between desire and necessity. Unlike nationalism, nationality cannot be refused altogether; it combines the voluntarist connotations of nationalism with the determinism suggested by "national origins." Since the establishment of "nation-ness" as, in Anderson's words, "the most universally legitimate value in the political life of our time,"[7] virtually every institution, ideological stance or identity must constitute itself in some relation to nationality, even if primarily in negative terms, as in Marxist internationalism.

Besides emphasizing the constructed and variable nature of even the most apparently "natural" aspects of nationality, this book argues that it is always characterized by conflict, multiplicity and contradiction. The model of the nation as imagined community does not always illuminate fully the struggles that surround it. Hegemonic versions of nationality often emerge after pitched battles over definitions and values, and are constantly haunted by the remnants of defeated constructions and threatened by the emergence of new alternatives. This is particularly true of the Ireland Yeats knew,[8] which gave him a keen sense of nationality as the subject of overt political struggle. That struggle was waged through various forms of Irish nationalism – cultural, parliamentary, revolutionary – and it was punctuated by savagely memorable events, including the land war, the Easter Rising, the Anglo-Irish War, and the Irish Civil War. Early in his career, Yeats helped found some of Irish cultural nationalism's most important institutions, he had personal relationships with nationalist radicals such as John O'Leary, Constance Markievicz and Maud Gonne, and he lamented the fall of Parnell and the subsequent disarray of the Irish parliamentary party. As a Free State senator, he participated in the postcolonial project of nation-building, ran some risk of being shot by republicans, and confronted his own isolation in the new Ireland.

Yeats's works also highlight the internal contradictions that mean nationality is never identical with itself. He had a complicated personal relation to several nationalities; a middle-class Irish Protestant by birth and upbringing, he sought to ally himself with invented versions of the Catholic Irish peasantry and the Anglo-Irish aristocracy. As an Irish poet heavily influenced by the English literary tradition and writing in English, Yeats had little purchase on or interest in a purist or exclusionary conception of Irish national culture. In "A General Introduction for my Work" (1937) he described the combination of love and hatred he felt for England and English culture and observed "Gaelic is my national language, but it is not my mother tongue" (*EI*, 520). His cultural nationalism also demanded a vigorous cultural internationalism. Homi Bhabha's work offers an influential and extensive formulation of the constitutive ambivalence of national discourses.[9] But Bhabha's largely textualist model sometimes tends to make the instabilities of all constructions of nationality look alike;[10] my analysis focuses on uncovering different kinds of ambivalence, various ways for nationality to lack identity with itself. Thus chapter 2 describes an ambivalence produced by the conflict between competing Irish nationalisms, chapter 3 discusses an ambivalence organized around the dangerous erotics of an intersubjectivity that threatens to dissolve the subject, and chapter 4 examines an ambivalence about the necessary repetition of a founding gesture.

By focusing on nationality, rather than nationalism, I hope to intervene in current debates about what is generally termed Yeats's "politics." These debates have gone hand in hand with an increasing interest in his "Irishness." Questions of nationalism and nationality have occupied a central but insufficiently examined role in the controversy which started with Conor Cruise O'Brien's famous essay[11] and continues today. Some critics follow O'Brien, characterizing Yeats's "true" nationality as Anglo-Irish Protestant and indicting his political opinions as elitist and authoritarian; others seek to exonerate him by reading him as an Irish nationalist, and/or by painting him as a liberal humanist and individualist. Still others map his transition from Irish nationalist to Anglo-Irish reactionary.[12] Some recent additions to the debate are informed by postcolonial theory, which casts a more critical and sophisticated eye on nationalism. Edward Said's reading of Yeats negotiates between a leftist critique of nationalism and praise for Yeats as a "poet of decolonization" by treating nationalism as a potentially regressive but necessary stage in struggles for national liberation.[13] In a related venture, another group, including Seamus Deane and Richard Kearney, base critiques of Yeats on the claim that he espoused a particularly damaging kind of nationalism, with tendencies towards mythology, mystification and blood sacrifice.[14]

Obviously, such differences have as much to do with a lack of consensus about the values and meanings of "politics" and "nationalism" in current literary and cultural studies as they do with Yeats's work, which is nevertheless varied and ambiguous enough to generate conflicting interpretations. In general I have tried to avoid the disabling project of either attacking or defending "Yeats's politics." Rather than emphasize the questions of partisanship and judgment that still inform much Yeats criticism – was Yeats a nationalist? was his nationalism liberatory or bloodthirsty? did he "mean it" when he embraced fascism and celebrated violence? – I suggest that in analyzing Yeats's nations and his politics it is more fruitful to foreground questions of form, quality, and complexity. Thus chapters 1 and 2 do not focus on the question of whether or not Yeats's early Celtic nationalism was complicit with British imperialism and

Anglo-Irish domination. They ask what shape that complicity took, what heuristic value it has, and how particular conceptions of gender and class functioned within it. Similarly, chapter 4 argues that as ambivalent as Yeats's views of the Protestant Ascendancy were, none of the several ambivalences in his Big House poems can be said to conduct a liberal political critique of aristocracy. The political interest of these poems lies elsewhere; they enable an analysis of how discourses of sexuality, family and genealogy often function to naturalize national claims and institutions. Of course, this approach does involve judgments about Yeats's politics, and some readers may find evaluations here that strike them as harsh. But such assessments are a small part of my analysis, rather than its goal. I have endeavored to sort out more and less politically and intellectually useful moments, strands and gestures in an extremely complex body of work. In that sense, this book is less about the politics or Irishness of Yeats the person or intentional author than it is about the rich, fascinating multitude of resources and problems his work offers to readers who are interested in the histories (and current formations) of those things.

This book also seeks to move beyond the terms of current thinking about Yeats's representations of women, gender and sexuality. Yeats belongs to a poetic tradition for which, as Mario Praz remarked, sex was "the mainspring of works of imagination"[15] and to a historical period during which the discourses of gender and sexuality in Ireland and England were more prolific and more sharply contested than ever before. He is famous for his many friendships with women, his early devotion to the conventions and ideals of romance, his unrequited love for Maud Gonne, his elaborate exploration of the metaphoric potential of gender difference and sexuality, his late preoccupation with "lust and rage" (*VP*, 591), and his vasectomy in search of sexual rejuvenation. But there has been surprisingly little serious feminist criticism of Yeats; Elizabeth Cullingford's ground-breaking *Gender and History in Yeats's Love Poetry* is an important exception.[16] Otherwise, there are a few archetypal studies that trace the appearance of such figures as femme fatale, queen, harlot and hag through his work, and a few discussions that chart a progress over time from idealized, romantic representations of women to supposedly more realistic and independent female figures.[17] Other critics explicate the work through references to Yeats's relationships with Katharine Tynan, Olivia Shakespear, Florence Farr, Maud

Gonne, Georgie Yeats, Lady Gregory, Margot Ruddock, Ethel Mannin and the other women who were important figures in his life.[18] While not denying the interest and importance of biography, this book suggests that if Yeats had not met Maud Gonne, he would have invented her. I argue that to explain the actual shape and texture of Yeats's representations of women, we must look to the culturally and historically specific interactions between gender, sexuality, and the other categories this study takes up.

Gender and nationality have an especially intimate relationship in the material analyzed here. They are not interdependent in the same way in all texts or moments. The exchanges between them are uneven, assume various forms, and are shaped by their relations to other categories. In addition, Yeats's works do not merely reflect the interactions between gender and nationality in larger cultural discourses; his engagement with them ranges from exaggeration to appropriation to resistance. But by the time Yeats began his career gender and nationality had acquired the status of "two of the most powerful global discourses shaping contemporary notions of identity,"[19] as the introduction to the recent collection, *Nationalisms and Sexualities*, puts it. So the fact of their intense mutual embeddedness was constant despite variations in its form. While the development of the two as discourses of identity did not occur entirely simultaneously or along parallel lines, in general they both began to acquire this status towards the end of the eighteenth century, and consolidated it throughout the nineteenth. Most historians agree that the modern conception of the nation has only been around since the late eighteenth century.[20] As the nineteenth century progressed, the nation came to be discussed and defined increasingly in terms of language, ethnicity, territory and historical memories.[21] In this sense, from the mid-nineteenth century on, virtually all nationalisms were "cultural" nationalisms.[22] Nationality became more than a matter of location, affiliation or loyalty; it was an essential fact of being. All aspects of an individual's life, behavior and circumstances became available as potential markers of nationality, including gender roles and sexuality. During this period discourses of gender also acquired an unprecedented relation to identity. As Foucault and other scholars have argued, the notion that one's sexual behaviors and preferences constituted an "identity" is largely an invention of the late eighteenth and nineteenth centuries.[23]

Most of the arguments in this book depend on discovering

intersections of various kinds between nationality, gender and class, rather than on drawing analogies between them. The act of constructing parallels between, for example, women and the Irish as corresponding oppressed groups or identities is part of the material to be analyzed here, not one of the conceptual tools to be employed. This is not to deny the heuristic value of noting that gender and nationality in particular share some features; clearly they do have much in common. Both gender and nationality are universally accepted categories of identity whose discursive organization involves claiming that they are based on innate differences; in fact, however, they are discursively constructed in relation to still other categories, and their precise organization and content varies nearly infinitely. Both have been instrumental in the emancipatory struggles of the groups they name, and have confronted them with the dilemma of choosing between asserting difference, which threatens to collude with hegemonic designations of otherness, and claiming sameness, which threatens to erase or deny the differences which have a very real existence and which form the basis for potential political solidarities. In addition, feminist and postcolonial theory often find or advocate similar means of representation and strategies of resistance, such as appropriation, mimicry, metonymy, and hybridity.

In other respects, however, nationality, gender and class operate differently as categories, and these differences have received less critical attention than their similarities. We need to be cautious and discriminating about drawing parallels lest they obscure more than they reveal. For example, Anderson comments on the "formal universality of nationality as a socio-cultural concept" by observing, "in the modern world everyone can, should, will 'have' a nationality, as he or she 'has' a gender."[24] Putting aside for the moment the question of whether everyone "has" a gender, it seems to me that having a nationality is constructed differently in several respects from having a gender. For one thing, there is a more prominent voluntarist strand in modern discourses of nationality. Immigrants are simultaneously promised and denied equal access to "national" status in their new homes, and expatriates often reject their native lands only to find their social identities determined by the "ex," the mark of that rejection. In both cases the process of assimilation or rejection is necessarily ambivalent and incomplete; on one level the modern discourses of nationality deny the possibility of exchanging one nationality for another. On another level, however, the hegemonic discourses of nationality, especially in the United States, do offer such mobility, largely through access to the universal, abstract rights of citizenship. Thus nationality has a network of connections to heavily naturalized categories such as race, ethnicity and family, but it also has links with the universalizing discourses of citizenship and human rights. Clifford Geertz has suggested that a similar tension between what he calls primordial and civic ties is both a central driving force in modern discourses of nationality and a major obstacle to their development and stability.[25] This dialectic between (to use Yeats's terms) the chosen and the fated operates differently in modern discourses of gender, and often involves designating sexuality and sexual orientation as the sphere of individual choice and variation.[26]

A related point is that modern discourses of gender are more rigidly binary than those of nationality. Both nationality and gender are constructed in relation to "others," but they use different techniques and structures of othering. While nations define themselves against a series of national others, or against several nations at once, in the modern period femininity has been discursively constructed in relation to masculinity and vice versa. While the definitions of each term are contested and changeable, in hegemonic discourses of gender the specular relation between them is much less so. Of course, in reality femininity is defined in relation to a number of categories besides masculinity, for example, class, race and nationality, but gender difference gets coded *as a binary* in a way that national difference, which can also be constructed as a global plurality of nations, does not.

Both gender and nationality are invoked in emancipatory struggles. It is less true, however, that both were instrumental in the oppression of the groups they name. While discourses of gender were always key instruments in enforcing the subordinate status of women, modern conceptions of nationality are, to a certain extent, bound up with modern ideas of rights, self-determination and territorial integrity, so that the notion of a nation of slaves or a nation, as opposed to a native population, subordinate to another nation is something of a contradiction in terms.[27] Of course, various states and powers have consistently oppressed groups who could or did claim to have a distinct nationality, but often the discourses of race, rather than those of nationality, served the purpose of designating difference that demanded political repression. While women were often said to merit second-class status because they were women, the Irish were said to merit it because they were members of an inferior race, and because they were not a "true" nation.

The specificities of class demand attention as well. While there have been a number of excellent studies of the cultural construction of bourgeois identity, such as Stallybrass and White's *The Politics and Poetics of Transgression*,[28] in some respects class functions differently in relation to identity than nationality and gender. Although socialist projects seek to mobilize oppressed classes on the basis of shared suffering, interests and aspirations, class struggles do not generally engage in the kind of identity politics that characterize political movements based on gender, race, nationality, or sexual orientation. In academic circles, identity politics are currently critiqued as often as they are embraced, and one could argue that gender, nationality and class are all categories whose usefulness to the struggles they name will end if those struggles are successful. However, critics who want to make this argument about gender or nationality often do it by comparing them to class.[29] In general, nationality and gender are more intimately moored, albeit unstably, to identity and culture than class. One reason for this may be that gender and nationality remain implicated, with varying degrees of mediation, in theories of biological determination.[30] In the material studied here, class lacks the naturalizing power of gender; falsely naturalized constructions of gender and sexuality are most often employed to guarantee class and other differences.[31] Yeats's representations of class often revolve more around the cultural productivity of material conditions like wealth and poverty than around questions of identity. Class also usually lacks the emotive and erotic mobilizing potential of nationality. Anderson comments dryly on the absurdity of trying to imagine the erection of a Tomb of the Unknown Marxist,[32] though the iconography of the Soviet Union, particularly during the early post-revolutionary period, suggests at least a partial exception. Class functions as an explicit and consciously held identity and as a hidden interest or agenda, a double role that is less important in the formations of nationality and gender here.

The intersections between nationality, gender and class I examine are more complex and more concrete than simple parallelism or homology between separate spheres. Fredric Jameson's controversial reading of third-world literature as national allegory both points the way towards the kind of mutual embeddedness I wish to describe and illustrates some of the less useful formulations I try to avoid. Jameson's proposed definition of allegory ostensibly does away with simple homologies in favor of a more complex interaction: in analyses of third-world literature, he suggests, "we must rethink our conventional conception of the symbolic levels of a narrative (where sexuality and politics might be in homology to each other, for instance) as a set of loops or circuits which intersect and over-determine each other."[33] However, in his readings of both first- and third-world literature, the libidinal and the political, while not homologous, are translatable into one another. In first-world litera-ture, Jameson argues, questions particular to the national, economic, public sphere are configured as manifestations of the private, sexual sphere: "in the west, conventionally, political commitment is recon-tained and psychologized or subjectivized by way of the public-private split."[34] In other words, first world literature tends to reconfigure political questions of nationality or class as the private and subjective dramas of gender and sexuality. Jameson argues his major thesis, that in third-world texts "the story of the private individual destiny is always an allegory of the embattled situation of the public third-world culture and society,"[35] by claiming that third-world texts effect a "radical reversal"[36] of the split between public and private spheres characteristic of first-world literature and culture. But the essay hesitates between two different versions of third-world reversal. On one hand, the public-private split is refused altogether; in one of Lu Xun's stories, he argues, "western anti-nomies – and most particularly that between the subjective and the public or political – are refused in advance."[37] On the other hand, Jameson also describes this third-world reversal as simply the inver-sion of the first-world's translation of the political into the sexual. In the third-world reversal, "psychology, or more specifically, libidinal investment, is to be read in primarily political and social terms."[38] While first-world texts translate nationality or class into gender and sexuality, third-world texts reverse the process. As Jameson's ac-knowledgment that "Such allegorical structures ... are not so much absent from first-world cultural texts as they are unconscious"[39] suggests, these two alternatives boil down to the same thing in important respects.

Reading the interaction between categories like gender, sexuality, nationality and class as (largely) ruled by the public-private split in this manner obscures important aspects of their interaction. Gender and sexuality are themselves intimate elements of Irish national discourses. In much Irish literature and culture, women represent national ideals or goals, particularly in figures like Cathleen ni Houlihan, Mother Ireland, Dark Rosaleen and the Shan Van Voght. But organizations like the Gaelic League also addressed themselves specifically to instructing women on how to take their proper places in the national struggle.[40] National discourses take up gender and sexuality as metaphors *and* as concrete realities with material resources and direct implications for political action. I also wish to emphasize the ways in which, for Yeats, the erotic and the irrational were part of the political rather than representations of it. Yeats's claim that "excess of love" (*VP*, 394) bewildered the men of 1916 does not (as Jameson might have it) translate political commitment into personal erotic devotion or vice versa. Rather, it indicates a central but often neglected component of Yeats's political thinking: that nationalist politics itself, for Yeats, is profoundly irrational and deeply eroticized. Similarly, chapter 3 argues that Yeats's occult interests offered him a set of practical political tools rather than merely metaphors through which to organize his thoughts and experiences.

In emphasizing Yeats the dialectician and self-critic over Yeats the totalizing system builder, and in claiming that Yeats's nations compel their own critiques and reveal their own instabilities, I am not arguing that this makes them either politically progressive or intellectually vulnerable. The constructions of nationality that are the most flexible and contradictory may well be the most powerful; Anderson notes the incongruity of "[t]he 'political' power of nationalisms vs. their philosophical poverty and even incoherence."[41] Instability and ambivalence do not lessen the persuasiveness or material effects of national discourses. While discourses that undermine themselves can offer useful tools for building a progressive politics – self-consciousness about the contingency of received truths and necessary assumptions, a suspicion of theological notions of purity, identity, or originality, an acceptance of limitation and partiality[42] – such discourses do not in themselves constitute a progressive politics, nor can they necessarily be said to "have" such a politics.

The point, then, of the kind of analysis this book undertakes is not to smuggle in a defense of Yeats's politics under the guise of the "subversive" nature of his representations of nationality. Instead, it is to recover a sense of the multiple possibilities and fluid constructions that characterize the discourses of nationality in any period, and of how such variation and complexity appears in Yeats's works. The purpose of this constructivist argument is not to reveal the extent or culpability of our boundedness in cultural determination; it is to make visible the possibilities for change and alternative construction that inhabit categories and formulations we might otherwise be tempted to surrender to the tyranny of the "natural" or the "inevitable." One limitation of the useful and influential *The Empire Writes Back* is that the book appeals frequently to the "inevitability" of the large structures it describes, as in "[a] characteristic of dominated literatures is an inevitable tendency towards subversion."[43] I do not wish to argue that such statements are false, but that the level on which they are true coincides with the book's aim of providing a general overview of postcolonial discourses rather than in-depth analyses of individual texts. This makes it difficult to address differences between constructions of nationality that fall into the same general category. It is just such differences that *Yeats's Nations* seeks to illuminate. In particular, I would like to emphasize the usefulness of thinking about differences among various forms of nationality as a set of possible alternatives within a particular period, rather than as a historical progression. Critics who emphasize the latter often picture a linear scheme in which early forms of nationalism, which are necessarily crude and inflexible, can give way to more sophisticated and progressive ones once the initial work of revolution or nation-building has been accomplished. This view of nationalism as an unfortunate but necessary "stage" in anti-colonial struggles has a long and respectable history. It is, for example, important to the work of Franz Fanon,[44] and has the virtue of allowing critics to reconcile a critique of the intellectual structures of nationalism with sympathy for its political aims.

Edward Said's otherwise excellent and provocative Field Day essay on Yeats is a good example. Said distinguishes between two stages of anti-imperialist resistance, "a period of nationalist anti-imperialism," which is in many respects regressive and reproduces imperialist structures of thought, and "an era of liberationist anti-imperialist resistance that often followed it," and which was more truly progressive and emancipatory.[45] One of Said's major points here is one that I wish to develop, that "nativism is not the only

alternative."[46] It is a point, however, that Said undercuts by outlining a teleological scheme of history in which it appears that, at a
particular (and temporary) stage in the national struggle, nativism *is*
the only alternative. Said concludes that, historically, "the nationalism that formed the initial basis of the second moment stood
revealed both as insufficient and yet as an absolutely crucial first
step."[47] Here tracing the existence of multiple alternatives merely
reveals in one moment the seeds of the next moment in a linear
progression. In contrast, my intention in mapping the relations
between hegemonic national discourses and their alternatives is to
question such schemes of necessity and progress. The problem with
designating nationalism as an element in a sequential historical
narrative is that it threatens to make critics too complacent about it
at one stage, and unproductively impatient at its very existence at
another stage when they think it has become outmoded.

While Yeats's nations are illuminating in relation to Irish culture
and current theories of nationality, they are not strictly representative or merely symptomatic. Yeats's work rarely offers simple
formulations, except perhaps in its insistence on the inevitability and
productivity of contradiction and change. Nearly all his critics agree
that Yeats's thought and works revolve around conflicts between
opposing desires, claims and tendencies. As he put it, "passion is
conflict, consciousness is conflict" (*EX*, 331). For every assertion there
is a counter-assertion; for every affirmation, a qualification. Each
answer multiplies questions, and every approach to unity and
reconciliation announces a fresh acknowledgment of disunity and
defeat. Such complexity makes it impossible to reduce his works to
exemplars of larger cultural discourses or theoretical precepts; I have
tried to put all three in dialogue with one another here.

Yeats's Nations is organized roughly chronologically, but I make no
claims for a strict periodization of Yeats's career; some of the various
conceptions of nationality I discuss appear more or less simultaneously in his works. Chapter 1 examines Yeats's engagement with
the Celtic movement and raises the question of how we should
describe its "dependence" on imperialist discourses. Chapter 2 takes
up the practice of representing the nation as a woman and reads *The
Countess Cathleen* as a complex national allegory of competing Anglo-
Irish and Catholic Irish nationalisms. Chapter 3 traces Yeats's
ambivalence about popular Irish nationalism as a specifically "mass"
politics in *Kathleen ni Houlihan* and his writings on the Irish theatre.

Chapter 4 analyzes some of Yeats's Big House poems, arguing that his formulation of Anglo-Irish nationality invoked and exposed the naturalizing functions of gender, kinship and sexuality in most national discourses. Chapter 5 argues that "A Woman Young and Old" constructs an alternative to the hegemonic middle-class version of Irish nationality that dominated the Irish Free State during the 1920s. Finally, chapter 6 examines the "race philosophy" in *Purgatory* and Yeats's later essays, which imagined Irish nationality as a normative ideal inspired by eugenics and enforced through state power.

CHAPTER I

That sweet insinuating feminine voice: hysterics,
peasants and the Celtic movement

That Ireland, more than any other country, is spoken of as a woman is probably due to the appearance in our national affairs of qualities which men call womanly. And this impression is not merely the cheap attribution of racial inferiority by the alien critic with which we are familiar, it is our feeling about ourselves.

Horace Plunkett[1]

You have been compelled by hags to spin
   gold thread from straw and have heard men say:
"There is a feminine temperament in direct contrast to ours,
which makes her do these things. Circumscribed by a
   heritage of blindness and native
     incompetence, she will become wise and will be forced to
       give in ..."

Marianne Moore[2]

For Horace Plunkett, the impression that the Irish are womanly charts the colonized subject's debilitating internalization of an imperial stereotype. Plunkett was a pioneer of Irish agricultural reform, a unionist MP for Dublin, and, later, a Free State senator. Like Matthew Arnold, he combined an enthusiasm for the virtues of Celts with a firm unionism. His comment invokes the common confluence of race and gender in imperialist discourses that equates femininity with racial inferiority and political subordination. Plunkett assumed this equation rather than questioning it, and his masculinism was widely shared among British imperialists and Irish nationalists alike. A major strand of British imperialist discourse labelled the Irish feminine and therefore inferior, dependent and weak; nationalists often disavowed femininity and asserted a compensatory and exaggerated masculinity.[3] What is at stake, of course, is not "femininity itself," but the ubiquity and tenacious force of the

linkages between femininity, racial or national character, and colonial status. The persistence of these linkages has shaped postcolonial
theory's formulations of the relationship between discourses of
resistance, especially nationalism, and the imperialist discourses they
resist, particularly in arguments which cast that relationship as one of
damaging dependence or complicity. The Celtic movement in
general and Yeats's Celticism in particular have often been theorized
in these terms. Celticism has entered traditional literary history as
aesthetically derivative, politically naive or suspect, and emotionally
immature: an effeminate, sentimental phase that Yeats cured himself
of or developed beyond. Recent studies of Irish cultural nationalism
often treat the Celtic movement as an example of neo-imperialist
nativism, a form of nationalist discourse that reinscribes colonial
power relations and structures of thought. What these critiques have
in common is that they often construct Celticism's failure, dependence or complicity as a form of femininity.[4]

This gendered construction of Celticism's political and aesthetic
shortcomings was sponsored not least of all by Yeats himself, who
consistently coded his move away from Celticism as a transition from
feminine to masculine and more truly national art. In 1903, after he
had begun making determined efforts to distance himself from the
Celtic Twilight, he told Lady Gregory, "My work has got far more
masculine" (*L*, 397). In a 1903 *Samhain* on "The Reform of the
Theatre" he insisted that art be "masculine and intellectual" (*EX*,
109), and in the next issue he called the English theatre "demora-
lising" because it rendered "the mind timid and the heart effeminate" (*EX*, 112). In 1904 he told George Russell that he had acquired
a positive aversion to Celticism, particularly to those aspects of it
associated with femininity:

I cannot probably be quite just to any poetry that speaks to me with the
sweet insinuating feminine voice of the dwellers in that country of shadows
and hollow images. I have dwelt there too long not to dread all that comes
out of it. (*L*, 434)

"That country" is the Ireland imagined by the Celtic movement, a
chimerical nation of shadows and hollow images whose lack of
national and artistic substance is equaivalent to its femininity.
Similarly, in the preface to the 1906 edition of *Poems, 1899–1905*,
Yeats claimed, "to me drama ... has been the search for more of
manful energy, more of cheerful acceptance of whatever arises out of

the logic of events, and for clear outline, instead of those outlines of lyric poetry that are blurred with desire and vague regret" (*VP*, 849).

This chapter will argue that Yeats's eventual rejection of Celticism as effeminate, blurred and melancholy represents a capitulation to imperial structures of thought rather than a move away from them. Yeats's Celticism was complicit with and dependent upon imperialism in a general and very important sense. But the shape of that generally complicit relation changed over time, and different aspects of Yeats's Celtic writings offered different forms of repetition, appropriation and critique in relation to imperialism. By breaking down Yeats's Celticism synchronically and diachronically, this chapter will distinguish between the moments or structures within it that gesture towards vigorous critiques and radical departures, and those that reinscribe imperialist structures of thought more uncritically. Yeats's earliest Celtic writings repeated, both overtly and covertly, the imperial gendering of the Irish as feminine, but in rejecting colonialism's (and Irish nationalism's) equation of femininity with inferiority and subordinate status they suggested a profound, though incomplete, departure from the axiomatics of imperialism. The incompleteness of that departure appears in the pervasive ambivalence about femininity that characterizes these writings. In Yeats's later Celtic writings, and especially in his eventual rejection of the "sweet insinuating feminine voice" of the Celtic Twilight, he tried unsuccessfully to resolve that ambivalence, abandoned the fragmentary radical possibilities of his earlier writings, and brought his representations of gender and nationality into greater harmony with the deep structures of imperialism. This transition also produced a version of Celticism structured more closely around the class interests of the Anglo-Irish.

Much has been written about the flexibility and complexity of British imperial discourses on race and on their mutual embeddedness with other categories, especially gender and health/illness.[5] Late Victorian representations of the Irish drew on a constellation of images, including simian savages, lunatics, women and children. This chapter will not survey them all; instead I will examine the relationship between Yeats's Celticism and the particular strand of imperialist discourses on Ireland associated with Matthew Arnold's liberal conservatism. This strand was shaped by several aspects of the colonial enterprise in Ireland. Their geographical proximity and racial and cultural similarity to the English rendered the Irish less radically "other" than the inhabitants of other British territories. The Irish were white, Christian and partially anglicized culturally; they upset what Franz Fanon called the "racial epidermal schemas"[6] that were crucial to imperialist discourses on Africa and India. While the Irish were sometimes compared to Africans, most representations of them, which contained some relatively positive and attractive features and which were not as obsessed with miscegenation as discourses on Africans, were more analogous to white representations of Native Americans.[7] In addition, the Irish represented "home" rather than "empire" in British thinking about emigration. Many nineteenth-century intellectuals argued that one potential benefit of empire was that emigration to the colonies, especially white settler colonies like Australia and Canada, provided a solution to the much discussed problems of poverty and over-crowding in Britain. It was largely in response to Irish over-crowding, and in an attempt to prevent the poverty-stricken Irish from emigrating to London, that the first systematic schemes for emigration and colonization were put forth in the 1820s and 1830s.[8] Thus in one important set of imperialist discourses, Ireland epitomized the domestic problems the British hoped the empire would help solve, rather than a foreign ground for expansion. Finally, in the nineteenth century British domination of Ireland entered a phase that relied increasingly on integrating the Irish into the state, resorting to coercion largely when conciliation and assimilation were perceived to have failed. Catholic emancipation made this development inevitable. Advocating integration was both a positive British strategy and a response to the economic and social integration for which Catholic emancipation paved the way.

Arnold's pronouncements on Ireland and the Irish in *On the Study of Celtic Literature* (1867) and the essays on Irish affairs written in the 1880s insisted that Ireland should remain within the empire, but they criticized England's treatment of the Irish and urged the British to become a people capable of "attaching" Ireland and the other Celtic territories under British dominion in order to form a peaceful union with "its parts blended together in a common national feeling."[9] There is a close relationship between his criticism of English attitudes towards Ireland and his criticism of British Philistinism in *Culture and Anarchy* (1869). The position Arnold and other liberal Victorian thinkers adopted was deeply indebted to the works of Edmund Burke. Burke's unionism involved criticizing the corruption and

brutality of the Protestant Ascendancy, calling for a "true aristocracy" to replace it, and protesting against the penal laws and other
forms of Catholic oppression. Later these positions became central to
nineteenth-century efforts to kill Home Rule with kindness.[10] Arnold
cited Burke frequently and even edited an anthology of Burke's
writings on Irish affairs. The publication of *On the Study of Celtic
Literature* coincided with an increase in "Fenian fever" in Ireland and
the United States, an outbreak of Fenian violence in Ireland and
England, an English crackdown on Irish unrest, and a rise in popular
and media attention to the Fenian movement.[11] In this political
climate its enthusiasm for Celtic culture and its relatively benign
form of imperialism made it a fairly radical document, and it made
little impression on Arnold's immediate contemporaries.

Arnold's emphasis on sympathy and integration, his preference for
conciliation over coercion, and the intermediate position the Irish
occupied in the British hierarchy of races all helped make a
particular version of nineteenth-century femininity a useful category
for his construction of the Celt: a cultured, sensitive, middle-class
femininity associated with hysteria.[12] Arnold's debts to the works of
Ernest Renan, Henri Martin and W. F. Edwards have been well
documented,[13] and critics have often noted the importance of the
Celt's femininity to the imperialist ambitions of Arnold's vision. Here
I wish to emphasize a few points about how this version of femininity
functioned in Arnold's argument. It provided crucial support to a
major aspect of Arnold's formulation of Celtic otherness – complementarity. Femininity marked the Celt's difference from the Saxon,
but also placed her in a relationship of natural complementarity to
him. Like man and woman, they were meant for each other, and
should acquiesce in the dictates of nature and history, combining to
form a more perfect whole. Both Celt and Saxon were radically
incomplete. The Saxon possessed precisely the qualities the Celt
lacked, and the Celt in turn could supply the Saxon deficiencies
Arnold outlined in *Culture and Anarchy*. The Celt's femininity stood,
not merely for racial difference, but for a combination of racial
difference and racial affinity in relation to the English. Robert Young
has analyzed Arnold's debts to nineteenth-century racial theory, and
argues that theories of race were also "covert theories of desire"
because they were largely based on the perceived results of sexual
unions between different peoples.[14] Arnold's essay contains a tension
between two related models of complementarity that reflects a major

nineteenth-century debate about the possibilities and results of racial hybridity. Arnold insists that the English race is a hybrid race, and that it already contains a Celtic element. Assimilation was prepared for by "affinity of race"[15] between Irish and English and was already underway. But while the essay lauds the mutual benefits of integrating Saxon and Celt, it also asserts their permanence as racial types.[16] Complementarity as a natural tendency to fuse into a new, homogeneous whole conflicted with complementarity as the existence of mutually enriching, interlocking characteristics that remained distinct and identifiable. The dialectic between hybridity as the elimination of difference and hybridity as the intermingling of distinct entities was central to the period's racial theory. Arnold's version of this dialectic enabled him to use an argument about racial and cultural separatism in the service of an argument for political integration. As he put it in 1887, the Irish could be "a nation poetically only, not politically."[17] The gendering of Celt and Saxon also revealed the important role sexuality played in Arnold's model of political integration as imperial romance and in his insistence that the English should become capable of "attaching" the Irish.

What Julian Moynahan has called the "confusion in the mid-Victorian mind ... between ideas of Celtic nature and of woman's nature"[18] often related them through a third term – illness, particularly nervous illness. The femininity of Arnold's Celt had affinities with some late nineteenth-century discourses on hysteria. While hysteria was known to afflict both sexes, for most contemporary analysts it was symbolically feminine. This femininity was associated with the middle and upper classes, and involved sensitivity, romance, idealism, and even genius. Freud and Breuer commented frequently on the gifted, cultured, morally sensitive natures of their patients in *Studies on Hysteria*,[19] and characterized hysteria as quite the opposite of degeneracy. According to Arnold, the Celt was "quick to feel impressions ... keenly sensitive to joy and sorrow"; she possessed "quick perception and warm emotion," and was subject to "penetrating passion and melancholy." The Celt was "impressionable," "sensuous," "extravagant," and "spiritual."[20] Above all, the Celt was, in a phrase of Henri Martin's which Arnold was fond of quoting, "sentimental – always ready to react against the despotism of fact."[21] These potentially attractive features shaded into the Celt's nervous instability, sexual pathology, lack of "balance, measure and patience," and "habitual want of success."[22] Renan's praise of the

Celt's ability to "conceive the ideal" of woman quickly gives way to
the charge that the Celt is dominated by this ideal, and then
progresses to images of drunkenness, insanity, and dizziness. "If it be
permitted us to assign sex to nations as to individuals," writes Renan,

we should have to say without hesitation that the Celtic race ... is an
essentially feminine race. No human family, I believe, has carried so much
mystery into love. No other has conceived with more delicacy the ideal of
woman, or been more fully dominated by it. It is a sort of intoxication, a
madness, a vertigo.[23]

Arnold's description of the Celt's feminine qualities contains the
same combination of the vaguely complimentary, the intriguingly
mysterious, and the pathological:

no doubt the sensibility of the Celtic nature, its nervous exaltation, have
something feminine in them, and the Celt is thus particularly disposed to
feel the spell of the feminine idiosyncracy; he has affinity to it; he is not far
from its secret.[24]

Other writers took the idea of the Celt's "nervous exaltation" more
literally, and grounded Irish identity in the physiological peculiarities
of the Celt's nervous system.[25] By linking the Celt's national
difference from the Saxon with clinical distinctions between masculinity and femininity, health and illness, Celticism described the Celt's
cultural value and simultaneously diagnosed the faults that marked
the limits of that value. The qualities that gave the Celt her exotic
worth were the same qualities that rendered her subtly inferior and
diseased.

A happy patriarchal marriage between the feminine and attractive
but inferior Celt and the masculine and superior Saxon, whose
domination was natural and inevitable but whose own existence
would be enriched by a feminine influence, provided a compelling
figure for the kind of imperial relation Arnold imagined. The version
of femininity Arnold ascribed to the Celt allowed him to express at
the same time the Celt's valuable uniqueness and crippling inferiority, spiritual strength and practical weakness, energetic passion
and the inability to govern it, imaginative richness and incapacity for
sustained and balanced logical thought. It enabled Arnold to construct a Celtic racial or national difference whose complementary
relation to the Saxon combined cultural separation and political
integration. The Celt alone was a specimen of maimed masculinity,
of illness and lack, while the Celt coupled with the Saxon could

become the angel in the British house of empire, sweetening and completing it. On the other hand, the Celt's femininity also expressed fears about integration, revolution, and English weakness. Behind Arnold's Celt lurk the degenerate, the hysteric, and the revolutionary. Arnold warned his fellow Englishmen, "perhaps if we are doomed to perish ... we shall perish by our Celtism [sic]."[26]

The Celt's sensuous nature and emotional excesses had several political implications. They indicated her material ineffectiveness and incapacity for self-government; both Arnold and Renan explicitly included political ineptitude in their characterizations of the Celt. But the Celt's sexuality and sentimentality also raised the specter of the revolutionary. From Edmund Burke through the nineteenth century, a number of thinkers had linked the French revolution (and political revolutions generally) to particularly feminine depravities and sexual pathologies.[27] Burke associated the excesses of the French revolution with "the horrid yells, and shrilling screams, and frantic dances, and infamous contumelies, and all the unutterable abominations of the furies of hell in the abused shape of the vilest of women."[28] Arnold described the Celtic political temperament as tending towards revolution and sexual pathology:

The Celt, undisciplinable, anarchical, and turbulent by nature, but out of affection and admiration giving himself body and soul to some leader ... is not a promising political temperament.[29]

Marx and Engels agreed about the Celt's revolutionary potential; they took up the imperial definition of the Celt as a combination of femininity, nervous illness and emotional excess, and linked these traits to a potential for political effectiveness. By the late 1860s, Marx had reversed an earlier position and had concluded that ending the oppression of Ireland was *the* necessary precondition for advancing the cause of the English working class.[30] Like Arnold, Engels saw the Celt as unbalanced, nervous, sensuous, and prone to failure; in his description of Ireland, the land and the people shared the same feminine changeability.[31] He claimed that "the Irish way of thinking lacks all sense of proportion,"[32] that "[w]ith the Irish, feeling and passion predominate," and that their "sensuous, excitable nature" rendered them unfit for the development of manufacturing.[33] Marx thought the Irish "more passionate and revolutionary in character than the English,"[34] while Engels rhapsodized: "Give me 200,000 Irishmen and I will overthrow the entire British monarchy."[35]

In the 1860s, then, femininity and nervous instability could acquire
political implications radically different from those Arnold attributed
to them, albeit in discourses outside the bounds of traditional political
theory. By the late nineteenth century, however, the cultural equation
of femininity with pathology – medical, political and sexual – was
even more firmly established than at mid century.[36] In addition, the
fact that the Celt's racial otherness sprang more from an excess of
civilization and culture than from a barbaric lack of it gave the
sensitive, brilliant and unstable Celt something in common with a
new figure that appeared on the late Victorian cultural horizon: the
decadent. The Celt's gender and the sexual excesses suggested by her
emotionalism and sensuousness reinforced that connection. Sexual
pathology and effeminacy were central to contemporary descriptions
of decadence, as were the decadent's similarities to the perceived
depravities of the New Woman.[37] Freud and Breuer notwithstanding,
the Celt's hysteria and decadence were also culturally linked to some
late nineteenth-century theories of degeneration; as Daniel Pick has
argued, such theories expressed fears about too much progress and
civilization as well as too little.[38] Many of Arnold's Celtic traits were
also the same qualities that were to characterize Max Nordau's 1895
portrait of the decadent artistic degenerate.[39] Although Nordau
acknowledged that degeneration afflicted both men and women, its
symptoms, which resembled and often occurred in conjunction with
those of hysteria, were particularly feminine. Arnold's feminization of
the Celt found further echoes in the work of Otto Weininger, whose
"anti-feminine"[40] and racist theories involved extensive comparisons
of Jews and women in his influential book, *Sex and Character* (1903).[41]
Like Arnold, Weininger linked femininity to necessary and natural
colonial status, insisting that the Jew, "like the woman, requires the
rule of an exterior authority."[42] His formulation of femininity as
racial inferiority lacks both Arnold's sympathy with the inferior race,
and his relative optimism about the causes and results of assimilation;
the racial meaning of femininity had become less ambiguous, more
decidedly damning.

Arnold's lectures were never reprinted during his lifetime. When
the elite cultural nationalism that became known as the Celtic
movement began in the 1880s, however, Arnold's definition of the
Celtic spirit became enormously influential, despite Yeats's anxious
claim, "I do not think any of us who write about Ireland have built

any argument upon it" (*EI*, 174).[43] Throughout the 1880s, 1890s and the first decade of the twentieth century, Yeats was intensely, if ambivalently, engaged with the Celtic movement and its imperialist precursors. Financial necessity provided one incentive; during this period Yeats wrote a number of journalistic essays and reviews, and he took up many of the phrases and ideas about Celts that were popular and saleable at the time. However, Yeats's interest in Celticism was not merely financial, despite his claim in a 1900 letter to D. P. Moran's *Leader* that he had never "used the phrases 'Celtic note' and 'Celtic Renaissance' except as a quotation from others" (*UPII*, 241). In fact, it was mainly through his attempts to write and rewrite Celticism that the early Yeats addressed one of the questions that would preoccupy him throughout his career, the question of Irish national identity and its relationship to the production of literature. During the 1880s, he liked to intone, "[t]here is no great literature without nationality, no great nationality without literature" (*LNI*, 30).[44]

The early Yeats was acutely aware of contemporary cultural connections between Celtic character and a cultured, nervous, bourgeois femininity. In his copy of Renan's *The Poetry of Celtic Races*, Yeats wrote three marginal comments next to Renan's description of the Celt's femininity: "Delicacy," "a feminine race," and "The Ideal of Woman."[45] Yeats did not begin his engagement with Celticism by accepting the equation of femininity with racial inferiority and colonial status put forth by Celticists like Arnold. In struggles between opposing political and cultural discourses, including imperialist and nationalist ones, some signs or values prove more "convertible" than others, like foreign currencies. In his earliest Celtic writings, Yeats struggled to construct an Irish nationality that incorporated, explicitly and implicitly, a trait that had become so closely associated with weakness and pathology that it was virtually impossible to convert it into a positive attribute: femininity. For a brief period, Yeats followed Arnold and Renan's gendering of the Celt without reproducing their political corollaries to it. In some of his earliest essays he outlined a version of the Celtic spirit that combined two contrasting models of Irish national character, one that was Arnoldian, feminine and particular, and another that was anti-Arnoldian, masculine and universalist.

This combination appears in Yeats's 1886 review essays about Sir Samuel Ferguson. Ferguson was a unionist, and many of his prose works offer a conception of the ameliorative and integrative possibilities of Irish culture that prefigures Arnold strikingly.[46] Yeats, however, claims Ferguson for Irish nationalism, an appropriation that suggests both how much Yeats's Celticism owed to the Arnoldian tradition and how boldly he was willing to alter the aspects of it that did not suit his purpose. The essays condemn the Dublin academic establishment, scorn Irish readers who are "servile to English notions" (*UPI*, 89), and present Ferguson as a poet who embraced the epic possibilities of Irish culture and legend. On one hand, Yeats emphasizes Ferguson's specifically Irish nature, lauding him as "the greatest Irish poet" (*UPI*, 87), claiming that he is "the most central and the most Celtic" (*UPI*, 103) and that his works "embody more completely than in any other man's writings, the Irish character" (*UPI*, 87). On the other hand, Yeats insists that this Irishness coincides with the virtues of other ancient literatures, especially the Greek tradition. As a result of his particular, feminine, Celtic nature, Ferguson produced works which were fundamentally continuous with ancient Greek epics, a tradition that Yeats characterized as both universalist and masculine. The essays revolve around the unacknowledged tension between these types of representativeness.

For the Celtic movement, the universalist claim alone was not enough; in fact, it threatened to neutralize the Celt's valuable and constitutive otherness. Yeats looked to the feminine when he wanted to emphasize the Celt's particular rather than universal nature. Yeats thought *Deirdre* "the greatest of Sir Samuel Ferguson's poems" (*UPI*, 92), compared it favorably to the work of Matthew Arnold, whose influence and legitimacy as a theorist of Celticism he was anxious to deny,[47] and claimed that Ferguson's superiority sprang from his mystical identity with essential Celtic nature: "In this Sir Samuel Ferguson was like the ancients; not that he was an imitator, as Matthew Arnold in *Sohrab and Rustum*, but for a much better reason; he was *like* them – like them in nature, for his spirit had sat with the old heroes of his country" (*UPI*, 92). He concluded:

No one will deny excellence to the Idylls of the King; no one will say that Lord Tennyson's Girton girls do not look well in those old costumes of dead chivalry ... Yet here is that which the Idylls do not at any time contain, beauty at once feminine and heroic. But as Lord Tennyson's ideal women will never find a flawless sympathy outside the upper English middle class, so this Deirdre will never, maybe, win entire credence outside the limits – wide enough they are – of the Irish race. (*UPI*, 95)

Yeats uses varying types of femininity as an index to the racial peculiarity of both work and audience. The "Irish race" is a community of readers capable of recognizing the representative Irishness of Deirdre's heroic femininity. Ironically, *Idylls of the King*, which was based on the Arthurian legends of Malory and the *Mabinogian*, put forth the Arnoldian view that Celtic elements were at the heart of British culture and race.[48] Yeats, on the other hand, characterized it as particularly English, and located its Englishness in Tennyson's representations of women. The contrast Yeats draws here allies femininity with racial specificity as such rather than with a specific race.

Ferguson's representation of heroic Irish femininity coexisted with and ultimately translated into a masculine universality. In an 1886 review of R. D. Joyce, written for the same series as the second Ferguson essay, Yeats contrasted poets who wrote out of their own peculiarities, "those who – like Coleridge, Shelley and Wordsworth – investigate what is obscure in emotion and appeal to what is abnormal in man, or become the healers of some particular disease of the spirit" (*UPI*, 105), with "the bardic class" who wrote of universal truths and spoke to all men, those "who sing of the universal emotions, our loves and angers, our delight in stories and heroes, our delight in things beautiful and gallant" (*UPI*, 105). While both classes of poet were necessary, the second was more valuable, "for they speak to the manhood in us, not to the scholar or the philosopher" (*UPI*, 105). Yeats's argument coincides with the classic humanist definition of "great" literature: great literature has no gender, no race; it arises out of the underlying humanity we all share, and speaks to all audiences equally by virtue of their common humanness. As feminist criticism has long recognized, this definition of universal humanity is not ungendered; it is masculine. As Yeats's equation of universal humanity and manhood suggests, there is no place for femininity in this definition of the common human essence, except as an illustration of its opposite, the diseased and particular.

Yeats's incoherent description of Ferguson sprang from the particular combination of indebtedness and departure that characterized the relationship between his earliest Celticism and Arnoldian imperialism. Rather than reject femininity as pathological or lock it into a hierarchical, complementary relationship with British masculinity, Yeats allied femininity with racial specificity, both Irish and English, and claimed that beneath Irish particularity lay a masculine universalism. This move was logically difficult but politically apt; it gave Yeats's Celticism claims to a version of cultural otherness he found appealing, and also to the political rights he wished to assert for the Irish. It gestured towards a revision of the national political implications of femininity by disrupting the imperialist equation of femininity with subordinate political status and by failing to establish a stable relationship between gender and Irish national character.

This formulation was short-lived, however. The cultural contra-dictions between femininity and masculine, heroic national culture proved too sharp for Yeats to maintain this combination, as his emphasis on the masculinity of the Fenians in "The Wanderings of Oisin" (1889) indicates. Yeats structured the poem around two related contrasts, each of which allies Oisin, the Fenians and truly vital Irish nationality with a version of masculinity. One contrast sets the physical and imaginative vitality of Oisin's pagan Ireland against the material and spiritual poverty of Patrick's Christian Ireland. It also sets Oisin's masculine prowess and "angry king-remembering soul" (*VP*, 36) against the "small and feeble populace" (*VP*, 58) and "bodies unglorious" (*VP*, 58) of Christian Ireland, and pits the "exultant faces" of pagan gods against Christ's "milk-pale face / Under a crown of thorns and dark with blood" (*VP*, 38). This contrast revolves around the relative presence or absence of virility; Oisin has "the Fenians' old strength" while the Christian Irish are "men waxing so weakly" (*VP*, 60).

The poem's second contrast opposes the masculine world of the Fenians and the national struggle to the feminine world of the Sidhe. The world of the fairies, presided over by Niamh, is a feminine realm of beauty, sexuality and romance. In 1895 Yeats emphasized the sexual excess implied by the world of the Sidhe by replacing Patrick's description of Oisin as "[t]rapped of an amorous demon" with his charge that Oisin has "known three centuries, poets sing, / Of dalliance with a demon thing" (*VP*, 2). This is also indicated by the poem's rhetorical preoccupation with heterosexual pairing in its descriptions of the first island, as in "men and ladies, hand in hand" (*VP*, 15), "men and ladies" (*VP*, 18), "girl and boy" (*VP*, 19), and "youth and lady" (*VP*, 29). The world of the Fenians, on the other hand, is a world of martial exploits and male comradeship. Oisin's descriptions of the Fenians are littered with references to hunting, weapons, blood and battles. For example, Oisin is first recalled to his Fenian loyalties by "a staff of wood / From some dead warrior's broken lance" (*VP*, 24). The Fenians (and even their dogs, Bran, Sceolan, and Lomair) usually come in comradely groups of three or more, such as "Caoilte, Conan, and Finn" (*VP*, 10) and "Blanaid, Mac Nessa, tall Fergus" (*VP*, 53),[49] rather than in the romantic pairs of the Sidhe.

By the time Yeats wrote "To Ireland in the Coming Times" (*VP*, 137–9) which first appeared in 1892 in *The Countess Kathleen and Various Legends and Lyrics*, the relationship between femininity and heroic national literature had become one of his Celticism's central problems rather than one of its distinguishing virtues. The poem's energizing tensions pit the speaker's assertion of his place in a masculine tradition of national literature against a series of anxious acknowledgments that his interest in the feminine, mystic Rose may preclude his inclusion in the nationalist brotherhood:

> Know, that I would accounted be
> True brother of a company
> That sang, to sweeten Ireland's wrong
> Ballad and story, rann and song;
> Nor be I any less of them,
> Because the red-rose-bordered hem
> Of her, whose history began
> Before God made the angelic clan,
> Trails all about the written page.   (*VP*, 137–8)

On one level, this central tension appears as a contrast between the imperative and conditional modes. In the first line, the commanding certainty of "know" is immediately undercut by the pleading uncertainty of the speaker's request. The negative phrasing of other assertions – "Nor be I any less of them" and "Nor may I less be counted one / With Davis, Mangan, Ferguson" – performs a similar function, asserting the speaker's community with the nationalist trio of Davis, Mangan and Ferguson by simultaneously calling up and banishing the specter of his isolation from them.

On another level, the poem's central conflict is a gender conflict. There are several different ways to characterize the problematic incompatibility the poem wrestles with – action versus contemplation, propaganda versus literature, empiricism versus mysticism, the particular versus the universal – all of which appear elsewhere in Yeats's work. While the tensions that inform the poem are not reducible to any one of these oppositions, they all offer contrasts between a position that is strongly allied with the intellectual or

material world of the "national," and one that is less so. The poem's
contrast between masculine and feminine represents and structures
the various forms of this central opposition; the national and the
masculine coincide, no matter how the national is defined.

The national identity the speaker tries to claim is definitional
rather than essential. As the poem's title suggests, whether or not the
speaker will be accorded a place in the nationalist brotherhood
depends upon how his future audience will write political and
cultural history. The poem affirms the value of the red-rose-bordered
hem and gestures towards the reconciliation between the feminine
and the national/heroic that Yeats sought in his early prose writings.
The poem's close does not achieve this reconciliation, however, and
acknowledges that it can only be granted by the future audience:

> I cast my heart into these rhymes,
> That you, in the dim coming times,
> May know how my heart went with them
> After the red-rose-bordered hem.

Yeats appealed to a future audience rather than a present one
partly because a number of contemporary observers rejected his
Celtic writings as not genuinely Irish precisely because they presented a version of Irish nationality that was too closely allied with
femininity. James Joyce's 1904 parody of "To Ireland in the
Coming Times" emphasized Celticism's femininity and stressed its
incompatibility with authentic nationalist community. Joyce por-
trayed Yeats as a whining, effeminate fool at the beck and call of a
bevy of women, probably Lady Gregory, Maud Gonne, and Annie
Horniman:

> But I must not accounted be
> One of that mumming company –
> With him who hies him to appease
> His giddy dames' frivolities
> While they console him when he whinges
> With gold-embroidered Celtic fringes –[50]

The poem characterizes the Celtic movement as a group of feminine
prudes, "sister mummers one and all" and "maiden[s], shy and
nervous."[51] Joyce invoked sisterhood to indicate a form of collectivity
that parodied true nationalist community, and equated nationalist
vigor with virility.

Joyce was not the only contemporary critic to accuse Yeats, and

Celticism in general, of two related failings which were in fact equivalent in most contemporary political discourses: effeminacy and the lack of a genuine national and cultural identity. In an essay on Fiona Macleod, the Celtic pen name of William Sharp, Paul Elmer More argued that "the new school of Celtic writers" engaged in a "confessedly feminine use of the imagination,"[52] and repeated Arnold's and Renan's equation of the Celt's femininity with a debilitating nervous disorder. More linked the Celtic movement with hysteria and decadence, accusing Macleod of an "inability to distinguish between an idea or even a genuine emotion and the fluttering of tired nerves."[53] More's criticisms of Yeats contrast the "virile passion"[54] and primitive vitality of ancient Irish literature with Yeats's feminine and decadent Celticism, which More compares to "the chattering of old women whose memory is troubled by vague and foolish superstitions."[55] For More, as for Joyce, Yeats's distance from true Irish culture is measured by his distance from virility. When Yeats finally rejected Celticism as effeminate, he was following a path that many of his contemporaries marked out for him in no uncertain terms.

Increasingly during the 1890s, Yeats addressed the Celt's femininity less often and less openly. In his only explicit response to Arnold's essay, "The Celtic Element in Literature" (1897), instead of allowing the particular (feminine) and the universal (masculine) to coexist or even conflict, Yeats replaces the former with the latter. The essay omits all overt references to the Celt's femininity, and its main purpose is to "re-state a little Renan's and Arnold's argument" (*EI*, 174) in order to substitute the word "primitive" for the word "Celtic." The connection is hardly startling, and, on one level, indicates how much Celticism owed to primitivism. Its function, however, was to refigure the racial specificity of Yeats's Celt as the embodiment of qualities that were more universal than particular. Yeats constructed the Irish folk tradition and the Celtic temperament as the most vital and immediate manifestations of the rich imaginative powers and access to the universal secrets of the Great Memory that all primitive traditions shared. Yeats writes of Arnold, "I do not think he understood that our 'natural magic' is but the ancient religion of the world" (*EI*, 176), and emphasizes that all folk literatures possess the properties Arnold ascribes specifically to the Celtic element in literature. Where Arnold uses "Celtic melancholy" Yeats prefers "primitive melancholy" (*EI*, 183) and where Arnold attributes English literature's "turn for natural magic" to a Celtic source, Yeats offers this corrective:

I will put this differently and say that literature dwindles to a mere chronicle of circumstance, or passionless fantasies, and passionless meditations, unless it is constantly flooded with the passions and beliefs of ancient times, and that of all the fountains of the passions and beliefs of ancient times in Europe, the Slavonic, the Finnish, the Scandinavian, and the Celtic, the Celtic alone has been for centuries close to the main river of European literature. It has again and again brought "the vivifying spirit" "of excess" into the arts of Europe. (*EI*, 185)

Passion, belief and excess were the cornerstones of Yeats's character-ization of the Celtic temperament. They were also important elements in Arnold's and Renan's portraits of the Celt. Yeats's description of Celts retained most of the qualities attributed to them by imperial Celticism, but had now dropped the attribute that appeared most damning and least convertible into a national virtue: femininity. The transition here from Celtic to primitive, from particular to universal, could only be made in the context of another transition – the one that the reviews of Ferguson had not made – from feminine to masculine.

This transition involved an increased emphasis on the Irish peasant, who had always been an important figure for Yeats anyway. After he abandoned his brief early efforts to include femininity explicitly in Celtic identity, Yeats increasingly emphasized the Irish peasant's masculine, heroic and primitive qualities as constitutive of Irishness. Celticism's focus on the Irish peasant was, of course, over-deter-mined. Nineteenth-century romanticism had long emphasized the exotic cultural worth and alternative wisdoms of the country folk and primitive peoples. Throughout the century, folklorists had been collecting material from the inhabitants of rural Ireland, and the equation of Irish culture with Irish peasant culture was already well-established.

Yeats's inadequacies as an accurate recorder of such sociological formations as the Irish peasantry have become cliches of Yeats criticism, and it is generally acknowledged that Celticism invented the versions of Irish peasant culture it claimed to have discovered.[56] Here I am interested in why Yeats invented the particular version of the Irish peasant that he did. While this increased emphasis on the peasant appears to be a move away from the imperial feminization

of the colonized and towards a more viable nationalism, a close
examination of Yeats's peasant suggests that it brought him into
greater harmony with the deep structures of colonial thought. Two
related projects can be discerned in Yeats's representations of the
peasantry. The first was to suppress femininity while retaining the
attributes associated with it, in an effort to negotiate the contemporary association of masculinity and viable political and cultural
nationhood. The second was to construct a version of Irishness which
accommodated the needs and interests of the Anglo-Irish as a class.
Yeats's representations of Irish peasants constructed them as heroic
and primitive figures whose cultural worth and uniqueness were
produced by their economic status, thus accomplishing both purposes at once. They demanded the maintenance of a poor peasant
class, thereby protecting the colonial interests of the Anglo-Irish, and
they transformed the "lack" which characterized the Celt from
femininity into poverty.

In focusing on the Irish peasant's representative Irishness, Yeats's
Celticism made the peasant's economic failure, poverty, exemplary
of the nation's heroic failure under British colonial rule. For Yeats,
Ireland produced a rich cultural tradition not in spite of such
failures, but because of them. "The spiritual history of the world,"
he wrote, "has been the history of conquered peoples" (*UPII*, 70).
Yeats's claim that the peasant's poverty produced his cultural value
was historically new in Ireland and accorded with the strategic
needs of Anglo-Irish Celticism. This becomes clear when we consider the manner in which nineteenth-century nationalist verse,
especially that of Young Ireland, the movement to which turn of the
century cultural nationalisms traced some of their origins, figured
the relationship between poverty, colonial status, gender, and Irish
cultural integrity.

In sharp contrast to Yeats's Celtic movement, much nationalist
verse of mid-nineteenth-century Ireland had emphasized the degrading effects of poverty and oppression, articulating a configuration echoed by Franz Fanon: "The poverty of the people, national
oppression, and the inhibition of culture are one and the same
thing."[57] James Clarence Mangan's "Words of Forewarning," for
example, asserts, "Slavery debaseth the soul, yea! reverses its primal
nature."[58] Womanly virtues had their place in the national tradition; nationalist rhetoric exhorted women to provide inspiration
and refuse unpatriotic dalliance to their warriors. "The Nation's

Valentine," addressed "to the ladies of Ireland," gives women the ultimate responsibility for the success or failure of their menfolks:

> Irresistible loveliness! wouldst thou but cherish
> The patriot virtues, at once we are free;
> But desert thou, or shrink, and as surely we perish –
> For man takes the tone of his spirit from thee.[59]

At the same time, nationalist writers also invoked womanish vices to criticize the faltering Irish male, and patriotic verses frequently represented the debilitating effects of slavery as feminization. "The Gathering of Leinster" evokes the same combination of melancholy, femininity and helplessness that Matthew Arnold would find so appealing twenty years later in 1867, but in quite a different tone:

> Serf! With thy fetters o'erladen,
> Why crouch you in dastardly woe?
> Why weep o'er thy chains like a maiden,
> Nor strike for thy manhood a blow?[60]

Another author castigates the Irish,

> Men! *Are* we men? We talk as such,
> Heav'ns, how we talk! but vain alarms –
> Nought masculine endures so much,
> Then brand our brows, as well as arms![61]

Such discourses continued in several turn of the century Irish nationalisms, including those of Horace Plunkett and D. P. Moran, who is often cited as an example of nationalist masculinism. For Moran, as for the Young Ireland writers, the essence of Irishness and the essence of masculinity were identical. Moran drew a heavily gendered contrast between the "feminine screech"[62] of his fellow Irish patriots, who he claimed were secretly content with Ireland's colonial status and ineffectual in their resistance to English rule, and the "real and virile national spirit"[63] that Ireland was losing. His vague but virile solution to this state of affairs was that "we mend our ways and do something masculine."[64]

Both the masculinist Irish nationalist and the English traditions linked Ireland's colonial status to femininity; poverty, slavery and failure suppressed rather than constituted true "masculine" Irish identity. David Lloyd has argued that nineteenth-century Irish nationalism, particularly that of Young Ireland, imagined national identity and individual identity as homologous; each individual replicated the sum of the national being on a smaller scale.[65] So did Yeats's Celticism, but with an important difference. While for Young Ireland, the spirit of the nation had been suppressed by colonialism and would emerge in its fullness after the nation was free, Celticism's Irishness was produced by the colonial experience. In Yeats's Celticism, with its emphasis on the peasant's poverty, the Irishman's fetters made him not a womanish slave, but a Celt. The Irish peasant's status as the embodiment of authentic national identity depended on his oppression. In contrast to Young Ireland, Yeats's Celticism no longer invoked freedom versus slavery for both nation and individual, but paradoxical liberty of the soul through earthly bondage. Material failure became a spiritual success rather than a shortcoming, poverty became a badge of moral superiority, and the Celtic peasant became imaginatively rich and vital precisely because he was literally poor and oppressed. Economic inferiority had replaced gender inferiority as the distinguishing mark of the Celt. Yeats's Celticism entered a new stage of dependence on imperialism, one which promoted the interests of the Anglo-Irish comprador class by transforming colonial discourses on nationality and gender into a discourse on nationality and class.

The idea that loss and defeat nurture creative life and beauty found its way into Yeats's thinking on a number of subjects. He recalls in his memoirs that he "chose deliberate poverty as a foppery of youth" (*Mem*, 32), he found in his first lover's beauty "the nobility of defeated things" (*Mem*, 85), and he built a major part of his early aesthetic on the principle that poetry was produced by failure and unfulfilled desire. He liked to quote Oscar Wilde's description of the Irish as "a nation of brilliant failures" (*UPI*, 250).[66] In his efforts to appropriate Irish history in the service of Celtic nationalism, Yeats constructed poverty and political failure as artistically productive and spiritually enabling. Like Arnold, Yeats created a definition of Irish cultural identity whose distinguishing features militated against the establishment of that identity as distinct and autonomous politically. This structure of thought was not merely a result of Yeats's Rosicrucian idealism or of his contempt for the petty material interests of party politics in Ireland. It also safeguarded the future of the Anglo-Irish as a caste by coding rural poverty, and the tenant system that helped perpetuate it, as a constitutive Irish material failure which actually produced Irish cultural difference.

Accordingly, in Yeats's characterization of the Irish peasantry,

"Celtic" and "primitive" tend to modulate into "poor," and Yeats imagines rural poverty, not merely as the setting for Irish temperament and imagination, but as their origin. The key to the Irish peasant's cultural worth was a mysticism illustrated in Irish folklore and spiritual belief and grounded in the material deprivation of the peasantry. Yeats linked every aspect of the Celtic spirit directly to the poverty and harshness of Irish peasant life, and constructed a series of antitheses between English success, vulgarity, and materialism and Irish failure, refinement, and spirituality. The "sordid compromise of success" would ruin the Celt's imaginative power and turn him into a cheap copy of his vulgar English conqueror. To strive for mere material prosperity was to become English; to compensate for material penury with imaginative wealth was to become Irish. According to Yeats's Celticism, there was no way to improve the peasant's lot materially while preserving his cultural integrity; in the Irish context, material success had been dependent on anglicization, and, as Yeats said, "anglicization has meant vulgarization" (*UPII,* 288).

For Yeats, "this strange Gaelic race lives between two worlds, the world of its poverty, and a world of wild memories and of melancholy, beautiful imagination" (*UPI,* 396), the latter a result of and compensation for the former. Yeats claimed that the imaginative world of the peasant, distinguished by belief in the supernatural, was:

that world of glory and surprise imagined in the unknown by the peasant as he leant painfully over his spade. His spiritual desires ascended into heaven, but all he could dream of material well-being and freedom was lavished upon this world of kings and goblins. We who have less terrible a need dream less splendidly. (*CT,* 205)

The harshness and poverty of rural peasant life produced the unconscious creativity that distinguished the primitive Celtic imagination from modern literature:

No conscious invention can take the place of tradition, for he who would write a folk tale, and thereby bring a new life into literature, must have the fatigue of the spade in his hands and the stupor of the fields in his heart. (*UPI,* 288)

The Irish peasant was less an artist than a vessel through which ancient traditions gave birth to new literary artifacts, and the material conditions of his peasant life performed the function of emptying the vessel of independent creativity. "Fatigue" and "stupor," which would interfere with the conscious creation of an autonomous subject, are the necessary grounds for the Celtic imagination, which consisted of a mediumistic access to other powers, other realms of thought.

Yeats himself combined piercing skepticism with a deep desire to believe, as he wrote in *The Celtic Twilight*, that "everything exists, everything is true, and the earth is only a little dust under our feet" (*CT*, 7). He wrote later that he "had noticed many analogies in modern spiritism" (*EX*, 30) to peasant belief, and attributed to the Irish peasant the simple, whole-hearted belief in the supernatural that he wished for in certain moods. The peasant's unconscious, mediumistic imagination enabled him to gain particularly intense beliefs in or perceptions of (Yeats was never sure which) the supernatural. As with the richness of the folk imagination, it was, in part, the harshness of rural poverty that produced these beliefs or perceptions:

the children of the poor and simple learn from their unbroken religious, and from their traditional beliefs, and from the hardness of their lives, that this world is nothing, and that a spiritual world, where all dreams come true, is everything; and therefore the poor and simple are that imperfection whose perfection is genius. (*UPII*, 190–1)

The imaginative wealth of the poor is not genius, however; it represents the raw materials out of which genius may be forged.

In some ways, Yeats's Irish peasant was the opposite of Celticism's Celt – masculine rather than feminine, simple and primitive rather than decadently civilized, vigorous rather than nervous. In this phase of Yeats's Celticism, however, poverty performed several of the same functions that femininity had performed in imperial Celticism; it designated an attractive cultural difference that also demanded material (political or economic) subordination. Not surprisingly, then, Yeats's characterizations of the Irish peasant are haunted by traces of the Celt's femininity, and his writings on Irish nationality continued to posit, persistently and ambivalently, a set of shifting relations between Irishness and femininity. In their relation to the occult and their access to forms of knowledge and artistic production not dependent on or confined by the limits of the individual self, women and peasants were interchangeable. Over and over again Yeats points to the limitations of modern rationalist thought and claims that, in contrast, "men who live primitive lives where instinct does the work of reason are fully conscious of many things we cannot perceive at all" (*EX*, 17).[67] Yeats described the Irish peasant's mysticism as a kind of instinctive knowledge available not only to primitive peoples, but to women:

Women come more easily than men to that wisdom which ancient peoples, and all wild peoples even now, think the only wisdom. The self, which is the foundation of our knowledge, is broken in pieces by foolishness, and is forgotten in the sudden emotions of women, and therefore fools may get, and women do get of a certainty glimpses of much that sanctity finds at the end of its painful journey. (*Myth*, 115)

Wild peoples like the Irish who cling to this alternative wisdom have a feminine, mediumistic ability to escape what Yeats saw as the modern preoccupation with the self, an ability which was a key element in the production of Irish national culture. Yeats had contrasted Ferguson's self-forgetful art, whose depictions of nature provided the reader with a "clear glass to see the world through" (*UPI*, 103), with the inferior works of modern bourgeois artists, in which descriptions of natural beauty were "only masks behind which go on the sad soliloquies of a nineteenth century egoism" (*UPI*, 103). One of Yeats's favorite phrases about an earlier time when literature and culture were imaginative and vital linked women and historically distant peoples as two groups whose ability to transcend the boundaries of the self enabled the production of vivid art:

The ancients and the Elizabethans abandoned themselves to imagination as a woman abandons herself to love, and created beings who made the people of this world seem but shadows. (*EI*, 196)[68]

Yeats sought this kind of knowledge through his occult studies, and he repeatedly compared Madame Blavatsky to an Irish peasant. Yeats wrote that she was a "sort of old Irish peasant woman" (*AY*, 117), and was "all primeval peasant" (*AY*, 119), and commented, "I knew that her imagination contained all the folklore of the world" (*AY*, 118). His description of her in an 1889 letter to John O'Leary evokes primitive mysteries to be admired rather than solved; Yeats writes that Blavatsky is "like an old peasent [sic] woman" and confesses, "I have no theories about her. She is simply a note of interregation [sic]" (*KLI*, 164).

Yeats's Celticism elevated the peasant to a position of great importance in national life – creator and guardian of the oral tradition that gave Irish literature its power and uniqueness – while insisting on the desirability of a poor rural class and its distinction from his bourgeois audience. Yeats styled himself "your Celt" when addressing his American readers in the *Boston Pilot* and the *Providence Sunday Journal*[69] and included himself in the Celtic tradition he claimed Matthew Arnold had not understood. However, when he was not immediately concerned with distancing himself from his American audience or his British precursor, his references to the Celt indicate that the Celt functioned as an exotic other to be contemplated and appropriated. Yeats strikes his characteristic tone, that of a Celticist rather than a Celt, about the barbaric simplicity and mysterious otherness of the Irish peasant when he describes an old seaman in *The Celtic Twilight*, appealing to a community of readers for whom the peasant is an foreign object of scrutiny and admiration:

Let us look upon him with wonder, for his mind has not fallen into a net of complexity, nor his will melted into thought and dream. Our journey is through other storms and other darkness. (*CT*, 161)

This separation was crucial to Yeats's theory of how vigorous national culture was produced. During the 1890s he began to elaborate a distinction between the artistic value of the peasantry – their supernatural beliefs and imaginatively rich folk traditions, both of which were compensatory responses to the harshness of rural poverty – and the literary achievements of the artists whose works embraced and celebrated peasant culture. Yeats's claim that the poor and simple are "that imperfection whose perfection is genius" made this distinction in a way that recast the complementary relation Arnold had ascribed to the English and Irish as a culturally productive complementarity between artist and peasant. Celts were, by definition, creatively enabling for other artists, but were imperfect artists themselves. In Yeats's early thinking, as in the major aesthetic traditions that produced him, the imperfect artist was often a feminine artist.

While in 1886 Yeats had described Samuel Ferguson's mystic identity with Celtic nature as the source of his genius, by 1897 his assessment of such an identification, like his assessment of heroic femininity, had become a central weakness in Celtic literature rather than a distinguishing strength. As a flaw, it was specifically aligned with femininity. Yeats's 1897 review of Fiona Macleod's *Spiritual Tales* illustrates this new formulation. Written the same year that "The

Celtic Element in Literature" sought to claim the universal/mascu-
line for Irish culture by replacing "Celtic" with "primitive," Yeats's
review reveals the structure of thought behind that gesture. The
strengths and weaknesses of the feminine writer are the tempera-
mental characteristics of the Celt.

William Sharp was a literary critic under his own name, and his
choice of Fiona for his Celtic identity underlines the links between
femininity and Celticism. Yeats's review is structured around the
differences between Macleod's feminine writing and the masculine
writing of male artists. It is also structured around the assumption
that the features which make Macleod particularly Irish are both the
signs of her valuable otherness and the marks of her artistic
inferiority. Yeats praises the Celtic movement as

one which is bringing new kinds of temperaments into our literature ... and
... is making countries like Ireland and like the Highlands ... begin to be
full of voices. (*UPII*, 43)

He finds Macleod as representatively Irish as he had found Sir
Samuel Ferguson: "And of all these voices none is more typical than
the curious, mysterious, childlike voice that is in these stories of Miss
Fiona Macleod" (*UPII*, 43). Yeats praises Macleod for her "absolute
absorption in the dreams and passions of her personages" (*UPII*, 43),
and attributes to her the same oneness with essential Irishness that he
had accorded to Ferguson:

she felt about the world, and the creatures of its winds and waters, emotions
that were of one kind with the emotions of those grave peasants, the most
purely Celtic peasants in Ireland, and that she had become their voice, not
from any mere observation of their ways, but out of an absolute identity of
nature. (*UPII*, 44)

Macleod's power as an artist, like Ferguson's, arises from her mystic
identity of nature with the Celts she describes. The boundaries of her
self have been broken. She does not merely observe Celts; she
becomes a Celt, and her voice now articulates their nature and their
emotions in articulating her own.

While this identity had contributed to Ferguson's unproblematic
status as the greatest and most Irish of Irish poets, in Macleod's case
it prevents her from achieving a similar status. In addition, now it
was explicitly gendered feminine. In the review, Yeats also praises
Kipling and Robert Louis Stevenson as other participants in the
movement to "recover the ancient trust in passion and beauty"

(*UPII*, 42), and he makes an important gender distinction. In contrast to Macleod's feminine absorption, Yeats says that Kipling and Stevenson write "as men write," and explains that they are

> too conscious of having been born to write of simple, passionate things to be themselves simple and passionate. They have never forgotten, and in this lies the very value of their art, that they have observed picturesque and barbarous things with the keen eyes of the people of a civilized and critical land; but Miss Macleod sees everything with the eyes of the personages of her tales. (*UPII*, 43)

That the value of art like Kipling's and Stevenson's is superior to the value of Macleod's is clear; their masculine detachment is the standard by which Macleod's weaknesses are measured. Macleod's feminine identity with Celtic nature is not only the source of her distinguishing strength; it is also the origin of her limitations as a writer. Her faults – a lack of distance from her creations and an inability to pay sufficient attention to craftsmanship – spring from the fact that she forgets herself as the conscious artist and gives herself wholly to the world she imagines:

> She forgets, in following some spectacle of love and battle, that she is using words and phrases, paragraphs and chapters, rhythms and cadences, and so "thou" and "you" get mixed together into her rushing sentences. (*UPII*, 43)

This distinctive combination of talent and technical ineptitude became Yeats's final stance on Macleod. In his last review of "her" work, written in 1899, Yeats found her technique at fault again, writing, "Miss Macleod has faults enough to ruin an ordinary writer. Her search for dim resemblances sometimes brings her beyond the borders of coherence" (*UPII*, 166).

It may be fairly objected that Samuel Ferguson was a better poet than Macleod, or that Macleod was in any case of limited talent. The important point here is not that Yeats found her work flawed, but that he invoked the rhetorical and intellectual structures of imperial Celticism to describe its flaws. Yeats's judgment that Macleod's distinguishing Celtic strength is also the source of her feminine weakness inhabits the contradictory structure of Arnoldian Celticism. Ultimately, her identity with the extravagant, feminine, volatile Celtic spirit that marks the Irishness of Macleod's writing leads it into incoherence and also signals its limitations. Behind Yeats's Celtic artist lurk the technical sloppiness of the poor craftsman, the hysterical outpourings and "rushing sentences" of an overly feminine

writer. In contrast to his earliest reviews, in which feminine peculiarity and masculine universalism appeared together, here he
follows Arnold's imperialist equation of femininity with racial inferiority and artistic imperfection.

Arnold's Celticism had produced a version of Irish nationality
whose cultural uniqueness and value demanded its political erasure.
Yeats's Celticism offered a similar construction of Irish cultural
difference, but claimed that it demanded political expression instead.
Yeats's vision of an harmonious alliance between a peasantry whose
material impoverishment made them rich in the raw materials of
national culture and an Anglo-Irish aristocracy capable of transforming those raw materials into finished cultural artifacts, evidence
of the genius of the race, gave him a stake in the cultural logic of
Arnoldian Celticism. Yeats's Celticism took up the imperialist construction of complementarity between Irish and English and mapped
it onto his construction of the relationship between "noble and
beggar-man."

Arnold had figured this complementarity as the Celt's femininity.
Although he masculinized Arnold's Celt by focusing on the rugged
Irish peasant, Yeats's writings on Irish identity continued to posit a
hidden femininity for the Irish in the Celt's mediumistic occult
knowledge, feminine self-forgetfulness, and secondary economic
status. While this hidden femininity constituted the Irish peasant's
status as the source of an epic national culture, it also provoked
Yeats's judgment of the inferiority of the Celtic/feminine artist, in
which Celticism and craftsmanship conflict and he values the very
Saxon self-consciousness that he praised the Celt for lacking. The
complex relationship between Irishness and femininity in Yeats's
early Celtic writings suggests a number of contradictory possibilities.
In national terms, the Celt's femininity occupied a site of irreducible
conflict between national difference and national inferiority, and
Yeats's construction of the Irish peasant was organized around
pursuing the impossible goal of retaining the qualities Arnold and
Victorian culture in general labelled feminine while rescuing the Celt
from the negative connotations of femininity. In class terms, the
Celt's femininity and its metonym, the peasant's poverty, inscribed
the continued dominance of the Ascendancy even while they claimed
a cultural difference that necessitated political nationhood.

However, merely to say that Yeats's acceptance, both overt and
covert, of the Celt's femininity indicates his alliance with Arnoldian

imperialism would be to succumb to Arnold's characterization of the relationship between race and gender in Ireland rather than to analyze it. On another level, it suggests a series of relations to imperialism that highlight one of the deep structures that often link colonial and anti-colonial discourses: the equation of masculinity with racial superiority and political nationhood. To the extent that his earliest Celtic writings included femininity in a definition of Irish nationality that was viable and valuable, not just culturally, but politically as well; that is, to the extent that he appeared, on one level, to be most derivative of Arnold's feminization of the Celt, Yeats was, in fact, revising the conventional political ramifications of such feminization. Conversely, Yeats was closest to adopting the confluence of race and gender in Arnold's sympathetic imperialism when he seemed to be most intensely engaged in revising Arnold. The complicity of Yeats's Celticism with imperialism appears less in his initial gendering of Celts as feminine than in his representation of the Irish peasant and in his rejection of Celticism as effeminate. What was truly radical and valuable in Yeats's Celtic nationalism was neither his idealization of the poverty-stricken and primitive Irish peasant nor his rejection of the Celt's femininity as a racial slur. Rather, it was his challenging, however partial, ambivalent, and implicit, of the period's equation of viable political nationality with masculinity.

CHAPTER 2

Fair Erin as landlord: femininity and Anglo-Irish politics in "The Countess Cathleen"

A nation and a woman are not forgiven the unguarded hour in which the first adventurer that came along could violate them. The riddle is not solved by such turns of speech, but merely formulated differently.

Karl Marx[1]

Tradition and custom, not philosophy, are the chief defenses of property.

Standish O'Grady[2]

In some of the Celtic writings examined in chapter 1, Yeats's representations of the Irish peasantry used class – the peasant's poverty – to refigure the necessarily subordinate political status that imperial Celticists like Matthew Arnold had most commonly figured through gender. Yeats's Anglo-Irish Celticism was, in part, the cultural nationalism of a native elite who advocated national independence but did not wish to alter the existing social order and distribution of wealth significantly. Celticism's claims to being a "national" movement required that it forge an harmonious nationalist alliance between aristocrat and peasant that would maintain the social and economic divide between them rather than erasing it. In addition, it had to compete with other versions of Irish nationality, struggling to appropriate desirable tropes and signs and structure them according to its needs. Yeats's early play, *The Countess Cathleen*, first written while he was still deeply but ambivalently engaged with the discourse of Celticism, arranges another configuration of class, gender and nationality towards these ends. This configuration appropriates the widespread tradition of representing Ireland as a woman.

Such representations are classic features of most nationalist discourses. In the conventional literary history of the Irish revival, figures like Fair Erin, Cathleen ni Houlihan, Dark Rosaleen and the

Shan Van Vocht have become hallmarks of the movement, and are often treated as the one thing its various competing literary and political movements had in common.[3] But, as the epigraph from Marx suggests, to a properly critical reader, a comparison between the nation and a woman should provide the beginning of an inquiry rather than a conclusion. We can only assess these figures by examining how various national discourses constructed the category "woman."[4] Rather than constituting a point of general agreement and certainty, the common practice of representing Ireland as a woman forms an important site of ambivalence and conflict in Irish national discourses. The particular way in which *The Countess Cathleen* figures the relationship between Cathleen and Ireland allegorizes the contradictory and embattled status of Anglo-Irish Celticism. The play constructs Cathleen as a Fair Erin figure whose "femininity" was particular to the kind of Irish nationality imagined by Celticism. This femininity inscribed the double-edged virtues of Celts: idealism, self-sacrifice and spiritual victory through material defeat and impoverishment, as well as the class hierarchies connected with them.

The Countess Cathleen was Yeats's most revised play; there are numerous published versions,[5] and the text did not assume its final form until 1913.[6] However, throughout the revisions, several central preoccupations remain constant and recognizable, though the text reconfigures or modifies them repeatedly. These preoccupations are functions of Anglo-Irish Celticism's major claims, questions and contradictions. Celticism claimed to be a movement based on recovery rather than innovation; it naturalized the version of ancient Irish culture it offered, claiming that it merely revealed the true national being. Celticism was also based on enlisting the Irish peasantry, both symbolically and literally, in a shared national project while continuing to dominate them politically and economically. These Celticist ambivalences help to account for what most critics have seen as the play's poor construction, unresolved tensions, and contradictory themes.[7] The text constructs a version of Irishness that derives from an originary and essential national character. At the same time, it also outlines the process through which this particular definition of national character struggles against and defeats a competing version. It presents national unity as the radical equality of all members of the nation, and it also imagines a national unity based on the maintenance of existing political and economic hierarchies. It suggests the possibilities for class conflict between

Anglo-Irish and peasant, but it also transforms class conflict into gendered conflict between colonizer and colonized. Such tensions reflect precisely those conflicts and divisions that Anglo-Irish Celticism both depended upon maintaining and needed to appear to transcend or resolve. Cathleen, and the Celticist conceptions of gender, class, and nationality she embodies, provide the structure for these contradictions and the vehicle for their apparent resolution: Cathleen as Fair Erin is inseparable from Cathleen as landlord.

From the outset, *The Countess Cathleen* was conceived, advertised, and read as a "national" work. The terms in which it poses its motivating conflicts and questions are drawn from and invoke contemporary nationalist discourses directly. Beginning with the earliest stages of its composition,[8] Yeats described the play as a representatively Irish text which would embody Irish national character and culture. Yeats thought the play "full of action and very Irish" (*KLI*, 148) and characterized it as an attempt to display a "feeling not less national, Celtic, and distinctive" than that found in his popular "The Wanderings of Oisin" and in ancient Irish songs and ballads (*VPI*, 1288). Its performance in May of 1899 inaugurated the Irish Literary Theatre, which Yeats and his collaborators hoped would help foster a new "Celtic and Irish school of dramatic literature."[9]

The controversy over the play revolved mainly around its claims to being a representatively Irish work; audiences and reviewers generally judged the play's failure or success according to whether or not it fulfilled their criteria for the representatively Irish. For many, it did not. The most famous (and the most intemperate) attack on the play was written by F. Hugh O'Donnell, who explicitly rejected its claims to being a national work:

Out of all the mass of our national traditions it is precisely the baseness which is utterly alien to all our national traditions, the barter of Faith for Gold, which Mr. W. B. Yeats selects as the fundamental idea of his Celtic drama![10]

Other, more reasoned responses also criticized the play most heavily for its claims to national or representative status. The reviewer for the *New Ireland Review* argued for a balanced view of the play, but acknowledged that there was room for criticism "when we touch on the national character of *The Countess Cathleen*."[11] He explained that while the impious acts and speeches to which critics had objected might prove allowable in drama under certain circumstances, "these things are fairly objected to when they are ascribed to ... an Irish peasant who is the leading type of Irish peasantry given us in the play."[12] In most nationalist discourses, the Irish peasant was the central locus of Irishness, so much negative criticism focused on the peasants as representative types. The *Daily Express* reviewer chided:

Mr. Yeats ... does not know the Irish peasant and what he believes and feels, and the Irish peasantry in this play are, and always were, totally incapable of the acts and sayings attributed to them.[13]

The protest signed by students at the Royal University (the young James Joyce refused to sign) denounced the play because it "offers as a type of our people a loathsome brood of apostates."[14]

While everyone agreed that the play was or should be national, there was little concensus about what that meant, and one source of tension in the play was that it actually drew on several conflicting nationalist discourses at the same time: Anglo-Irish Celticism, Young Ireland's romantic nationalism, and a more popular, Catholic nationalism. This conflict produced a series of disjunctions between the play's Celticist politics and its popular nationalist thematics. The play is set in "famine-struck" (*VPI*, 5) Ireland, and Yeats chose themes that were prevalent in the literature of Young Ireland and had enormous resonance for Irish audiences: landlords and tenants, sacrifice, and spiritual betrayal for material gain. These elements invoked the kind of Irish nationalism that was associated with the land war and militated against the harmonious and complementary relationship between landlord and tenant that Yeats's Celticist version of nationality demanded. Throughout the nineteenth century, sympathetic unionists had advocated such a benign partnership between noble and peasant. Yeats's play was unusual (one could substitute incoherent or contradictory) in that it drew so resolutely on nationalist traditions that were anti-Ascendancy in order to promote Ascendancy interests. It used a famine setting and nationalist thematics usually associated with criticism of the grim social reality created by the exploitative tenantry system as the setting for the play's central affirmation of an idealized version of that very system, presided over and represented by Cathleen.

The play's representation of Cathleen appropriated nationalist narratives about spiritual betrayal for material gain – selling souls for gold – and restructured them. Much of the controversy over the play involved the representations of characters selling their souls. Such representations could certainly be read as affronts to Irish Catholic doctrines and sensibilities (Grattan Freyer points out that the story did not offend French Catholics, and that "in France the story was apparently regarded as an improving one for Lent"[15]). However, to make sense of the specifics and intensity of a reaction that now tends to generate bemusement among critics,[16] we must note the importance of souls and their sale in nationalist discourses as well as theological ones. Although the original tale on which Yeats based the play was not Irish, the political theme of souls for gold was a well-established one in Irish literature, dating back at least to the eighteenth century and continuing through the poems of Young Ireland and into turn of the century nationalist literature. It was intimately connected with the history and mythology of souperism, a term invoking the alleged proselytizing activities of Protestants who ran soup kitchens in times of famine; peasants who converted in exchange for material gain or mere sustenance were labelled soupers. In the *Spirit of the Nation* volumes, selling one's soul for gold meant selling it to the English by working for the government or in the army, or by converting to Protestantism, in exchange for material prosperity, the notorious "Saxon shilling." As one poem put it: "All slaves and starvelings who are willing / To sell yourselves to shame and death – / Accept the fatal Saxon shilling."[17] Such a sale constituted a simultaneous betrayal of self and country, and many authors emphasized the national betrayal over the personal, as in "Go! Traitor and cow'rd, in our deadliest danger, / Sell country and soul to the Saxon for gold."[18] Here the syntax indicates that the more important crime is the collective one. Other poems used souls for gold as a figure for Irish complicity in colonization, in particular for the Act of Union, to which the Irish parliament had agreed:

> How did they pass the Union?
> By perjury and fraud,
> By slave who sold for place or gold
> Their country and their God ...[19]

Padraic Colum wrote an anti-recruiting play in 1902 entitled *The Saxon Shillin'*, which won the first prize in a one-act play contest sponsored by Cumann na Gaedheal and was accepted for production by the Irish National Theatre Society. Maud Gonne, who praised Colum's play as "good from national point of view" (*GY*, 160), and to whom Yeats dedicated *The Countess Cathleen*, also used this theme in her 1904 play *Dawn*.[20]

In the Young Ireland nationalist tradition, which imagined the individual and the nation as necessarily homologous, this sale always represented self-enslavement and the concomitant betrayal of the national cause. The inner essence represented by the soul was national as well as theological: that precious portion of the individual that participated in the national being. Over and over again in nationalist discourses, what is most interior to the individual, the soul, also represents the individual's exterior relation to the national community, so that to sell one's soul was also to sell one's country. Yeats's representation of the misguided, materialistic peasants who sell their souls accorded with this formulation, but provoked nationalist fury because Irish peasants on stage were generally understood to be representative Irish peasants.

On the other hand, *The Countess Cathleen* offers the sale of Cathleen's soul as something quite different – self-sacrifice in the service of the national cause. It presents an alternative version of Irish nationality, one that was Celticist in its equation of true nationality with feminine self-sacrifice, heroic failure, and spiritual victory through material defeat. In the discourse of Anglo-Irish Celticism, the soul of the Celt and the Irish nation was constituted by an absence whose metonyms included colonial status, poverty, femininity, and practical failure. The very act which in nationalist discourses would represent Cathleen's betrayal of her country represents instead her decision to take up the national cause and sacrifice herself for it. This conception of the national import of souls and sacrifices became increasingly prevalent as the revival progressed, appearing in Yeats's later works and the writings of patriots like Pearse.

The play does more than construct an Ascendancy nationalism in a context that invokes the logic of a competing nationalism. The text dramatizes a struggle between this Celticist construction of Irish national identity, which suppresses class conflict between Irish landlords and peasants and promotes the continued dominance of the Anglo-Irish, and a more popular peasant nationalism which excludes the Anglo-Irish and demands a class struggle against them. As Yeats revised, the quarrel between Shemus and Mary in the opening scene became more and more closely allied with this conflict. Mary Rua's attitude towards Cathleen is that of a humble peasant who knows and accepts her place in the social hierarchy and whose respect for nobility parallels her reverence for God and her support for the community's traditions. Her husband Shemus represents the grasping, petit-bourgeois materialist who resents his betters and is willing to sell his soul, his national traditions, and his intended place in the social hierarchy for material gain.

This is particularly true of versions after the 1912 revisions. The dialogue between husband and wife and their subsequent behavior towards Cathleen upon her entrance outline class relations under each position and place each one in a particular relation to Irish national identity. Shemus criticizes the rich for their indifference to the plight of the poor ("My curse upon the rich!" [*VPI*, 15]), while Mary counters by asserting that their superior economic status necessarily breeds contempt for those less fortunate:

> God's pity on the rich!
> Had we been through as many doors, and seen
> The dishes standing on the polished wood
> In the wax candle light, we'd be as hard,
> And there's the needle's eye at the end of all.   (*VPI*, 15)

The contrast between "My curse" and "God's pity" indicates which view the play endorses as part of a divinely sanctioned order. As Cathleen approaches, Mary wants to prepare by straightening up the house, while Shemus plans to "call up a whey face and a whining voice" (*VPI*, 15) to plead for money. When Shemus interrupts Mary's welcoming speech to beg, he alerts Cathleen that the stable feudal relationship suggested by Mary's words is threatened, and Cathleen comments, "So you are starving even in this wood, / Where I thought I would find nothing changed" (*VPI*, 19).

The text represents Shemus's conflictual attitude towards the rich as part of an emergent bourgeois culture which is materially successful but spiritually impoverished and whose dangers, vulgarities and limitations Yeats would describe with increasing frequency and hostility in the years to come. Shemus's invocation to the devils is a rejection of both human and divine morality. Above all, from the very first drafts, it represents a capitulation to sheer materialism (*VPI*, 16). He invites to his house any creature, no matter how inhuman or unholy, "So that they brought us money," as Teigue says (*VPI*, 10). The text represents the devils as merchants who "travel for the Master of all merchants" (*VPI*, 12). The play also participates in Celticism's rejection, not just of materialism, but of the material as such in favor of the spiritual or ideal. The merchants' very material substantiality is part of what makes them sinister. As one of the merchants notes, "there is nothing on the ridge of the world / That's more substantial than the merchants are / That buy and sell you" (*VPI*, 13). Similarly, Teigue decides to barter his soul on the grounds of its insubstantiality: "I'll barter mine. / Why should we starve for what may be but nothing?" (*VPI*, 14), and he later speculates, "And maybe there's no soul at all" (*VPI*, 22). The exchange of souls for gold means the rejection of the ideal and immaterial and therefore of Celticism's version of nationality.

As James Flannery and other critics have noted, the text also allies the merchants, and all who collaborate with them, with British imperialism.[21] Though Yeats specifies that the devils are dressed as "eastern merchants," no one reading or watching the play could have failed to make the equation between England and materialism that was prevalent in Ireland at the time. England is, after all, east of Ireland, a geographical fact whose symbolic resonance Joyce exploited in *Dubliners*. The merchants are foreign conquerors who travel through the land, posing as saviors but offering damnation instead through the materialism associated with anglicization. As a result of the way in which the text manipulates the opposition between materialism and idealism, gold and souls, Shemus's hostility towards Cathleen in the first scene appears as a species of bourgeois English materialism, closely allied with English imperialism, and foreshadows his complicity with the merchants. Shemus's set of values revolving around merchandise, class struggle, imperial domination and spiritual betrayal threatens to supersede an older order, associated with Mary and Cathleen, which the text constructs as more Irish and more worthwhile, and which promotes harmony between peasant and noble.[22]

For Mary, Home Rule will mean the chance to occupy the place intended for her in a social order exemplified and dominated by Cathleen, who represents the ideal of a benevolent aristocracy, and whose status is ostensibly based less on material superiority than on a custodial relation to tradition. The purpose of Mary's conversation with Cathleen in this scene is to present the particular unequal social and economic relationship between Mary and Cathleen as a constitutive part of Irish national identity. The text accomplishes this by placing her in opposition to Shemus and by emphasizing the ancient origin and historical continuity of that relationship. As Standish O'Grady observed (apparently with no conscious irony) in one of the epigraphs to this chapter, "Tradition and custom, not philosophy, are the chief defenses of property."[23] Yeats originally conceived Shemus Rua as the innkeeper of an inn called The Lady's Head after the countess. In an early prose draft of the play, Shemus says that his inn is "The Lady's Head, called this to honour her ladyship, the Countess Kathleen O'Shea. We and all men hereabouts belong to her and were her father's men before."[24] Cathleen's proprietary relationship with her tenants has the support of tradition, and so is honored by them; she is the emblem of their means of livelihood and their patron. This gives the social order the status of a cultural artifact, a tradition to be preserved along with other traditions of the Irish peasantry.

Subsequent versions retain this characterization of Cathleen, but they make an increasingly clear distinction between Mary, who supports her, and Shemus, who opposes her. In the 1892 text Shemus merely relates that the inn is " 'The Lady's Head,' / Called from the Countess Kathleen" (*VPI*, 22). In the 1895 version, Yeats further sharpened the contrast between Mary's Irish traditionalism and Shemus's anglicized contempt for the traditional, omitting Shemus's speech about the name of the inn and his role as innkeeper, and contrasting Shemus's obsequious begging with Mary's simple offer of hospitality. In later versions, Mary welcomes Cathleen to her house on the basis of a long tradition of service:

> ... sit down and rest yourself awhile,
> For my old fathers served your fathers, lady,
> Longer than books can tell – and it were strange
> If you and yours should not be welcome here.   (*VPI*, 19)

This cultural tradition is truly originary; "Longer than books can tell" suggests that it dates back to oral peasant culture, which Irish cultural nationalism privileged as the source of the purest Celtic culture. It also suggests an origin of a more absolute nature, one whose unique status as the source of all subsequent culture means that no secondary cultural inscription can adequately capture it. Since, by the end of the nineteenth century, virtually every variety of Irish nationalism was a form of cultural nationalism, and usually characterized the expression of authentic national culture as a return to an originary, pre-colonial Irishness and as the recovery of buried continuities between pre-colonial purity and the present, Mary's respect for tradition casts her position as the only viable expression of nationality available.

The contrast between Shemus and Mary in their relation to Cathleen (and therefore to genuine Irish national identity) is closely associated with another contrast, which pits Mary's respect for various Irish traditions, both pagan and Christian, against Shemus's rejection or violation of them. In the 1892 version, Mary warns Shemus not to burn a branch of quicken wood, which in Irish folklore is "[a] spell to ward off demons and ill fairies" (*VPI*, 20), and laments that they have "no milk to leave o'nights / To keep our own good people kind to us" (*VPI*, 20). Shemus, on the other hand, asserts that he's not afraid of spirits and casts the quicken branch into the fire at the urging of the merchants (*VPI*, 26). The 1895 version supplements the conflict over folkloric belief with a more explicit disagreement over Christian belief. In this text, Mary prays to a shrine of the Virgin (*VPI*, 7) while Shemus kicks it to pieces (*VPI*, 31), an act that drew heavy criticism from the play's contemporary detractors. The text does not acknowledge the obvious contradictions between Christian and pagan belief, though its early readers were quick to do so; what is important about all Mary's pieties – her belief in Cathleen's rightful superiority, in Irish folk wisdom, and in Catholic doctrine – is that the play casts them as traditional Irish beliefs, the basis for a national culture, and as opposed to English materialism and imperialism.

Although the play scorns Shemus's point of view and aligns it with English imperial culture, it also contains the fragments of a counter-narrative that legitimizes Shemus's claims. The conversation between Mary, Shemus, and Cathleen in the opening scene is framed by and shot through with images of violence, change, and fear. The social and cosmic orders have been disturbed; sinister supernatural beings and distorted, half-human creatures have been seen, and, as Teigue observes, "the whole land squeal[s] like a rabbit under a weasel's tooth" (*VPI*, 9). Mary suspects evil omens and fears accidents. The poor turn on one another; Shemus has been driven from the crossroads by the other beggars, who "would not have another share their alms, / And hunted me away with sticks and stones" (*VPI*, 11). Shemus recounts other horrors he has seen while out foraging, "There were five doors that I looked through this day / And saw the dead and not a soul to wake them" (*VPI*, 13). In this scene, the text vacillates between presenting a threatened feudal order (which Mary and Cathleen want to preserve) and suggesting the oppressiveness of that order (which Shemus criticizes). The potential conflict between prosperous landlord and starving tenant is hinted at in the 1895 version by Cathleen's unprovoked plea, "Do not blame me, / Good woman, for the tympan and the harp" (*VPI*, 21) and made explicit in subsequent revisions by Shemus's bitter reaction to Aleel "mocking us with music" (*VPI*, 13) to soothe Cathleen's sensitive nerves and spirits. Cathleen explains, "The doctors bid me fly the unlucky times / And find distraction for my thoughts, or else / Pine to my grave" (*VPI*, 21). Cathleen is no doubt the only person in the vicinity in danger of pining to her grave; as Shemus reports, the peasants face death by starvation in their cottages. Aleel's defiant song and insulting gesture (he snaps his fingers in Shemus' face) indicate his superior position as Cathleen's retainer and threaten Shemus with physical violence:

> Were I but crazy for love's sake
> I know who'd measure out his length,
> I know the heads that I should break,
> For crazy men have double strength.   (*VPI*, 23)

Shemus' bitter comment, "Why should the like of us complain?" (*VPI*, 23) makes the divide between powerful landlord and powerless peasant clear.

The second scene also suggests the possibilities for conflict created by this divide. In the 1892 and 1895 versions Cathleen's gardener reports that "a crowd of ugly lean-faced rogues" (*VPI*, 48) have scaled her garden wall, eaten all the apples, trampled and broken the vegetable garden and orchard, and murdered the gardener's dog (*VPI*, 48–50). The whole incident, and the death of the dog in particular, recalls nineteenth-century descriptions of the "outrages" committed in times of rural unrest, many of which involved maiming or killing livestock. The herdsman also reports that his sheep have been stolen by hungry peasants (*VPI*, 56). The later version of the play retains these incidents, but makes them less brutal, dropping references to the dog, and emphasizing Cathleen's forgiving response that "starving men may take what's necessary, / And yet be sinless" (*VPI*, 69). By presenting themes and incidents that evoke the land war, the play repeatedly raises the possibility that peasants like the Rua family do have grounds for complaint against their landlord Cathleen, a possibility that is consistently defeated, but not expunged.

After Cathleen's departure in the opening scene, the disagreement between Shemus and Mary escalates into a quarrel in which Shemus strikes his wife "to show who's master" (*VPI*, 29). Shemus's characterization of the quarrel, which culminates in his invitation to the devils, represents it as a power struggle between husband and wife over domestic authority:

> There had been words between my wife and me
> Because I said I would be master here,
> And ask in what I pleased or who I pleased.   (*VPI*, 35–7)

As their previous behavior has shown, however, neither Shemus nor Mary is master in their house. Both Mary's invocation of a tradition of service and the mask of servility Shemus assumes to beg indicate the material truth that the master is the landlord Cathleen. The domestic violence that follows is a displacement of the violence inherent in the relationship between landlord and tenant and suggested by Aleel, and its function is to transform potentially divisive class conflict into colonial conflict, preserving the alliance between peasant and noble demanded by Celtic nationalism. Having cast Shemus as a bourgeois, anglicized villain complicit with British imperialism and materialism, the text represents Shemus' abuse of Mary and his assertion of a traditional domestic hierarchy of husband over wife as the suppression of Celtic and Catholic idealism and faith, with Mary as suffering and martyred Erin. The play links Mary and Cathleen as supporters of Irish traditional culture, insulted and abused by vulgar English materialism and brutality.

Yeats's text emphasizes the harshness of Irish rural life in famine times, hints at the obvious tenant-landlord conflict that such a subject suggests, but ultimately focuses on another villain, English materialism. As Adrian Frazier observes, "A social contradiction (harmony of aristocracy and peasantry in time of scarcity) is turned into an imaginary unity by means of gathering the potentially opposed classes together against an external enemy: under the leadership of the Protestants, Ireland will be saved from England."[25] The substitution of Celtic nationalism for peasant nationalism, a substitution which the play gestures at repeatedly but never makes completely, finds its vehicle and correlative in another substitution: class conflict is displaced by gender conflict, evoking the long tradition of sexual metaphors for relations between Ireland and England and offering a disrupted family structure as a model for Ireland under British rule. Cathleen functions as the idea of the nation; their relation to her determines the peasants' relations with each other and their inclusion in either the traditionalist or the materialist communities. Those who support Cathleen adopt a stance which focuses the conflict in the play on the clash between (masculine) commercial English vulgarity and (feminine) spiritual Irish purity, suppressing the class differences within Ireland whose eruption would threaten Celticism's nationalism. While the text ambivalently posits two sources for threats to the integrity of Irish character – English commercialism or Anglo-Irish domination – the figure of Cathleen ensures the primacy of the England/Ireland conflict by erasing class divisions within Ireland. As the herdsman in the 1892 and 1895 versions of the play phrases it, "When gazing on your face the poorest, Lady, / Forget their poverty; the rich their care" (*VPl*, 58, 65).

As her name suggests, the text places Cathleen in a well-established and much discussed Irish nationalist tradition that represented Ireland as a woman in distress.[26] Cathleen embodies the idea of the nation: an idealized set of beauties and virtues, a continuous link to a pure and originary past which awaits revelation in the present, that which must be protected and venerated at all costs. She also embodies the ideal of self-sacrifice in the service of that idea, a role played by devoted male followers in most nationalist narratives about such female figures. Cathleen's double representative function sets her apart from other constructions of Ireland as a woman; this doubleness, which includes an emphasis on her self-sacrifice, is structured around the particular needs of Anglo-Irish Celticism.

Many commentators have read the play's emphasis on self-sacrifice as an expression of Yeats's feelings about Maud Gonne's political commitments. Yeats himself encouraged the notion that Cathleen was modelled on Gonne, and he certainly wrote the play with her very much in mind. His memoirs recall:

I told her after meeting her in London I had come to understand the tale of a woman selling her soul to buy food for a starving people as a symbol of all souls who lose their peace, or their fineness, or any beauty of the spirit in political service, but chiefly of her soul that had seemed so incapable of rest. (*Mem*, 47)

Similarly, Yeats's explanatory letter to the *Morning Leader* in 1899 read: "The Countess herself is a soul which is always, in all laborious and self-denying persons, selling itself into captivity and unrest that it may redeem 'God's children,' and finding the peace it has not sought because all high motives are the substance of peace" (*L*, 319). In citing Gonne as his inspiration for the play, Yeats repeatedly emphasized self-sacrifice as the quality which she and Cathleen shared.[27] But as several critics have pointed out, Cathleen resembles neither Gonne's own characterization of her activities nor Yeats's other characterizations of Gonne as enslaved by hate and fanaticism.[28] For example, Cassandra Laity remarks that "Yeats's tearful Countess failed to convey 'her soul that had seemed so incapable of rest,'" and claims that Yeats was "unable or unwilling to characterize the vehemence of Gonne's dedication to politics."[29] Recognizing the inconsistencies in Yeats's claim that Cathleen was modelled on Gonne is important, but not (as Laity claims) because it allows us to see in Cathleen's character Yeats's failure to represent Gonne accurately. Rather, it enables us to read the figure of Cathleen as a product of Yeats's engagement with the structure of Anglo-Irish Celticism, which demanded a feminized heroics of failure and self-sacrifice.

Cathleen's self-sacrifice and material erasure specify her femininity as the version demanded by the discourse of Celticism. In contrast to many other Cathleen figures of the revival, including Yeats's own Cathleen ni Houlihan, this Cathleen does not demand that her followers rescue her by sacrificing themselves. Instead, she sacrifices herself for them and then is rescued by God. Cathleen's sacrifice involves complete self-effacement; she renounces her wealth, her love for Aleel, and, finally, her soul. She renounces not only the notion of owning anything, but also the possibility of having any emotions whose meaning is interior to herself, of interiority as such. All versions after 1892 contain assertions like "From this day for ever / I'll have no joy or sorrow of my own" (*VPI*, 77), and "From this day out I have nothing of my own" (*VPI*, 79). Other statements such as "I will pay all" (*VPI*, 68, 73) and "sell all I have" (*VPI*, 70, 75) also suggest the absolute nature of Cathleen's commitment and sacrifice. The more Cathleen erases herself from the material world of the text, the more potent she becomes as a symbol of the spiritual victory, through earthly sacrifice and defeat, of Celtic virtue. In addition, the play's deus ex machina ending suggests that Cathleen's victory occurs on a supra-worldly level, and compensates for, but does not erase, her worldly death. As in the discourse of Celticism, material failure produces spiritual triumph. The play's representation of Cathleen's sacrifice as the ultimate act of selfless devotion contradicts the souls for gold tradition in patriotic Irish literature, in which the "soul" constituted an inner essence that was allied with the essence of nationality. But it accorded with the discourse of Anglo-Irish Celticism, which imagined material poverty and failure as the necessary ground for spiritual triumph and constructed an ability to break the boundaries of the self as a crucial, but problematic, element of feminine/Celtic nature.

Accordingly, reviewers who liked the play appealed to the discourse of Celticism to describe its virtues and read it as illustrative of the combination of femininity and heroic failure that distinguished the Celtic spirit. Such assessments emphasized the feminine virtues of the Irish; sympathy, charity, self-sacrifice; and focused on the figure of Cathleen herself as the Celtic center of the play. She was Fair Erin incarnate. In his introduction to the work, Lionel Johnson said that Cathleen "makes, like Iphigenia, but in a loftier way, the sacrifice of herself," and displays "a divine excess of charity."[30] In 1904, Horatio Krans wrote a book on the Irish literary revival and Yeats's role in it for the English Contemporary Men of Letters series. He found feminine Celtic traits to be the key to the play's Irishness as well as to its power and general literary merit. No play in Ireland, claimed Krans, had ever been "so inspired with the spirit of the race and so subtly and beautifully steeped in national dyes."[31] He praised *The Countess Cathleen* as "unmistakably Irish in setting, in subject, in characterization, in sentiment, style, and literary allusion,"[32] and his assessment of the play's power and Irishness hinged on Cathleen's sacrifice:

the personages, like everything else in it, are distinctively national; – Cathleen herself by virtue of that active sympathy for suffering, her ruling passion, out of which grows the self-sacrifice that is the master-motive of the play. This touching spirit of true charity she inherits from that company of noble Irishwomen who in famine times have sold their goods and served the poor ...[33]

Krans found this "spirit of charity" to be "one of the most distinctive of Irish characteristics."[34] Renan had said that "Sympathy ... is one of the deepest feelings among the Celtic peoples,"[35] and Yeats described the countess as "intoxicated with compassion" (*UPII*, 297).

Capacity for suffering and sympathy for the suffering of others had long been a part of the discourse of Celticism, as had what Yeats called "a barbarous gift of self-sacrifice" (*EI*, 248). For these critics, the play's national character was equivalent to Cathleen's feminine virtues.

Besides establishing her as a Celtic opponent of English materialism and providing a series of sacrifices within which to read the sacrifice of her soul, Cathleen's emptying out has an additional significance: it opens the way to an analysis of her allegorical status as an image of the nation. She embodies the idea of the nation, but the play reveals that the "nation" is a category that is universally meaningful but empty of stable content. She becomes, as she says, an "empty pitcher" (*VPI*, 89) whose essence lies in her lack of essence and her status as a potential receptacle for various essences or meanings. Many commentators have expressed surprise and disapproval that the play does very little to represent Cathleen's inner conflict over her decision to sell her soul.[36] It is certainly true that, on the level of character, Cathleen's choice appears as always already made. But this is because Cathleen has nothing that is properly interior to her; the conventional language of character is not appropriate to explain her significance in the text. Her meaning lies not in her inner conflict, but in the fact that she is at the center of the conflicts the play does present – materialism versus idealism, class war versus class harmony, peasant nationalism versus Celtic nationalism. Questions such as whether Cathleen is a benevolent aristocrat or an oppressive landlord, whether she will sell her soul or keep it, whether she will abandon the contemporary social and political world or engage with it, are, in the absence of anything like a visible decision-making process on her part, questions of essence. They are questions less about what she will do than about what she is, and the definition of the national essence or being is precisely what is at stake in the play.

After Cathleen's death, a series of characters make elegiac statements about her: Aleel, Oona, and some generically labelled peasants. The peasants lament her beauty and the feelings Cathleen roused in them:

> A Peasant. She was the great white lily of the world.
> Another Peasant. She was more beautiful than the pale stars.
> An old Peasant Woman. The little plant I loved is broken in two.
>
> (*VPI*, 48)

Aleel calls for the apocalyptic end of all things, and Oona expresses a wish to "die and to go her I love" (*VPI*, 169). No one in this final scene speaks Cathleen's name. This further individualizes and disperses her meaning/essence. There is no Cathleen, on both the literal and symbolic levels, only the multiple and varied meanings she has for the individual speakers. Phrases like "she" and "her I love" suggest both identity and anonymity, a particular woman and an abstract generalization. In other words, they suggest Cathleen's role as image of the nation, a category to which everyone in the play has a definite relation, but to which no two characters have the same relation. By privileging Cathleen as the saintly heroine who allegorically represents the nation and simultaneously emphasizing her "emptiness," the play both claims originary status for its version of nationality and enacts the emergence of that claim out of multiple possibilities and competing conceptions of national character.

The other major aspect of Celticism's construction of Cathleen's identity as "woman" is that this identity belongs to a particular social and economic class. While her name claims her status as an embodiment of a transcendental, essential Irishness whose political institutionalization is the goal of the national movement, her title, countess, gives her a class specificity which suggests Anglo-Irish Celticism's preoccupation with forging an harmonious alliance between peasants and aristocrats. The text repeatedly points to and shores up her economic and political domination of the peasants. While the differential valuation and purchase of souls is the devil's work, the text upholds the principle of a social hierarchy that is linked to and sanctioned by a metaphysical hierarchy. In direct contradiction to all versions of Christian doctrine, everyone in the play except Cathleen believes her soul to be worth more than the souls of the starving peasants. The merchants know that only her soul is worth the price she asks, and several peasants offer themselves instead. One pleads, "Do not, do not, for souls the like of ours / Are not precious to God as your soul is. / O what would Heaven do without you, lady?" (*VPI*, 149–51). Another peasant cries, "O Queen of Heaven, and all you blessed saints, / Let us and ours be lost so she be shriven" (*VPI*, 161–3). Oona offers her own soul instead, and laments, "O that so many pitchers of rough clay / Should prosper and the porcelain break in two!" (*VPI*, 159). Cathleen alone asserts the priceless uniqueness of each soul:

> There is no soul
> But it's unlike all others in the world,
> Nor one but lifts a strangeness to God's love
> Till that's grown infinite, and therefore none
> Whose loss were less than irremediable
> Although it were the wickedest in the world. (*VPI*, 69–71)

Cathleen embodies a truth this speech contradicts: within the play's economy, her soul is in fact worth more than others.

At the end of the play, Cathleen ascends to heaven, while the peasants kneel upon the ground, a closing image that embodies the play's combination of national unity and class hierarchy. On one hand, as James Flannery has observed, the play's ending suggests a nation unified by the common worship of the national symbol, Cathleen; "Ireland – symbolized by the kneeling peasants with Aleel among them – is mystically transformed into the perfect nation of Yeats's dreams: a community of people sharing the one religious, cultural, and aesthetic ideal."[37] On the other hand, the scene offers an exaggerated version of the initial contrast between revered landlord and humble peasant. From the 1912 revisions onwards, the last line of the text emphasizes the renewed subjugation of the peasants to a now angelic Cathleen and the social order she represents: "The vision melts away, and the forms of the kneeling Peasants appear faintly in the darkness" (*VPI*, 169).

Cathleen's journey down among "unnumbered hovels" (*VPI*, 125) and subsequent ascension to heaven illustrate Celticism's efforts to establish a double-edged relationship between Anglo-Irish and peasant, one which is both an egalitarian national unity and a class hierarchy. The play constructs its version of Irish nationality, which involves erasing class conflict between peasant and noble, by manipulating a series of other oppositions: gold and souls, materialism and idealism, English and Irish, masculine and feminine. Cathleen's feminine virtues, all of which helped constitute Celticism's definition of Irishness: charity, idealism, Christian egalitarianism, and, most important, self-sacrifice, efface her economic dominance over the peasants and substitute her selfless national unity with them. But the text reinscribes Cathleen's superior status in the suggestions of class conflict, the last scene, the excessive value of her soul, and Aleel's extravagant assessment of her worth. These two narratives conflict, but both are proper to Anglo-Irish Celticism. Indeed, Celticism's claims to being a national discourse depended on maintaining this contradiction.

Yeats's Celticism rested on a similar contradiction in relation to the production of national culture. After the opening scene, Shemus and Teigue go into business like any other bourgeois father–son team, Mary starves to death, her soul pure, events bring Cathleen closer and closer to her final fateful act, and a good deal of the action revolves around the apparently extraneous Aleel. Yeats added the poet figure who eventually became Aleel after a two-year hiatus in his work on the play, during which time he gave most of his energies to editing his edition of Blake with Edwin Ellis, and almost immediately after Maud Gonne refused his first proposal of marriage.[38] The most striking feature of Yeats's revisions of the play over the years is the progressive enlargement of Aleel's role, until he appears in every scene of the final version. Critics have generally seen Aleel as significant in two respects. They assume that Aleel represents Yeats to Cathleen's Gonne,[39] which is arguably true without being particularly revealing, and they cast Aleel as the representative of the world of dreams, art and love which is opposed to the world of politics, responsibility and self-sacrifice that Cathleen chooses.[40]

On the contrary, in the context of the play as part of Yeats's troubled engagement with the discourse of Celticism, Aleel represents the utter interdependence of "art" and "politics." This interdependence is played out in accordance with the discourse of Celticism, as the text aligns Aleel repeatedly with two things that Celticism imagined as interdependent: a strong national culture, in which all members of the nation participate, and continued Ascendancy hegemony, symbolized by Cathleen's place at the pinnacle of earthly and heavenly hierarchies. In relation to Cathleen's choice, Aleel represents, not art as opposed to politics, but a particular Celticist version of national art that demands a particular political organization, the benevolent tyranny of noble over peasant. As Yeats acknowledged in his memoirs: "The fascination of the national movement for me in my youth was, I think, that it seemed to be an image of a social ideal which could give fine life and fine art authority" (*Mem*, 180).

Aleel's significance lies not simply in his status as an artist, but in his status as a national artist whose art depends upon and articulates Irish peasant culture. From the earliest versions of the play onward, Aleel's identity as an artist derives from his intimate

connections with the world of Irish myth and legend. He distracts
Cathleen from her sorrows by telling her stories about Queen
Maeve (*VPI*, 55), and sings songs about the fairies. Aleel has the
kind of immediate and semi-mystical relation to the ancient essence
of the Celt that Yeats ascribed to writers like Ferguson and
Macleod; he even converses directly with the spirit world of the old
Celtic gods, who urge Cathleen, through Aleel, to abandon her
peasants and live in the hills until the famine is over. In intermediate versions, Mary refers to Aleel as one "who has talked with
the great Sidhe" (*VPI*, 29). Aleel's importance in the play grew as
Yeats began to elaborate a distinction between Celts, who were
"that imperfection whose perfection is genius," and artists, inspired
by and devoted to Celtic culture, who were capable of perfection.
In chapter 1 I argued that this distinction represented Yeats's
refiguration of Arnold's complementary relationship between Saxon
and Celt and that its aesthetic judgments revealed themselves as
political imperatives. Similarly, Aleel's role as guardian and articu-
lator of the world of Irish folklore and peasant culture involves a
rejection of the material interests of the peasants themselves. He
urges Cathleen to "leave all things to the Builder of the Heavens"
(*VPI*, 151). In earlier versions, Yeats was more explicit about exactly
who Cathleen would be abandoning: "Leave the peasants to the
builder of the heavens" (*VPI*, 151). According to Aleel, in order for
Cathleen to embrace the world of folklore and peasant culture she
must abandon the peasants who ostensibly produced it.

The contrast between Aleel and Cathleen helped lay the foundations for a major part of Yeats's later philosophical system. It is a
contrast between poetic and religious genius, artist and saint, a
contrast between hierarchical and democratic politics. In Yeats's
autobiography, George Russell exemplifies religious genius:

to the religious genius all souls are of equal value: the queen is not more
than an old apple-woman. His poetical genius does not affect his mind as a
whole, and probably he puts aside as unworthy every suggestion of his
poetical genius which would separate man from man. The most fundamental of divisions is that between the intellect, which can only do its work
by saying continually "thou fool," and the religious genius which makes all
equal. (*AY*, 315)[41]

Cathleen, who asserts the radical equality of souls, is a religious
genius; Aleel, who claims Cathleen's queenly superiority over the
peasants, a poetic one. Or, to use the terms Yeats would adopt later

in *A Vision*, Cathleen's character is primary, Aleel's antithetical. The religious genius envisions a democratic society and spiritual equality, and the poetic genius "separates man from man" to create hierarchies. "Russell," wrote Yeats to Katharine Tynan in 1906, "cannot bear anything that sets one man above another" (L, 477). Yeats preferred the poetic genius, writing to Russell in the same year, "you have the religious genius to which all souls are equal. In all work except salvation that spirit is a hindrance" (*L*, 466).

Many varieties of Irish nationalism imagined their work as the work of salvation. Cultural nationalism demanded that each individual member of the nation manifest his or her nationality, not merely or even primarily in terms of practical choices or political opinions, but as an essential fact of being. The nationalist literary traditions which represented the sale of a soul as the betrayal of the nation constructed the "soul" as the very core and essence of an identity that was, above all, a national identity. The soul was the nation manifested within the individual self. The very idea of the nation, as it was imagined by the period's cultural nationalisms, demanded homogeneity among its members and equality in their access to and representativeness of the national being. The national ideal suppresses class differences by invoking shared nationality and obliterates historical change by making visible the continuity of the national essence from past to present. The boundaries of individual selves become permeable and irrelevant; they are boundaries separating essences that are identical to one another and to the larger entity (the national being/God) of which they are a part. This construction coincides with the Christian doctrine of the radical equality of all souls, a doctrine that Cathleen upholds rhetorically while embodying its opposite. In other words, Cathleen's status as a "religious genius" coincides with her role as the embodiment of both the essence and the invention of the nation.

Cathleen's transcendental status as the spirit of the nation, her "religious genius," conflicts with the social and economic station denoted by her title. As Yeats's comments on George Russell and the character of Aleel both suggest, it also conflicts with the production of culture, which provided cultural nationalism with its foundation and which was, according to Yeats, only possible in the context of social hierarchies like the one that ensures Cathleen's superiority. Thus Cathleen's religious genius is in direct contrast to the possibilities of embracing Irish culture. Cathleen does give up the dreamy world of Irish folklore and myth in order to engage with the responsibilities of contemporary social and political issues. But the national position she takes up – defender of Irish traditions and Irish peasants – belongs to a cultural nationalism which in turn claimed its origins in the very world of Irish folklore that she renounces. We might say, then, that while the nationality of Yeats's Celticist cultural nationalism demanded religious genius and democratic politics, the culture of his Celticist cultural nationalism demanded poetic genius and authoritarian politics. If the play does indeed enact a conflict between dreams and responsibilities, it also illustrates the necessary interdependence that Yeats would articulate between them with increasing frequency, most famously in the epigraph to *Responsibilities*: "in dreams begins responsibility" (*VP*, 269).

In *The Countess Cathleen*, the nation is embodied in the figure of a woman. Which is to say that Cathleen embodies the series of conflicts and contradictions that constituted Anglo-Irish Celticism's version of Irish nationality. Cathleen is a complex national allegory that points in a number of conflicting directions. Her identity is made up of various elements: her feminine virtues, such as self-sacrifice, charity, sympathy and piety, the social and political power denoted by her title, her relation to other characters – Mary, Shemus, Aleel, and the other peasants, and her position vis-a-vis the various binaries that structure the play. Each of these elements creates different structures and possibilities for her role as representative of the nation. Cathleen and the Celticist conceptions of gender and class that organize her character embody a neo-imperialist Anglo-Irish nationality that suppresses conflict between peasant and aristocrat and focuses on gendered colonial conflict instead. She embodies both an egalitarian national unity and a social and political hierarchy dominated by the Anglo-Irish. She figures the essence, unity and emotional force of the idea of the nation; she also figures the national as a category that is constitutively empty and whose content therefore varies widely and must be constantly re-invented and contested. Cathleen allegorizes a particular interested definition of Irishness. At the same time, she also allegorizes that definition's secret lack of identity with itself. Analyzing such female figures as complex national allegories reveals the power struggles, contradictions and ambivalences beneath an apparently unified national tradition.

CHAPTER 3

When the mob becomes a people: nationalism and occult theatre

A nation should be like an audience in some great theatre – "In the theatre," said Victor Hugo, "the mob becomes a people".

(*VP*, 836)

Superstition is knowledge, because it sees together the ciphers of destruction scattered on the social surface; it is folly, because in all its death-wish it still clings to illusions: expecting from the transfigured shape of society misplaced in the skies an answer that only a study of real society can give.

Theodor Adorno, "Theses Against Occultism"[1]

Yeats was a nationalist who longed for community but hated crowds. In both versions of *A Vision* he described the men of Phase 17, his own phase, as men who dedicate themselves to work in the public sphere but hate precisely the things that make it public:

men of this phase are almost always partisans, propagandists and gregarious; yet because of the *Mask* of simplification, which holds up before them the solitary life of hunters and of fishers and "the groves pale passion loves", they hate parties, crowds, propaganda. (*V*, 143)

Yeats cites Shelley as his major example, but he was equally describing his own conflicted relationship to nationalist political work. Parties, crowds and propaganda are associated with a particular kind of politics that emerged as an increasingly important paradigm of politics in general during the nineteenth century: mass politics. Like the men of Phase 17, Yeats was both fascinated and repelled by crowds. Much of his ambivalence about popular Irish nationalism revolved around the fact that it involved crowds, that it was, inescapably, mass politics. The theoretical and practical structures of Yeats's early Irish theatre embody his conflicted engagement with the idea of national politics as mass politics and his attempts to come to terms with the (potentially) mass character of Irish nationalism in a productive way. These structures were profoundly indebted to one of Yeats's lifelong interests: the occult.

Yeats's gradual rejection of Celticism and the intensification of his interest in the theatre signalled a shift towards a mode of engagement with the question of Irish nationality that emphasized the creation and definition of national community. Of course, national identity and national community are inextricably intertwined, and Yeats never relinquished his efforts to find and define the former, but between about 1899 and 1910, Yeats's Irish theatre represented, in part, an effort to forge and simultaneously theorize about the nation as a collectivity. What kind of collectivity was a nation? What kinds of intersubjective connections among people made them a nation, and how could one foster them?

Yeats first announced the inauguration of the Irish Literary Theatre in January of 1899. One does not have to agree with Conor Cruise O'Brien's negative judgement of Yeats's political "cunning"[2] to see that, especially where the theatre was concerned, Yeats frequently made calculated and relatively skilled interventions into the Irish public sphere, and that he conceived of the theatre as very much a "public" project. He followed the initial announcement with a barrage of essays and activities designed to help publicize it. Two days later he published an essay outlining some of the project's major goals and methods. He addressed the Irish Literary Society in April, wrote "Plans and Methods" for the first issue of *Beltaine* in May, and published "The Irish Literary Theatre" two days before the first performance. Yeats had no illusions about achieving instant popularity; he distinguished his theatre carefully from the commercial theatre and maintained that he and his collaborators had "appealed to the imaginative minority and not to the majority which is content with the theatre of commerce" (*UPII*, 163).[3]

However, these early, self-consciously public statements about the theatre make it clear that Yeats viewed the theatre as a potential means of mobilizing and "nationalizing" the masses, something he recognized any successful nationalism in the age of mass politics must do.[4] The theatre was to foster Unity of Being and Unity of Culture in Ireland.[5] Although he rejected the strands of Irish nationalism that allied themselves explicitly with Catholicism, Yeats recognized that as a means of mobilizing and unifying large numbers of people, nationalism operated much like religion. He observed, "There is no feeling, except religious feeling, which moves masses of men so powerfully as national feeling, and upon this, more widely spread among all classes in Ireland to-day than at any time this century, we build our principal hopes" (*UPII*, 140). In 1891 he was more explicit about the relationship between dramatist and audience in such mobilization, writing in a review of a play by John Todhunter, "Many people have said to me that the surroundings of *Helena* made them feel religious. Once you get your audience in that mood, and you can do anything with them" (*LNI*, 51).

This mobilization was to spread from the original audience, who had been transformed by the dramatist, to the populace at large. In "The Irish Literary Theatre" Yeats speculated hopefully, "It may happen that the imaginative minority will spread their interests among the majority, for even the majority becomes imaginative when touched by enthusiasm" (*UPII*, 163). Yeats's major models for his theatre were Antoine's Theatre Libre in Paris, the Independent Theatre in London, and the Scandinavian theatre.[6] In a lecture on the "Ideal Theatre" Yeats claimed: "The Scandinavian theatre was the nearest approach to an ideal theatre in modern Europe. It was the only theatre whose plays were at once literary and popular" (*UPII*, 155). He measured the Scandinavian theatre's success by the fact that "Heroic ideas and interest in great passions spread abroad among the mass of the people" (*UPII*, 155). In December of 1899, after the first performances of *The Countess Cathleen* and Edward Martyn's *The Heather Field*, Yeats predicted, "their success means, as I think, that the 'Celtic movement,' which has hitherto interested but a few cultivated people, is about to become a part of the thought of Ireland" (*UPII*, 184). Yeats hoped that the limited audiences of "a few cultivated people" would pave the way to a mass audience coincident with the Irish nation; such popular mobilization was the ultimate goal of the Irish theatre as he first conceived it. To create plays that would be both literary and popular would be to bridge what Andreas Huyssen has called the Great Divide between high art and mass culture that informed so much of literary modernism,[7] and would create an alternative mass culture to the commercialized popular theatre Yeats hated. This alternative mass culture would be a truly national culture.

Yeats's Irish theatre was intended, not merely to express the Irish nation, but to help create it, to "give Ireland a hardy and shapely national character" (*EX*, 76). In the theatre Yeats wanted to "recreate the ancient arts ... as they were understood when they moved a whole people" (*EI*, 206), and thereby render the Irish a whole people, a nation. This meant not just creating unity, but a particular kind of unity, and Yeats often compared the kind of national unity he sought to the organic oneness of a single mind. In the project that prefigured the Irish theatre, his efforts to create an Irish nationalist equivalent to the Hermetic Order of the Golden Dawn, he hoped to provide a basis for national collectivity that would help produce "an Irish literature which, though made by many minds, would seem the work of a single mind" (*AY*, 170). In "Magic" (1901) he claimed that the ancient enchanter created or revealed "the supernatural artist or genius, the seeming transitory mind made out of many minds," and continued, "He kept the doors, too, as it seems, of those less transitory minds, the genius of the family, the genius of the tribe ..." (*EI*, 43–44). Even in 1909, when his disillusionment with the theatre was running high, Yeats wrote in his journal,

All creation requires one mind to make and one mind for enjoyment; the theatre can at rare moments create this one mind for an hour or so, but this grows always more difficult. Once created it is like the mind of an individual in solitude, immeasurably bold – all is possible to it. (*Mem*, 215)

Although there were a number of other models of national unity available – the family, an army, a voting public, a brotherhood – Yeats consistently chose the model of a group mind that was comprised of many minds but looked and functioned like a single consciousness. This image emphasized the permeability of individual subjects, unconscious[8] connection rather than conscious choice, and the creation of an organic whole rather than a constructed aggregate or an abstract relation between individuals.

For Yeats, this organic national unity must arise not out of homogeneity or conformity, but out of a paradoxical combination of deep, non-rational, mystical community and flourishing individual creativity and will. This formulation provides a crucially important structure for Yeats's theory of the theatre and its relation to national culture, and it appears in a number of guises.[9] He wrote in 1904 that to "create a great community" (*EX*, 28) would be to return to conditions under which "the finest minds and Ned the beggar and Sean the fool think about the same thing, although they may not think the same thought about it" (*EX*, 28). The Irish theatre and the national community it fostered would be thoroughly national and thoroughly international, as Yeats's injunctions to playwrights to study both the European masters and Irish folk culture indicates. Even though he theorized extensively about the theatre's effect on the reader or spectator, Yeats also liked to distinguish genuine art from nationalist propaganda by insisting that artists must not try to express anything but themselves and their individual visions, and that they must not write with the effect on their audiences in mind.[10] Yeats also observed, "Literature is always personal, always one man's vision of the world, one man's experience, and it can only be popular when men are ready to welcome the visions of others" (*EX*, 115). For the personal vision of literature to move masses of people, the masses must achieve a psychic receptivity that would enable them to embrace the visions of others.

Yeats's earliest attempt to foster an Irish collectivity that would resemble a single mind was a set of occult rituals, devised as part of his ill-fated effort to create the Celtic Mysteries, modelled on the Golden Dawn. Yeats pursued this project off and on between 1895 and 1903, and planned to use an empty castle on an island in Lough Key to create "an Irish Eleusis or Samothrace" (*Mem*, 123). It was partly a way of courting Maud Gonne, who helped Yeats with it for several years, and who remembered the Castle of the Heroes as a place where nationalists "might through lonely meditation on Ireland harmonise their individual effort with national endeavour."[11] The Celtic Mysteries were to form a school in which the artists and intellectual leaders of Ireland could organize a "common symbolism, a common meditation."[12] Yeats and Gonne devised twelve Irish initiation rituals, two sets of six, modelled on the rituals used by the Golden Dawn. They also obtained "in vision" (*Mem*, 125) long lists of symbols related to Irish tradition and myth for use in the Celtic Mysteries.

The line from the Celtic Mysteries to the early Irish theatre runs remarkably straight, as critics have often observed.[13] They were parallel means to similar ends; Yeats wanted to write plays for the theatre which would have a "secret symbolic relationship" (*Mem*, 124) to the Castle of the Heroes. Like the Irish Mysteries, Yeats's Irish theatre relied heavily on ritual and symbol and sought to produce a meditative, visionary experience for the audience. Yeats pursued this effect through a set of now famous theatrical techniques. His theory of the theatre was stridently anti-realist, and he insisted that drama was "essentially conventional, artificial, ceremonious" (*EX*, 172). He wanted his theatre to approach the condition of ritual, emphasizing that "the theatre began in ritual" (*EI*, 170), and claiming that ritual remained "the most powerful form of drama . . . because everyone who hears it is also a player" (*EX*, 129). The acting style Yeats favored, with its slow, formalized gestures and conscious artifice, was designed to bring the stage closer to ritual, as were his largely unsuccessful efforts to get the actors to speak the lines of his own plays in a melodious, chant-like incantation.[14] He chose the names Beltaine and Samhain for the periodical associated with the theatre because they denoted seasonal Irish festivals and he hoped that Irish theatre performances would acquire the status of these annual rituals and become part of a "season of a great racial gathering" (*UPII*, 163).[15] Throughout the 1890s, Yeats's scenery was dominated by patterns intended to parallel rhythm in poetry. After 1902, when he discovered the set designs of Gordon Craig, Yeats moved from explicit ritual and pattern to an emphasis on spatial relations and contrasting color schemes as the better way to achieve the effect he sought. Equally important were symbols that could evoke the desired response in the audience, and Yeats's early symbolism of the theatre had much in common with the French symbolist theatre.[16]

The beginning of Yeats's theatre was marked by a basic conflict: the desire to move "the mass of the people," and the recognition that in their current state the masses were not receptive to the kind of theatre he was creating. The masses needed to be transformed into a nation. For Yeats the theatre was both the agent and the paradigm of this transformation, and the mode of transformation was more magical than evolutionary. As he wrote in an essay on "The Irish Literary Theatre, 1900," "Progress is miracle, and it is sudden, because miracles are the work of an all-powerful energy" (*UPII*, 199). The first epigraph to this chapter is one of Yeats's favorite misquotations about the potential power of the theatre to effect this transformation by creating plays that were at once literary and popular. In the essay that followed his announcement of the Irish theatre, he wrote,

Victor Hugo has said that in the theatre the mob became a people, and, though this could be perfectly true only of ancient times when the theatre was a part of the ceremonial of religion, I have some hope that, if we have enough success to go on from year to year, we may help to bring a little ideal thought into the common thought of the times. (*UPII*, 141)

He used this saying again in 1902[17] and in 1934. This exact quotation does not appear in Hugo's writings. In the passage Yeats was probably referring to, Hugo does not distinguish between the mob and the people, and he figures the relationship between the writer and the crowd as reciprocal.[18] Yeats's construction of this passage emphasizes two important elements of his national theatre. First, his ideal of the nation was organized in relation to a dangerous alternative form of collectivity: the specter of the crowd both enabled and haunted Yeats's nation as theatre audience. Second, Yeats's desire for a national unity that combined mystical communion and heroic individuality often modulated into a formulation in which the heroic individuality of the artist produced mystical communion in the people, and he emphasized the dramatist's transformative power over the masses, figured as a passive audience. Both elements arose out of his anxious engagement with the idea of Irish nationalism as mass politics.

Many turn of the century nationalisms imagined national community as a deep emotional bond among men united in the service of a country or cause personified by a woman. Freud thought all group ties were libidinal, and writers like George Mosse have argued that such nationalisms often rely on the creation of homoerotic ties among men, ties which then have to be carefully policed, contained and deflected onto more acceptable heterosexual objects.[19] The degree to which this particular ambivalence about male-male relations structures specific nationalisms varies, however, as Mosse notes.[20] While he eventually rejected Celticism for its "femininity" and worried about his possible exclusion from the brotherhood of Davis, Mangan and Ferguson, Yeats's Irish nationalism during these years paid little specific homage to the manly virtues and male comradeship that were important features of other nationalisms. His anxieties about Irish nationalism did not, as a rule, lead him to scrutinize the border between the homosocial and the homosexual. His model of the nation, which resembled a single, group mind, offered another eroticized danger: the dissolution of the individual subject.

Yeats's early negotiations with the erotics of Irish national community were organized around a heterosexual relationship between a male subject and an eroticized goddess figure who was both the embodiment of a transcendent national unity and a potentially devouring mother. Works like the Rose poems of the 1890s inscribe an erotic relationship between the speaker and the Rose that is aesthetic, occult and national; the multiple and varied symbolism of the Rose has been well-documented in Yeats criticism.[21] Like the erotics of the crowd, the erotics of the Rose entail the dissolution of the individual subject into a larger whole. The Rose is outside the symbolic order, linear time, and narrative. It stands for the negation of conflict, distance, desire and individuation – all the painful lacks that Yeats thought produced poetry. The Rose represents an erotic death that is also a return to origins. In religious terms, it represents apocalypse; in psychoanalytic terms, the pre-oedipal. In "The Rose of Peace" (*VP*, 112–13) the speaker accords the Rose the power to effect the ultimate reconciliation, "A peace of Heaven with Hell." In contrast to "God's wars" which preoccupy God and "Michael, leader of God's host," the Rose of Peace represents non-violence, gentleness and quiet; its followers are "led on by gentle ways" and God will "softly make a rosey peace." But this peace coincides with the annihilation of the quotidian world through its absorption in the divine. Similarly, "Into the Twilight" (*VP*, 147–8) presents Ireland as a benign mother – "Your mother Eire is always young" – and invites the "outworn heart" of the speaker to return to a symbiosis with her: "Come clear of the nets of wrong and right / Laugh, heart, again in the grey twilight, / Sigh, heart, again in the dew of the morn." But the poem also depicts the twilight realm of mother Ireland as disturbingly devoid of human beings and human emotions like love and hope:

> And God stands winding His lonely horn,
> And time and the world are ever in flight;
> And love is less kind than the grey twilight,
> And hope is less dear than the dew of the morn.

In "The Rose of the World" (*VP*, 111–12) the Rose existed before God made humanity, the stars and the "labouring world" and will remain after they have passed. "To the Rose Upon the Rood of Time" (*VP*, 100–1) pits the seductions of the Rose against the fear of erotic dissolution into it: "Come near, come near, come near – Ah, leave me still / A little space for the rose-breath to fill!" In "The Secret Rose" (*VP*, 169–70) the Rose, itself "inviolate," has the power to "enfold" the most disparate of beings, and deliver them all to the "sleep / Men have named beauty." At the end of the poem, the speaker equates the Rose with the apocalyptic end of the world:

"When shall the stars be blown about the sky, / Like sparks blown out of a smithy, and die? / Surely thine hour has come, thy great wind blows, / Far-off, most secret, and inviolate Rose?"

One could argue that anxiety about male homoeroticism and about engulfing female figures often go together, especially in an era that stigmatized homosexual men as improperly, monstrously feminine, or that the former lies "behind" the latter. Such a reading, however, makes it difficult to focus on the ways in which different nationalisms produce different sexual imperatives and anxieties. Instead, I want to argue that the link between Yeats's anxiety about Irish nationalism as a mass movement and his ambivalent representations of idealized but potentially destructive female figures lies in an ambivalence about the potential dissolution of the subject. At stake are the boundaries of the subject, rather than its relation to a forbidden object, a pleasurable/threatening dissolution that positions him in a pre-oedipal symbiosis with the mother, rather than in an Oedipal narrative.[22] For Yeats, the erotics and problematics of national community in the age of mass politics lay precisely in the desirable and frightening aspects of an intersubjectivity that promised or threatened to deepen into the paradoxically re-unifying dissolution of the subject.

This is illustrated in *Cathleen ni Houlihan*, which originated in a dream of Yeats's and was written collaboratively by Yeats and Lady Gregory. First performed in April of 1902, the play stages a moment in the ongoing transformation or nationalization of the masses. As Yeats's only really popular play, it also represents his only successful effort to achieve that transformation, or something vaguely like it, in the theatre. The central (but unstaged) transformation in the play occurs when the old woman metamorphoses into a young girl with "the walk of a queen" after Michael Gillane agrees to join the national movement and sacrifice himself for her. But this transformation is contingent on another one that is equally significant, if not as dramatically striking. Michael changes from an individual preoccupied with his own personal happiness, symbolized by his impending marriage, to a selfless, boundary-less element in a larger whole – the national movement – in which he has no meaningful individual existence. The play is often read as an allegory about the conflict between public duty and private hopes, love of country and love of family, individual happiness and the collective good.[23] This is true enough; more important for my purposes here is how the conflict is staged and resolved. The conflict the text presents between these pairs of values is actually quite minimal; to the extent that Michael struggles with his "decision" to follow Cathleen, that struggle takes the form of a feeble and temporary resistance to the trance-like state into which he is falling.[24] Cathleen does not reason with Michael or persuade him; she bewitches or hypnotizes him. The text emphasizes his lack of comprehension; he says, "I do not know what that song means, but tell me something I can do for you" (*VPI*, 228), and Bridget comments, "he has the look of a man that has got the touch" (*VPI*, 229). This impression is strengthened by the fact that it is the song Cathleen sings, rather than her conversation, that proves decisively compelling for Michael:

> They shall be remembered for ever,
> They shall be alive for ever,
> They shall be speaking for ever,
> The people shall hear them for ever.   (*VPI*, 229)

The song's patterns of repetition give it the status of a ritual incantation, and it works on Michael not through reason, or even through appeals to identifiable personal or national emotion, but by putting him into a trance. He does not renounce Delia so much as forget her, asking "What wedding are you talking of?" (*VPI*, 230) and recalling her only partially and with difficulty. Two points are particularly important here. First, Michael's transformation into a follower of Cathleen erases his individual aspirations, subjectivity and life altogether. As Cathleen says, "If any one would give me help he must give me himself, he must give me all" (*VPI*, 226). Second, the play casts his transformation not as the expression of his conscious will, whether intellectual or emotional, but as a consequence of its suppression.

Patrick Keane has done a provocative and insightful reading of Cathleen as a devouring mother, and argues that Yeats's play inscribes both the attractions and the dangers of Irish popular nationalism by emphasizing that answering the siren call of country is invariably fatal and by depicting Cathleen as a vampire who demands a blood offering.[25] I want to suggest, further, that *Cathleen ni Houlihan* embodies Yeats's historically specific anxieties about Irish nationalism as mass politics. The text suggests these anxieties through the other figure in which it embodies national unity – the ever present but never visible cheering crowd. The play's opening line draws attention to the crowd: "Peter. What is that sound I hear?" (*VPI*, 214), and the crowd "reappears" frequently throughout the text, forming a consistent aural backdrop to the central action. Patrick observes "They are cheering again down in the town" (*VPI*, 219) and is sent to discover the cause. Michael remarks, "They're not done cheering yet" (*VPI*, 220). Peter asks the old woman if she has heard it, and she replies, "I thought I heard the noise I used to hear when my friends came to visit me" (*VPI*, 223). Later she says "I have good friends that will help me. They are gathering to help me now" (*VPI*, 227). Obviously, the crowd is a figure for the national movement that serves her. At the end of the play Patrick returns to report that "the boys are all hurrying down the hillside to join the French" (*VPI*, 230).

On a literal level, of course, as we learn at the end of the play, the cheering crowd hails the arrival of the French forces in support of an Irish insurrection. On another level, as an image of the national unity that such resistance necessarily involves, the crowd complements and comments on the play's central image of such unity, Cathleen. The moment of Michael's sacrifice, Cathleen's transformation, and the revelation of her true identity is also the moment when we learn the true cause of the cheering crowd. These two revelations are versions of the same revelation. Both signify the individual's entry into the larger whole represented by the national movement. Symbolically, Cathleen and the crowd are equivalent. The crowd's cheers even perform the same hypnotic function as Cathleen's song. Michael, half-remembering his wedding, begins to break the spell, but the crowd re-ensnares him: "He looks at the clothes and turns towards the inner room, but stops at the sound of cheering outside" (*VPI*, 230). A moment later, "The clothes slip from Michael's arm" (*VPI*, 230) and he looks at his bride-to-be "like a stranger" (*VPI*, 230). As Michael's sacrifice (or more accurately, his forgetting) of his entire private existence and his trance-like submission suggest, the figure of Cathleen as a mythic devouring mother in this play is specifically a figure for the dissolution of the individual subject into the larger unity of a crowd.

The structure and particular nature of the anxieties expressed in the Rose poems and *Cathleen ni Houlihan* owe much to the fact that Yeats was a nationalist who hated crowds. Maud Gonne, who played the role of Cathleen in the first production of *Cathleen ni Houlihan*, later recalled that during their political work together in the 1890s, "he hated crowds; I loved them."[26] From the late 1890s through the Easter Rising, he and Gonne carried on a sporadic debate about crowds, politics and the "popular" in their correspondence. Gonne praised the Dublin crowds, even when they attacked her after she divorced MacBride, and she cast herself less as their dominating leader than as their representative. In 1903, after she had told Yeats she planned to convert to Catholicism, she wrote to him, "You say I leave the few to mix myself with the crowd while Willie I have always told you I am the voice, the soul of the *crowd*" (*GY*, 166). Gonne did not argue that the masses were the rational political actors theorized by liberalism; for her the source of their positive power was unconscious thought and a capacity for intense feeling. She admonished Yeats, "there is more good than you admit in the unconscious thought of the masses of the people" (*GY*, 221), and said "How I love & *reverence* the Dublin crowd. They are always fearless & heroic whenever a national or religious ideal is before them" (*GY*, 346).[27] Gonne also repeatedly drew distinctions between her political work, which plunged her into the crowd, and Yeats's literary work, which separated him from it, writing, "You have a higher work to do – With me it is different I was born to be in the midst of a crowd" (*GY*, 73). During these years, Yeats associated crowds with the nationalist activities and views that drove various wedges between himself and Gonne; for him, Gonne and crowds were linked in much the same way that *Cathleen ni Houlihan* links Cathleen and the cheering crowd.[28]

One of the most threatening features of the crowd was its ability to allure, not just Gonne, but also the unwilling Yeats. His record of the 1897 Jubilee Riot combines many of his ambivalent feelings about nationalist crowds:

That evening there was a meeting of our council in the City Hall, and when we came out after it the crowds were waiting for us all round the Hall. We were going to the National Club in Rutland Square, and they came too. Outside the National Club a magic lantern was to show on a white screen statistics of evictions, deaths from starvation, etc., during Victoria's reign. Somewhere in front of us was a mock funeral Maud Gonne devised, a coffin with "The British Empire" printed upon it, and black flags with the names of all those who had been hanged for treason during Queen Victoria's reign. Presently they began breaking windows where there were decorations. Maud Gonne was walking with a joyous face; she had taken all those people into her heart. I knew she would not interfere. I knew her principle. If a crowd does anything illegal and you try to stop it, you may succeed, but you are certain to seem to have done it to keep from danger yourself. I tried to speak and could only whisper. I had spoken too much through a disorderly debate at the council, and my voice had gone. Then I too resigned myself and felt the excitement of the moment, that joyous irresponsibility and sense of power. (*Mem*, 112–13)[29]

The police charged the crowd with batons, and in the ensuing violence one person was killed and over two hundred people were injured. Yeats's description illustrates the major characteristics he (and many other contemporary observers) associated with crowds. The crowd needed a leader; they cheered and followed Gonne, who had given an inflammatory speech earlier in the day, a speech at which, Yeats reports, "the whole crowd went wild" (*Mem*, 112). The crowd was destructive and violent, and resulted in property damage, injury and even death. It was incited most effectively by spectacle – the magic lantern show and the mock funeral. Finally, the crowd was profoundly seductive, and surrender to it brought a "joyous irresponsibility and sense of power."

During the Jubilee Riot, Yeats sought to lead the crowd, but ended up succumbing to it instead. These two possibilities structured important aspects of his Irish theatre's negotiation with the idea of nationalism as mass politics. On the one hand, as his revision of Victor Hugo and *Cathleen ni Houlihan* suggest, Yeats cast the artist and the theatre as the powerful agents of a transformation visited upon a largely passive audience. He wrote in his autobiography, "All civilisation is held together by the suggestions of an invisible hypnotist – by artificially created illusions" (*AY*, 326), and Yeats imagined himself as such a hypnotist, creating the illusions that would unify the nation. On the other hand, Yeats found the dissolution of the individual subject this transformation seemed to suggest for the audience or nation deeply threatening, all the more so because it was potentially seductive, and he worked to define the Irish nation as a collectivity that nurtured rather than suppressed the individual will. Thus Yeats began his theatre project wanting mass mobilization into one kind of collectivity, a nation, and fearing mass mobilization into another kind of collectivity, a crowd or mob. The problem was that they looked unnervingly alike.

Yeats was not alone in his anxiety over the problematic bases of national collectivity in the age of mass politics. By the 1890s, a number of thinkers had concluded that mass politics were based on mysticism, symbolism, the irrational and the emotional. As Eric Hobsbawm observes, after the 1870s, "The intellectual study of politics and society was transformed by the recognition that whatever held human collectivities together it was not the rational calculation of their individual members."[30] In one form or another, this recognition influenced states, resistance movements, and social scientists. It led governments to invent and strengthen official nationalisms through an unprecedented flurry of public ceremonies, monuments and symbols like national holidays, flags, songs and statues. In the Irish resistance movement, this recognition appears slightly earlier – in the 1840s – in the transition from O'Connell's rational, constitutional nationalism to the romantic, emotive nationalism of Young Ireland.

While crowds, protests and riots had been a feature of political thinking since Plato, the mid-nineteenth century represents a watershed in the history of ideas about such unruly collectives.[31] Before that, crowds were aberrant political entities that required policing, but not theorizing. They stood for everything that politics and collectivities should not be, and everything they were not if politics and society were operating the way they were supposed to. "Before," observes J. S. McClelland, "the crowd does not appear to have forced political thinkers to re-examine the assumptions of their own political theorizing."[32] After 1848, and certainly after 1871,[33] the crowd forced just such a re-examination. Now the crowd was not what happened when politics broke down; instead, the crowd offered a compelling model of how politics and collectivity worked all the time.[34]

Placing the crowd at the center of social and political theory involved several important ideas. For most theorists during the late nineteenth century, the crowd was not merely the sum of its individual parts; it had become a new, unified entity – a single, distinct group mind. The idea of the group mind was one of the cornerstones of crowd theory. The widely read but intellectually derivative Gustave Le Bon, who popularized much crowd theory and was, in the words of one historian, "the supreme scientific vulgarizer of his generation," theorized it as the Law of the Mental Unity of Crowds.[35] The group mind was unconscious, irrational, emotional, easily led, incapable of complex thought and particularly susceptible to image, symbol and spectacle. An individual in the midst of a crowd resembled Michael Gillane under Cathleen's spell, and followed the impulses of the group mind in blind, unreasoning obedience, or even revelled in the sense of "joyous irresponsibility" and "power" that Yeats experienced during the riot. Crowd theorists discussed the intersubjective relationships between members of crowds in various terms – most commonly, suggestion, imitation, contagion and hypnotism. What they all had in common was their conviction that the group mind broke down the barriers between individual minds, and swept away individuality, will and reason. All crowd theorists (until Canetti[36]) agreed that crowds needed leaders, and theorized the relationship between the leader and the group as a kind of hypnosis.[37] Hypnotism suppressed the conscious will and usual restraints of the subject, and brought to the surface thoughts, emotions and desires that were unconscious.[38] It also lifted the normal restraints on behavior.

Most crowd theory was highly conservative politically; it feared the masses and the crowds they might form and associated crowds with unreasoning violence and savage destruction. Le Bon's widely known book *The Crowd* (1895) was intended partly as a handbook for political elites who needed to learn the techniques of mass manipulation and crowd control, and indeed by about 1910 Le Bon had achieved the position he had aspired to – that of "a senior advisor to contemporary rulers."[39] The techniques he recommended were similar to those of the hypnotist, the advertiser, the magician and the theatre manager. Le Bon argued that "a crowd thinks in images,"[40] and is most influenced by "illusions and words."[41] He compared the art of using "words and formulas" to evoke images and stir crowds with that of a magician: "Handled with art, [words and formulas] possess in sober truth the mysterious power formerly attributed to them by the adepts of magic."[42] He claimed that "Nothing has a greater effect on the imagination of crowds of every category than theatrical representation."[43] For Le Bon, as for Yeats, the public sphere in the age of mass politics was a theatre, and the skillful politician/artist could wield a power over his audience akin to the transformative power of the hypnotist or magician.

These developments in crowd theory had profoundly troubling implications for the middle classes who viewed the masses as a potential threat. Several decades earlier, the masses and the crowd had been closely allied; the middle and upper classes worried about how to defend themselves against the masses, who could form mobs under the right circumstances, but they generally did not express anxiety about the possibility of becoming members of crowds themselves. For writers like Le Bon, however, while some people, like the working classes, women, and foreigners were more likely to succumb to the group mind than others, anyone and everyone could become part of a crowd. Yeats learned this lesson in a very personal way during the Jubilee Riot. The irrational, unconscious group mind did not characterize just certain sections of society; theoretically, it could appear in society as a whole. For Le Bon, mass society was crowd society,[44] and, as McClelland observes, by the 1890s "crowd theory was confident enough of itself to advance a serious claim to *be* social theory."[45] In addition, Le Bon claimed that physical proximity was not necessary for crowd formation, which meant that the possible magnitude of crowds and the circumstances under which they could form were vastly multiplied. A crowd, like Benedict Anderson's imagined national community, could be composed of individuals who were physically disparate but mentally joined by psychic reciprocity and shared emotions and rituals.

Crowd theory offered a new theory of politics and society by positing a new and worrisome kind of political subject. As McClelland observes, "By no means all crowd theorists took the idea of the group or crowd mind as literally as Le Bon did, but they all speak of the present or imminent crisis as a crisis of individualism."[46] In contrast to the autonomous, rational actor of liberal political theory, this political subject was motivated by unconscious, irrational and emotional forces. The boundaries that separated it from other subjects were permeable and subject to sudden disintegration; it threatened to dissolve itself into the larger, unified subjectivity of the group mind.

This subject also had very specific gender and class valences. The kinds of individuals who were most likely to be drawn into crowds were the working classes and women: Le Bon associated the modern age of crowds with socialism and feminism.[47] Yeats's gendering of the threatening unity represented by the crowd as feminine was echoed in crowd theory; crowd theorists routinely compared the crowd to a woman.[48] Other constructions of femininity, such as the emergent discourses on hysteria that occupied an oblique relation to the Celtic movement, were resoundingly middle class and figured femininity as a pathological hyper-refinement and sensitivity. The hysteric's pathology expressed itself largely in her estranged relation to her "self," or to a portion of her own psychical activity, rather than in her relation to other selves. For Freud, hysterics were divided, conflicted creatures whose illness sprang from a paralyzing internal clash between an affect and its suppression.[49] The feminized subject of the crowd, however, like Yeats's image of impossible, apocalyptic unity and reconciliation, the Rose, expressed its pathology in its singular lack of inner conflict, having been liberated from the constraining effects of will, conscience, and the super-ego. Far from being paralyzed, it was frighteningly capable, and was likely to engage in violent and destructive behavior that individual subjects would shrink from. It was a "mass" subject whose threatening "feminine" features lay in its lack of autonomy, its inability to maintain subject boundaries, its slavish devotion to a strong leader, its changeability, and its precipitation of the crisis of individualism.

While a national culture could obviously be theorized as a group mind, most crowd theorists cast the nation as the opposite of the crowd, a more civilized, non-destructive form of collectivity in contrast to the irrational, atavistic barbarism of the crowd. Crowds, at least in their pure form, were temporary; nations were not, and therefore were capable of providing social stability.[50] For Le Bon, race (by which he meant something like national culture) was virtually the only thing capable of preventing society from regressing to a crowd. But while national culture provided a major bulwark against the crowd, it was also a version of the crowd. Many of their deep structures and mechanisms were essentially the same. In Le Bon's evolutionary scheme for the history of nations, a people emerged out of an original barbarian crowd, and when their civilization declined into decadence, it returned to that state.[51] Although much crowd theory opposed the crowd and the nation, insofar as crowd theory offered itself as a model of social theory in general, it posited less an opposition than a frightening continuum as the relationship between the crowd and the nation.[52]

This is not the only way to theorize the nation in the age of mass politics, but in important respects it was Yeats's way. The 1890s saw a flurry of influential books about crowds,[53] and over the next few decades Le Bon in particular influenced a wide range of European nationalists and politicians, including Charles DeGaulle, Theodore Roosevelt, Mussolini and Hitler.[54] He also influenced Freud's *Group Psychology and the Analysis of the Ego*.[55] Like the thinkers who had begun to suspect that the crowd provided the paradigm for mass society, that crowd theory was social theory, Yeats wondered "Was modern civilisation a conspiracy of the subconscious?" (*AY*, 177). Like crowd theory, Yeats's ambivalence about Irish nationalism in texts like *Cathleen ni Houlihan* often recognized, overtly or covertly, the possible continuum between the nation and the crowd, even while he insisted on their opposition.

Yeats, always the anxious defender of the heroic individual, recognized that the group mind with which he figured his ideal national unity precipitated a crisis of individuality and threatened to converge with contemporary descriptions of crowds that emphasized their mental unity, their dissolution of individual subjects and the feelings of boldness and invulnerability which made them capable of ghastly acts of destruction. The tension between Yeats's nation, which fostered individuality, and the crowd, which erased it, could not be managed by appealing to crowd theory, liberal political theory, or the varieties of mainstream Irish nationalism that demanded homogeneity. It was the occult doctrines and practices Yeats favored, particularly theosophy, that seemed to offer him a way to negotiate his ambivalences about Irish nationalism as mass politics by combining organic, mystical unity and heroic individuality. The nationalist politics of Yeats's Irish theatre demanded magic.

Contemporary criticism usually views any combination of politics and the occult, the supernatural or magic with deep suspicion. The general trend in Yeats studies has been to treat the occult as either a symptom or a cause of what is less than desirable about Yeats's politics. Some critics cast Yeats's occult politics as mystical, elitist politics, and read them as the unfortunate but logical political outgrowth of modernist aesthetics.[56] Others see Yeats's occult pursuits as an attempt to translate the messy and frustrating realities of the Irish public sphere into the false but orderly world of the occult.[57] More recently, some critics have attempted to generate a fuller assessment of the relationship between politics and the occult in Yeats's work by examining its historical context and pointing out that in the 1880s and 1890s interest in magic and the supernatural came in many forms and could acquire a wide range of complex political resonances, few of which were consonant with the political implications it is generally assumed to carry today.[58]

What all these approaches fail to note is that many of the things Yeats understood by the term "magic" formed an explicit and important part of his practical, material political thinking about the problems he associated with mass politics. While in contemporary analyses of nationalism, it has become standard to point to nationalism's reliance on religious modes of thought[59] and to unmask the particular structures of its metaphysics,[60] the metaphysics of Yeats's nationalism of the theatre do not need unmasking; they are explicit and insistent. He repeatedly articulated the common structures, methods and appeal of nationalism and religion, writing in 1901 that the two "passions" artists would find ready to hand in Ireland were "love of the Unseen Life and love of country" (*EI*, 204). Instead, I want to emphasize that the registers on which the occult was meant to operate were more literal than metaphorical and that in important respects Yeats's occult was more of a technology than a realm or system. In theory and in practice, the occult offered him a way of organizing his thoughts about groups: the sources and structures of more and less desirable forms of collectivity, the attractions and dangers of the kind of subject required or created by them, the theatrical (and more generally poetic) techniques and spectacles most likely to foster them, and the intersubjective relationships among members of a group and between leaders and followers. Critics who accuse Yeats of escapism or who, like Adorno, see the occult as an attempt to solve metaphorically problems that can only be solved socially and materially, take insufficient notice of the ways in which occult techniques like ritual and symbol have material existences and effects in the social and political world. Yeats, threatened by the fact and the idea of the crowd, turned to the occult in order to intervene more effectively in a potentially hostile public sphere, rather than to escape it. This is not to say that Yeats's practical occultism was effective on a mass scale: it was not. But in an age that was discovering the unconscious and irrational bases of politics and collectivity in important ways, it had significant affinities with the secular theories and technologies offered by more respectable political analyses like crowd theory and more successful attempts at mass mobilization. In this respect, Seamus Deane's claim that for Yeats, "fascism was the political form of occultism,"[61] has the virtue of reminding us that one reason fascism was successful in mobilizing masses of people was that it took the irrational and unconscious foundations of politics and society and the "occult" technologies needed to manipulate them seriously.

In 1892 Yeats wrote to a censorious John O'Leary, "It is surely absurd to hold me 'weak' or otherwise because I chose to persist in a study which I decided deliberately four or five years ago to make, next to my poetry, the most important pursuit of my life" (*L*, 210). During the period when he was most engrossed in the idea of a popular theatre, from the late 1880s until about 1910, Yeats's occult studies and groups took up an enormous amount of his time and energy. Yeats's interest in the occult was extremely diverse and wide-ranging; I am concerned here with an important but not exhaustive strand in the concatenation of terms, concepts and activities that he organized under the sign "magic." The essay "Magic" offers a helpful starting point:

I believe in the practice and philosophy of what we have agreed to call magic, in what I must call the evocation of spirits, though I do not know what they are, in the power of creating magical illusions, in the visions of truth in the depths of the mind when the eyes are closed; and I believe in three doctrines, which have, as I think, been handed down from early times, and been the foundations of nearly all magical practices. These doctrines are: –

(1) that the borders of our minds are ever shifting, and that many minds can flow into one another, as it were, and create or reveal a single mind, a single energy,

(2) that the borders of our memories are as shifting, and that our memories are a part of one great memory, the memory of Nature herself, and

(3) that this great mind and great memory can be evoked by symbols. (*EI*, 28)

The permeability of individual minds, their access to one another and to some larger entity, and the importance of symbols in realizing that access were crucial components of the occult for Yeats. So was the conviction that the profoundest truths were to be found in the unconscious "depths of the mind," where "no mind's contents [were] necessarily shut off from one another."[62] These depths revealed both the individual's most genuine uniqueness and his or her deepest connections with other individuals. Although theoretically all minds were potentially connected to the great mind, Yeats's magic demanded a magician, an adept who had the power of creating "magical illusions" and who knew what symbols to employ, just as a crowd needed a leader.

Despite the fact that Yeats read a good deal of arcane occult material (he acquired the status of an expert on such material in the Golden Dawn), in important respects the occult was not only or even primarily about an individual's private communion with his own intellect, vision or the spirit world. For Yeats, the occult provided a way of thinking about and fostering intersubjectivity and social groups. Most of the visionary and occult experiments and experiences Yeats recorded in his memoirs and essays were highly social, not just practically but theoretically as well. Seeing visions was something he preferred to do in groups, or at least in pairs. The student of magic engaged in a project that created intersubjective connection; according to the doctrines of the Golden Dawn, the adept has a duty to help others, and "has been sent among them to break down the walls that divide them from one another and from the fountain of their life, and not to build new walls."[63] Yeats spoke of the theatre's effect on the audience in similar terms, writing that "Tragedy must always be a drowning and breaking of the dykes that separate man from man" (*EI*, 241). In general, as the three precepts from "Magic" suggest, for Yeats the content of individual visions was less important than the fact that visions could be shared, illustrating "the power of many minds to become one" (*EI*, 36).[64]

Around the turn of the century, the Golden Dawn was rocked by a series of debates and power struggles among its members.[65] Subjects of discussion and conflict included the degree of centralization and hierarchy that should characterize the group, the question of whether or not members would be allowed to form separate study groups, and proposed changes in rituals and requirements for advancement. Such issues had great significance for Yeats, who believed that the Order's social structure should mirror the structures of the immaterial world they sought. According to Yeats, a mystical order should ideally form a collective that was more than the sum of its aggregate parts or members; it should create a new group mind with a distinct personality. During the debates within the Order, Yeats, who sided with Annie Horniman and against Florence Farr and many other members, wrote several essays and letters to the group to make his views clear. These documents, especially "Is the Order of R.R. & A.C. to remain a Magical Order?", which George Mills Harper calls "perhaps the most careful analysis he was ever to make of his fundamental religious convictions,"[66] outline his theory of the proper collectivity for a magical order. Yeats protested Farr's desire to form a separate group within the order, predicting dire results:

The members of the chief "group" have certainly formed themselves into a magical personality made by a very formal meditation and a very formal numerical system. Unless magic is an illusion, this magical personality could not help, the moment it came into contact with the larger personality of the Order, from creating precisely the situation it has created. It was a formal evocation of disruption, a formal evocation of a barrier between its own members and the other members of the Order, a formal intrusion of an alien being into the conscious and what is of greater importance into the super-conscious being of our Order ...[67]

Yeats also took care to distinguish a magical order from other kinds of groups. In his debates with Farr, he repeatedly stressed the importance of maintaining the unity and personality of the order, so that the group did not dwindle into a mere crowd of chance comers drawn together by a mutual interest in occult pursuits. He argued that if Farr had her way the order would become simply "a society for experiment and research," whereas a Magical Order was "an Actual Being, an organic life holding within itself the highest life of its members now and in past times."[68]

Yeats's organicist language of personality, mystical community, being and potential alienation cast the Golden Dawn as a collectivity similar to a nation or a group mind and distinguished it from a mere aggregate of autonomous individuals brought together by chance, choice or rational calculation. He also figured the nation as a collection of minds sharing complementary elements of the same occult vision. In his autobiography he wondered,

Seeing that a vision could divide itself in divers complementary portions, might not the thought of philosopher or poet or mathematician depend at every moment of its progress upon some complementary thought in minds perhaps at a great distance? Is there nation-wide multiform reverie, every mind passing through a stream of suggestion, and all streams acting and reacting upon one another no matter how distant the minds, how dumb the lips? A man walked, as it were, casting a shadow, and yet one could never say which was man and which was shadow, or how many the shadows he cast. Was not a nation, as distinguished from a crowd of chance comers, bound together by this interchange among streams or shadows; that Unity of Image, which I sought in national literature, being but an originating symbol? (*AT*, 176)[69]

This mystical version of a group whose minds have become permeable, offering access to other minds and to the great mind, approached the group mind of crowd theory: an intimate, mystical intersubjectivity, impelled by suggestion rather than rational choice, dependent not on physical proximity but on emotional unity and a common relation to an instrumental symbol or spectacle. But it differed from crowd theory's group mind as well because it explicitly

accommodated individual variation, gesturing towards the paradoxical structure that underlay Yeats's Irish theatre. Nation-wide reverie
could be "multiform," and individual visions could be "complementary," rather than identical with one another. Although Yeats hated
censorship and endorsed the maintenance of a public sphere which
allowed the free and open exchange of conflicting views, such a
public sphere had little relevance to his construction of the particular
kind of collectivity represented by the nation during this period. This
version of the Irish nation demanded a kind of sacred public sphere
similar to a collective unconscious whose existence and functioning
were not immediately accessible to the rational consciousness of
citizens.

While crowd theory addressed the merging of minds and the
threat of crowds through scientistic concepts like hypnotism and the
law of the mental unity of crowds, Yeats addressed them through
occult doctrine. These approaches were not as disparate as they
might seem. Far from being anti-science, theosophy was deeply
interested in and quite compatible with important aspects of late
Victorian science. Tom Gibbons has argued that the ultimate effect
of Darwin's *On the Origin of Species* was to help replace the high
Victorian period's emphasis on the mechanistic physical sciences
(like physics), and a related view of the universe as "dead, material
and atomistic," with a new emphasis on evolutionary biology, which
encouraged a view of the universe as animated by an all-pervading
life force.[70] This was also the world view offered by theosophy, and
one of its most compelling features was that it claimed to reconcile
religious belief with important contemporary developments in the
physical sciences. The sub-title of Madame Blavatsky's *Isis Unveiled*
claimed that it was "a master-key to the mysteries of ancient and
modern science and theology." Although the Society for Psychical
Research had accused Blavatsky of fraud in 1885, its existence and
activities illustrate that a range of discourses possessing varying
degrees of scientific legitimacy was constructing narratives about
"occult" phenomena that could be classified under the merging of
minds.

For Yeats, this occult intersubjectivity was clearly erotic; he tended
to see visions with women, especially his lovers, and later he and
Gonne entered their "spiritual marriage" which substituted metaphysical connection for the physical contact she refused to grant him.
In Yeats's early poetry, occult practice and contemplation were

inseparable from sexual life.[71] This was not necessarily true for other occult enthusiasts. British spiritualists, embarrassed by the associations with free love that American spiritualism had acquired, emphasized sexual purity and respectability.[72] Madame Blavatsky demanded chastity of her students (*AY*, 120), and among the theosophists "an unwritten rule pronounced love and the spiritual life incompatible" (*AY*, 164). In the Golden Dawn Yeats incurred Florence Farr's wrath by suggesting what she called the "loathesome idea" that some kinds of occult meditation were used by lovers to make their love more intense.[73] The dangerous erotics of Yeats's occult activities coincided with the dangerous erotics of national community; both offered an intense, intimate intersubjectivity whose logical extreme was the dissolution of the individual subject.

The major aspects of Yeats's theory of the theatre – ritual, symbol, pattern, rhythm – were all important elements of occult theory and practice. Yeats praised Johnson's phrase, "life is ritual" (*AY*, 201) and he spent a good deal of his time in the Golden Dawn attending or participating in rituals; he went through that organization's rituals hundreds of times. He reports in his memoirs that ritual inspired him to national feeling and public work: "After I had been moved by ritual, I formed plans for deeds of all kinds I wished to return to Ireland to find there some public work; whereas when I had returned from meetings of the Esoteric Section I had no desire but for more thought, more discussion" (*Mem*, 27). For Yeats, the theatre as occult ritual could inspire audiences to practical work in the public sphere precisely because it accessed the intersubjective unconscious, instinct and the emotions. More cerebral occult studies, on the other hand, remained interior and private experiences and would not mobilize people for collective endeavor because they only engaged the conscious intellect.

Symbolism was also an important part of Yeats's public theatre because it transported the audience or reader to an alternative, visionary, unconscious realm or reality. As Yeats wrote in his 1909 journal, "The more unconscious the creation, the more powerful" (*Mem*, 248). A major strand of Yeats's early theory of symbolism was organized around the symbol's relation to occult vision, intersubjectivity and national community. Between 1896 and 1900 Yeats wrote a series of essays in which he examined the nature and function of symbols: the essays on Blake and Shelley, "Symbolism in Painting," "A Symbolic Artist and the Coming of Symbolic

Art," and "The Symbolism of Poetry." There are many possible
sources for the structures of Yeats's early symbolism, and these
structures themselves come in several varieties. But these essays
return repeatedly to a theory of the symbol that is occult rather
than literary.[74] They often cast the poet as an "enchanter" (*EI*,
141), or mystic visionary, and symbols as magic "talismans" (*EI*,
148). This theory of the symbol is instrumental; it emphasizes what
the symbol does rather than what it is or represents. It differs from
more familiar literary theories of symbolism because the symbol
itself does not describe or re-present a vision. Rather, as in the
occult sessions in which Yeats used symbols to produce visions, and
in crowd theory's conception of how images and spectacles incited
crowds, it provides access to some deep truth, state of mind, or
intersubjective connection.[75]

In their occult aspect, then, symbols did not simply express the
person who used them; they also had a signifying or evocative life of
their own, independent of his or her will or imagination. Yeats
reported that when he invoked visions in other people, it was the
symbol itself and not the power of his own imagination that
determined the content of the vision; if he used the wrong symbol by
mistake, he would evoke the wrong vision (*AY*, 173).[76] In "Magic" he
admitted that "It was a long time before I myself would admit an
inherent power in symbols" (*EI*, 48), but he insisted that symbols'
ability to invoke visions could not be explained by "the power of one
imagination over another, or by telepathy" (*EI*, 48). Yeats posited an
"objective" immaterial reality as the subject of occult study in the
sense that the Great Memory or the spiritual world were not, for
him, simply projections of individual emotions or thoughts: "images
well up before the mind's eye from a deeper source than conscious or
subconscious memory" (*AY*, 124). Thus Yeats's instrumental symbol
was not simply the passive instrument of the individual poet or
magician; it was equally the instrument of the impersonal, eternal
forces represented by the Great Memory. The symbol had its own
properties, its own powers, its own meanings which sprang from the
Great Memory or from long association; the individual could tap
into them, but not control them. During one of the debates among
members of the Golden Dawn, Yeats wrote:

It is a first principle of our illumination that symbols and formulae are
powers, which act in their own right and with little consideration for our
intentions, however excellent. Most of us have seen some ceremony

produce an altogether unintended result because of the accidental use of some wrong formula or symbol.[77]

The independent life of the symbol meant that evocation always carried the risk of unexpected or unwanted results. While in literary terms such results threatened only misunderstanding or a plurality of interpretation, the occult and political ramifications were much more serious, and ranged from black magic to mass riots. The symbolism of the Irish theatre was meant to give the audience access to the deep, mystical intersubjectivity of nationhood, but it risked provoking other responses. When he looked back on the controversy over *The Countess Cathleen*, Yeats adopted a pose similar to that of a magician who had chosen the wrong formula or symbol: "the disturbances were in part my own fault. In using what I considered traditional symbols I forgot that in Ireland they are not symbols but realities" (*AY*, 279). Yeats had chosen symbols that the audience did not recognize as such; instead they interpreted them literally. While Yeats thought *The Countess Cathleen* offered them evocation and transformation, the audience saw only representation.

Symbols, and by extension poetry, were most fully perceived and experienced by a mind which had temporarily abandoned reason and logic and entered a trance-like state analogous to hypnotism: "the soul moves among symbols and unfolds in symbols when trance, or madness, or deep meditation has withdrawn it from every impulse but its own" (*EI*, 162). Pattern and rhythm were the primary agents which induced this state. In 1898 Yeats wrote that in the arts, "pattern and rhythm are the road to open symbolism" (*UPII*, 133; *Mem*, 283), and in "The Symbolism of Poetry" he explicitly compared their work to the work of hypnosis:

The purpose of rhythm, it has always seemed to me, is to prolong the moment of contemplation, the moment when we are both asleep and awake, which is the one moment of creation, by hushing us with an alluring monotony, while it holds us waking by variety, to keep us in that state of perhaps real trance, in which the mind liberated from the pressure of the will is unfolded in symbols. If certain sensitive persons listen persistently to the ticking of a watch, or gaze persistently on the monotonous flashing of a light, they fall into the hypnotic trance; and rhythm is but the ticking of a watch made softer, that one must needs listen, and various, that one may not be swept beyond memory or grow weary of listening; while the patterns of the artist are but the monotonous flash woven to take the eyes in a subtler enchantment. (*EI*, 159)

As late as 1910, Yeats wrote that the tragic theatre should bring the viewer "almost to the intensity of trance" (*EI*, 245) and that it does this by using "rhythm, balance, pattern, images that remind us of vast passions, the vagueness of past times, all the chimeras that haunt the edge of trance" (*EI*, 243).[78]

In the theatre symbol, ritual, rhythm, and pattern were designed to foster national unity by accessing the unconscious and emotions of the audience through a process like hypnotism and transporting them to an alternative psychic realm. Yeats's wish to nationalize the masses led him to cast the playwright and stage as magicians with the power to transform the audience as Cathleen transforms Michael. In *Cathleen ni Houlihan* and in the crowd theory that used hypnotism as the model for the status of an individual in a crowd, hypnotism was a state in which individuality and will were completely submerged or suspended. According to Yeats, however, a poet or visionary entered the state he sought by cultivating his own uniqueness and personality rather than by suppressing them.[79] Although Yeats repeatedly compared it to hypnosis or trance, he was also careful to distinguish the state of psychic receptivity or "reverie" he thought necessary for symbolic vision and mystical community from them. Hypnotism, trance and mediumship represented threatening states of receptivity or intersubjectivity that were equivalent to passivity and suppressed the individual will. Reverie was active and depended on the assertion of the individual will. This distinction was an occult distinction; it was a crucial component of many of the occult doctrines and traditions Yeats favored, especially theosophy. It was also a gender distinction.

In recounting his own occult experiments, Yeats drew distinctions between his own state of visionary "reverie" and the "partial or complete hypnosis" he often induced in other people (*Mem*, 27), and he seems to have preferred the role of evoker or mesmerist to the role of the subject. Yeats also distrusted mediumship, theorizing it as a passive, feminized state that suppressed the will and threatened the temporary dissolution of the subject. When Yeats met MacGregor Mathers and Mathers helped him to see visions, he recalled, "Sight came slowly, there was not that sudden miracle as if the darkness had been cut with a knife, for that miracle is mostly a woman's privilege, but then rose before me mental images that I could not control" (*AY*, 125). The first time Yeats attended a seance he went into a trance, his body moved violently against his will, and he broke the table. Yeats remembered, "Everybody began to say I was a medium, and that if I would not resist some wonderful thing would happen. I remembered that Balzac had once desired to take opium for the experience's sake, but would not because he dreaded the surrender of his will" (*AY*, 69). He began reciting the opening lines of Milton's *Paradise Lost*, the nearest thing to a prayer he could think of. This experience frightened him so badly he loathed seances for years afterwards, although beginning in 1911 he attended them regularly for a few years. Many of the hermetic traditions he favored took a dim view of seances and mediumship.[80] Blake disapproved of seances. Blavatsky held that "Mediumship is the opposite of adeptship; the medium is the passive instrument of foreign influences, the adept actively controls himself and all inferior potencies,"[81] and she warned Yeats against mediumship, calling it "a kind of madness" (*Mem*, 25).[82] Swedenborg was against everyone's mediumship except his own, especially the "passive kind which wipes out instead of heightening the will."[83] The doctrine of the Golden Dawn proclaimed that "man's Higher Self must wake, not sink into sleep. Any trafficking with the gods or the disembodied dead must be in full, not muted consciousness."[84] Yeats and Annie Horniman added a new section to the by-laws of the Order which stipulated, among others things, that "members are forbidden to permit themselves to be mesmerized, hypnotized, or to lose control of their thoughts, words or actions."[85] He wrote in his memoirs, "It is always inexcusable to lose one's self-possession" (*Mem*, 138). Yeats's accounts of his occult activities are riddled with references to the actual or potential dangers that accompanied them. Central among those dangers was the suppression of the will, the dissolution of the individual subject.

Culturally, mediumship was associated with the two groups who embodied the crowd's tendency to dissolve subject boundaries and lift the usual restraints on behavior – women and the working classes. In contrast to more elite and esoteric pursuits, spiritualism drew many of its mediums and enthusiasts from the working and lower middle classes. Spiritualist doctrines drew heavily on conventional conceptions of femininity in defining mediumship, for which they claimed women were uniquely gifted. Spiritualists praised the Victorian womanly woman, emphasizing women's supposed spiritual superiority and domestic virtues. Their conception of mediumship equated passivity with power, thereby offering women a form of power, though a very limited one.[86] The conventionality of spiritualist doctrine was often subverted by spiritualist practices in seances, however; seances offered opportunities for mild titillation and transgression of sexual and gender norms. Mediums frequently flouted conventional definitions of femininity and respectable behavior, and Alex Owen speculates that "possession and spirit ratification act as strategies for obtaining attention, social standing, and privileges that are otherwise denied."[87] For women, spiritualism and seances could function as a way of both preserving their femininity and violating it in a manner that carried few risks of rejection or reprisal. Mediumship, or anything approaching it, was much more problematic for men; there were far fewer male mediums, and they were sometimes accused of effeminacy.[88] Throughout his life, passivity was one of the things Yeats feared most, primarily because he also found it appealing. As he wrote in "An Acre of Grass," "My temptation is quiet" (*VP*, 575). Theosophy's adept, who achieved vision and intersubjective connection through a heightened will, offered Yeats a model of the merging of minds that was compatible with the autonomous subject and with his ideas of masculinity. Occult proscriptions against losing control sought a model of the subject that was both firmly individuated and mystically merged.

The by-law forbidding hypnotism to members of the Golden Dawn encapsulates the ironies and contradictions of the kind of autonomy Yeats insisted upon for the individual subject engaged in the occult merging of minds he thought necessary for national unity: a totalitarian edict that demands individuality, something like "I command you to be your own person." Yeats resolved the crisis of individualism by salvaging a very specific (and very limited) definition of the individual. This individuality has little to do with the pluralism of liberal political theory; it mandated autonomy, not in the content of the individual psyche (expressed, say, in conflicting interests or ideologies), but in its form: the bounded subject. The heightened individual will that Yeats's occult theatre posited as a complement to mystical mental unity demanded less personal individuality than psychic individuation. This individuality was compatible with Yeats's wish to occupy the role of the leader or magician who transforms the masses.

Yeats's audiences refused to transform themselves into a nation or to welcome and celebrate the unique visions of his favorite artists; they insisted on displaying versions of collectivity and autonomy Yeats disapproved of. The Irish Literary Theatre and its successors did become quite popular; Adrian Frazier claims that popular involvement in the activities surrounding the writing and staging of plays "amounted to a mass movement."[89] But it was not the mass movement Yeats had sought to create and influence. As Frazier puts it, "Drama now was under way in Ireland, under the control not of a few Anglo-Irish authors but of a vast national apparatus."[90] The controversies and riots over *The Countess Cathleen, In the Shadow of the Glen* and *The Playboy of the Western World* brought Yeats into contact, sometimes face to face contact, with the unruly crowds whose possible formation haunted his writings on the national theatre. As he became increasingly disillusioned with the theatre, Yeats continued to ponder the relationship between the nation and the crowd, writing in 1909, "Are there not groups which obtain, through powerful emotion, organic vitality? How do they differ from the mob of casual men who are the enemies of all that has fineness?" (*Mem,* 250). He came to believe that the kind of organic unity he sought was not possible for a modern nation, even Ireland. Increasingly, his representations of the threat of the crowd emphasized, not its seductive ability to dissolve the subject, but the frustrated leader/magician's inability to control it.

For Yeats, the failure of his theatre to be at once literary and popular was a symptom of the fact that the public sphere in the age of mass politics was dominated by the crowd: during the early years of the twentieth century, he increasingly referred to his opponents in these controversies as "the mob." Obviously, Yeats's construction of the mob was highly idiosyncratic, and bore only tenuous resemblances to the sociological formations and phenomena he sought to describe. The important point here is that during these years "the mob" became his catch-all phrase for people and events that he found disturbing in the Irish public sphere. Yeats's earlier works had expressed anxieties over the possible continuum between the nation and the crowd by meditating upon the attractions and dangers of the dissolution of the subject. In contrast, Yeats's constructions of the mob figured it as the opposite of the nation, rather than its logical and threatening extension. While the nation combined mystical unity and flourishing individuality, the mob was both fragmented and homogeneous. The mob resembled Le Bon's group mind in that it enforced homogeneity and conformity among its members, and suppressed individual will and creativity. On the other hand, Yeats also claimed that members of a mob lacked any deep and genuine connection with each other. A mob was "held together not by what is interior, delicate and haughty, but by law and force which they obey because they must" (*Mem*, 251). The Irish mob was embodied in the Catholic church (a competing master of the mobilization of the masses through occult technologies) and the newspapers, and Yeats, encouraged by his reading of Nietzsche, which he began in 1902,[91] repeatedly linked "pulpit and press" as its twin manifestations.[92] Rather than the working classes, Yeats's mob was associated with the materialistic middle classes.

Like the Rose poems and *Cathleen ni Houlihan*, Yeats's excoriations of the mob figured the threatening form of collectivity as feminine; as late as 1934, Yeats associated women and crowds as parallel entities: "the logic of fanaticism, whether in a woman or a mob is drawn from a premise protected by ignorance and therefore irrefutable" (*VP*, 837). However, because the mob posed a different threat Yeats figured it through a different form of femininity. The mob's "femininity" was no longer the femininity of a seductive devouring mother or goddess figure, but the maimed masculinity of a castrated male. Yeats claimed that "the political class in Ireland" had "suffered through the cultivation of hatred as the one energy of their movement, a deprivation which is the intellectual equivalent to the removal of the genitals. Hence the shrillness of their voices. They contemplate all creative power as the eunuchs contemplate Don Juan as he passes through Hell on the white horse" (*Mem*, 176).

This castrated mob was both insufficiently passionate and overly excited. Yeats's earlier negotiations with his ambivalence had dealt with the problematic erotics of crowds; now an erotics of any sort was one of the important things the mob lacked. The erotics of the crowd had coincided with the erotics of occult intersubjectivity, and Yeats explained the mob's sexual dysfunction through magical paradigms as well:

Certainly evocation with symbol has taught me that much that we think of as limited to certain obvious effects influences the whole being. A meditation on sunlight, for instance, affects the nature throughout, producing all that follows from the symbolical nature of the sun. Hate must, in the same way, make sterile, producing many effects which would follow from the meditation on a symbol capable of giving hate. Such a symbol would produce not merely hate but associated effects ... Hatred as a basis of imagination, in ways which one could explain even without magic, helps to dry up the nature and makes the sexual abstinence, so common among young men and women in Ireland, possible. (*Mem*, 176–7)

The form of collectivity designated by the term mob resembled a group of adepts who have meditated on the wrong symbol, in effect practicing black magic on themselves.

The gradual process of Yeats's disillusionment with the Irish theatre and the growth of his conviction that "the dream of my early manhood, that a modern nation can return to Unity of Culture, is false" (*AY*, 196) coincides with a transition from one kind of crowd threat to another. The first volume of poetry to document Yeats's disillusionment with the theatre, *The Green Helmet and Other Poems* (1910) enacts this transition. The volume begins with a seldom discussed poem called "His Dream" (*VP*, 253–4). The poem depicts a speaker who finds himself swept up in the ecstatic, erotic group mind of a crowd against his will. Initially, the speaker is isolated from the crowd, both physically and mentally; he is alone on a boat, a sort of human island, and the crowd surrounds him. He "saw wherever I could turn / A crowd upon a shore." In addition, he does not share the crowd's ecstatic state of mind; he "would have hushed the crowd" if he could have.

The crowd have been incited to this state by a spectacle, the "figure in a shroud / Upon a gaudy bed." They exhibit the frenzied behavior contemporary descriptions of crowds emphasized, as the repetition of "running," "crying" and "cried" suggests. Their frenzy is also an erotic one; they cry with "ecstatic breath." Their ecstasy is an ecstasy over a dead body, a figure they call "By the sweet name of Death." This indicates that the crowd is erotically drawn to dissolution and death, and that the kind of collectivity it represents spells the erasure of the individual. As in Yeats's account of the Jubilee Riot, the speaker's inability to control the crowd leads to his participation in it: "Though I'd my finger on my lip, / What could I but take up the song?" This crowd embodies the erotic promise and threat of the dissolution of the subject in the Rose poems and *Cathleen ni Houlihan*.

The rest of the volume, however, presents crowds whose main feature is their refusal to cooperate with the poet, magician or leader, rather than their seductive threat to engulf him. Unlike Yeats's earlier volumes, *The Green Helmet and Other Poems* is full of crowds: the "ignorant men" and "little streets" which rise up in violence in "No Second Troy" (*VP*, 256–7), the implied audiences of "Reconciliation" (*VP*, 257), "Against Unworthy Praise" (*VP*, 259–60) and "The Fascination of What's Difficult" (*VP*, 260), the agitators of "On hearing that the Students of our New University have joined the Agitation against Immoral Literature" (*VP*, 262), the "hundreds" of "At the Abbey Theatre" (*VP*, 264–5), and the crowd of "At Galway Races" (*VP*, 266). These crowds are middle-class materialists, "the merchant and the clerk" who "Breathed on the world with timid breath" (*VP*, 266), and they can neither appreciate nor experience the erotic ecstasy of the crowd of "His Dream." Instead, they seek to enforce moral conformity, presenting the spectacle of "youth / Restraining reckless middle age" (*VP*, 262).

Yeats turned the passage in his memoirs about eunuchs and Don Juan into "On those that hated 'The Playboy of the Western World', 1907" in 1909 (the poem appeared in *Responsibilities* [1914] rather than *The Green Helmet and Other Poems*, however). The passage and the poem were based on Charles Ricketts' painting of Don Juan in Hell,[93] and Yeats put it out around Dublin that he had Arthur Griffith, once a friend and now an enemy, specifically in mind.[94] The Playboy controversy represents the height of Yeats's disillusionment with the theatre; he called the audience's failure to understand Synge's play "the one serious failure of our movement" (*EX*, 229). The poem illustrates Yeats's new construction of nationalist crowds:

> Once, when midnight smote the air,
> Eunuchs ran through Hell and met
> On every crowded street to stare
> Upon great Juan riding by:
> Even like these to rail and sweat
> Staring upon his sinewy thigh.   (*VP*, 294)

The spectacle before the crowd provokes a frenzy, but a frenzy of sexual dysfunction and sexual jealousy rather than an ecstatic or erotic one. The anti-erotic crowd is represented by an anti-man, an eunuch, rather than a woman. The individual confronting the crowd, Don Juan, is the opposite of the hapless Michael Gillane; he towers over and is impervious to the crowd rather than being mesmerized by it.

The difference between *Cathleen ni Houlihan* and "On those that hated 'The Playboy of the Western World', 1907" is the difference between a theory of the theatre that needs crowds because it seeks to move the masses and a theory of the theatre that rejects such a project. While Yeats began the Irish theatre in the hopes that he could create plays that were at once literary and popular, his experiences with Irish audiences taught him to see literary and popular as necessary polar opposites, and that celebrations of heroic individual creativity would not produce mystical national community. In "J. M. Synge and the Ireland of his Time," Yeats wrote, "ideas and images which have to be understood and loved by large numbers of people must appeal to no rich personal experience, no patience of study, no delicacy of sense" (*EI*, 313).

This opposition structures the 1916 essay on "Certain Noble Plays of Japan," written after Yeats discovered the Noh drama, in which he claimed "I have invented a form of drama, distinguished, indirect, and symbolic, and having no need of mob or Press to pay its way – an aristocratic form" (*EI*, 221). The "popular arts," on the other hand, should seek a "more complete realism" (*EI*, 228). The same opposition between the popular theatre and Yeats's new theatre informs the 1919 essay "A People's Theatre," in the form of *A Vision*'s opposition between subjective and objective. In the modern world, because "great crowds, changed by popular education with its eye always on some objective task, have begun to find reality in mechanism alone" (*EX*, 245), only an objective theatre could be popular with audiences. Yeats saw the Abbey's successful peasant plays as "the making articulate of all the dumb classes each with its own knowledge of the world, its own dignity, but all objective with the objectivity of the office and the workshop, of the newspaper and the street, of mechanism and of politics" (*EX*, 249). The age of crowds has spelled the demise of a theatre that could be both literary and popular; the subjective artist could no longer "draw the crowd" (*EX*, 251). Yeats argued that the "Popular Theatre should grow always more objective" (*EX*, 257), but he envisioned a different kind of theatre for himself: "I want to create for myself an unpopular theatre and an audience like a secret society where admission is by favour and never to many" (*EX*, 254).

While Yeats began his work with the Irish theatre by theorizing that a popular nationalist theatre would be by definition an occult one, by 1919 he desired a theatre he described as occult precisely because it was not popular. Yeats's description of the audience as a mob undergoing a magical transformation into a people and his

portrait of an audience like "a secret society" were both occult in
that they took seriously the idea that the foundations of politics and
society were shaped by the unconscious and nonrational, by ritual
and symbol. In "A People's Theatre" the subjective art Yeats
wishes to turn to involves the same anti-realist emphasis on ritual,
vision and meditation as his early Irish theatre, "doing its work by
suggestion, not by direct statement, a complexity of rhythm, colour,
gesture" (*EX*, 255). The major difference between the two was the
scale on which they operated – the nation versus the aristocratic
drawing room. Yeats's ambivalent embrace of the idea of nationalist politics as mass politics produced one version of the crowd in
the Rose and *Cathleen ni Houlihan*; his rejection of that idea
produced another version in *The Green Helmet and Other Poems* and
Responsibilities.

If the continuum between Yeats's nation and the crowd embodies his discomfort with the masses and mass politics, it also
embodies some important insights into the nonrational bases of
mass politics and modern collectivity. When Yeats confronted the
mass character of modern nationalism, he drew on a widespread,
largely conservative conception of mass politics as a politics of the
irrational, the unconscious, the erotic and the feminine. As Andreas
Huyssen puts it, "The fear of the masses in this age of declining
liberalism is always also a fear of woman, a fear of nature out of
control, a fear of the unconscious, of sexuality, of the loss of
identity and stable ego boundaries in the mass."[95] But Yeats
appropriated this discourse without any nostalgia for the rational
politics of liberal theory. Instead, Yeats's early Irish theatre explicitly desired, feared and theorized about the nonrational bases of
collectivity and the occult technologies required to establish and
strengthen those bases. The forthrightness with which Yeats recognized the inadequacy of rationalist assumptions and liberal political
theory for thinking about collectivity offers an important reminder
that criticizing nationalism on the grounds of its nonrationality
alone is a critical and political dead end. Mass politics are "occult"
(in Yeats's sense of that term) in a number of important ways, and
it is far more useful to draw distinctions between different versions
of occultism than to lament that fact. Yeats's early theory of the
Irish theatre often has troubling political implications because too
often Yeats could only figure the audience as a collection of
feminized, passive mediums or hypnotic subjects, rather than as a

CHAPTER 4

In the bedroom of the Big House: kindred, crisis, and Anglo-Irish nationality

Black fortress of ascendancy,
    Beneath whose wasting sway
Sprang crime and strife, so deadly rife –
    What rests of thee to-day?

John O'Hagan[1]

Tradition is kindred.

(*EX*, 312)

Yeats's engagement, in the works of his great middle period, with Anglo-Irish nationality and culture is one of the best-known and most controversial aspects of the "politics" of his work. His imaginative construction of the Irish eighteenth century as "that one Irish century that escaped from darkness and confusion" (*EX*, 345); his praise of Burke, Swift, Goldsmith and Berkeley as iconoclastic figures who represented the flowering of an Ascendancy culture which resisted the modernizing, mechanistic, democratic ideals of the enlightenment; his partial embrace of his own Anglo-Irish heritage; and his interest in the declining political and economic fortunes of the Irish Big Houses have generated a wide range of conflicting critical assessments.[2] For Yeats, Anglo-Irishness was by definition a nationality in crisis, the nationality of an ex-ruling elite whose displacement was already an accomplished fact and an important aspect of their cultural heritage. Most versions of nationality reveal themselves as constructions, despite their efforts to naturalize and conceal their own invention. Yeats's Anglo-Irish nationality, on the other hand, deliberately and elaborately exposes itself as a construction. In fact, its uniqueness as a national identity and its strength as a cultural tradition depend upon that exposure. Anglo-Irishness is a willful, imaginative response to the erosion of material power, the rupture of historical tradition and continuity, and the absence of a stable

group of masculine adepts who achieved mystical intersu[b]
through the exercise of an active and heightened wil[l]
constructions are occult; they differ in their gender an[d]
encodings and the degree to which they succumb to or man[age]
crisis of individualism.

identity. Yeats's Anglo-Irish meditations offer an analysis of the ways in which gender and sexual discourses are often used to naturalize and legitimize political relations, structures and ideologies.

Yeats's Anglo-Irish nationality was a contradictory one whose very foundations contained the corrupting seeds of its demise, and whose most valuable strengths and reassuring continuities were also the sources of its debilitating weaknesses and fragmentations.[3] He imagined the Anglo-Irish as a noble and worthwhile tradition, one capable of providing Ireland with the cultural continuity, political leadership and artistic integrity that he thought middle-class Catholic Ireland lacked. However, he also imagined Anglo-Irishness as a nationality founded on crime, perpetually in crisis and inherently subject to degeneration and decay. Its essence lay in this combination of coherence and crisis. Critics often read Yeats's emphasis on aristocratic families in his Anglo-Irish meditations and his related claim that "tradition is kindred" as emblematic of ar of a national tradition whose essential naturalness, self-perpetuation meant that it approached the cond On the contrary, in the context of Yeats's constructions of Anglo-Irish nationality, "tradition is kindred" means quite the reverse; the phrase expressed the disintegration of Anglo-Irish tradition rather than its coherence. Yeats's Big House poems represent Anglo-Irishness as crisis by embedding it in constructions of gender, sexuality, genealogy and family that were unstable, defamiliarized and denaturalized.

Most discourses that employ languages of family, sex and gender to characterize a national community or national identity do so in order to transfer a set of natural and desirable qualities from the former to the latter. To say that the nation arises out of the family is usually to claim that it forms a natural unit, that the ties which bind members together are as original, deep and enduring as the ties of kinship, that the individual's devotion to the nation itself is as natural and passionate as sexual love, and so forth. Other national discourses in which gender or sexuality and politics are mutually embedded seek to borrow constructions of natural inferiority or essential weakness. For the imperialist discourses examined in chapter 1, to claim that the Irish were like women was to assert their inherent inferiority and incapacity for self-government. In other moods Yeats imagined relationships between gender and nationality that follow both these patterns. For our discussion here, the important feature of both is that they accord gender, sexuality, genealogy and family structures the status of natural, essential and stable entities in order to confer a similar status on nationality through comparison.

As Yeats became increasingly interested in Anglo-Irish tradition and identity, however, he began to elaborate an alternate model of gender, sexuality and family, one which asserted the mutual embeddedness of sexuality and politics differently. The gender and sexual structures involved in this version of nationality center around what Freud called the victory of the race over the individual. They emphasize issues of origin and continuity: sexual reproduction is reproduction of the nation, and the purpose of sexual desire is to motivate choice of a mate. Femininity represents a passive, reflective principle whose primary function is mimetic and reproductive. But the nation does not sustain itself by simply relying on sexual reproduction as a "natural" process. Reproduction and the definition of femininity devoted to it are inseparable from the political sphere – the victory of the race over the individual demands regulation and enforcement. Yeats's Big House poems define the Anglo-Irish as a nationality in crisis by refusing the hegemonic conceptions of gender, sexuality and family as elements in a natural and stable economy of wholeness, continuity and reproduction. By repeatedly separating reproduction and genealogy from "nature," these poems reveal that the continuity of the nation depends, not on sustaining or passing on some founding essence or energy, but on a repeated crisis of foundations that demands that each generation begin anew amid isolation and adversity. In this alternate model, kindred *is* crisis.

Many of Yeats's poems about Anglo-Irish tradition enact the shattering of individual and collective illusions of wholeness, continuity and purity and the recognition of Anglo-Irish complicity in their own denigration and decline. Yeats's Anglo-Irish works are preoccupied with dismantling distinctions between external threats and internal corruption, public political catastrophes and private sexual crises, and repeatedly posit the former only to reveal their identity with the latter. Yeats drew on Edmund Burke's definition of the state as a partnership between the dead, the living and the unborn and focused on continuity (and its lack) between past and present rather than on the "deep, horizontal comradeship" that Benedict Anderson observes characterizes most modern imagined communities.[4] At the same time, these poems figure such genealogical inheritance, not as the biologically assured transmission of tradition, but as a crisis in reproduction which stands for the failure of such transmission. While most conceptions of nationality construct homologies between the individual and the group, Yeats's Anglo-Irish meditations refuse the notion of a nation or tradition in which each individual replicates, on a smaller scale, the national being. Instead, they emphasize a concept of nationality or "race" which is constantly at war with the individual and for which the social construction and management of sexual identities and desires represents the necessary but sometimes violent subjugation of individual to nation or family.

As this contradictory portrait of nationality suggests, Yeats's Big House poems are deeply ambivalent in several respects. Ambivalence comes in many forms, and the two particular forms that appear in these poems are crucial in defining his construction of Anglo-Irish nationality. The first is an ambivalence best summed up by Richard Gill's characterization of "Ancestral Houses" as an elegy for "the house as a lost community" which is an "ambiguous compound of eulogy and satire."[5] Many of Yeats's Anglo-Irish meditations look back to the Anglo-Irish of the eighteenth century and lament the gap between what the Ascendancy once was and what it has become, alternating between elegizing the virtues and lifestyles that are gone and castigating the current Anglo-Irish for not possessing them. The second structure of ambivalence in these poems acknowledges that Anglo-Irish civilization is based on barbarism, that its rich cultural identity originates in crime and violence. This ambivalence is in the mode of irony rather than indictment; for the Yeats of this period, violence and greatness, blood and power go together. Yeats found those who imagined things were otherwise hopelessly utopian, and he criticized this lack of a vision of evil in a range of thinkers, from socialists to Shelley to Whitman.[6]

Both varieties of ambivalence place Yeats's Anglo-Irish nationality in a deeply conservative political tradition. For over a century, writers in England and Ireland had been lamenting the gradual, perpetual decline of the political and economic power of the Anglo-Irish, and had cast this decline as a major cause for the deplorable state of Ireland as a whole. Most descriptions focused on the internal degeneration of the Anglo-Irish and on such destructive abdications of responsibility as absenteeism. Although writings in this tradition often mention the threats posed by restless Irish peasants and an indifferent London government, examination of such external threats is generally eclipsed by their concentration on the internal corruption of the Anglo-Irish themselves.

But such discourses did not see the decay of the Anglo-Irish as a corruption inherent to the inequalities of the landlord system. The problem with the Anglo-Irish aristocracy, in other words, was not that they were an aristocracy, but that they were a weak aristocracy; it was not the landlord system as such, but the preponderance of bad landlords over good ones. For this tradition, the internal corruption of the Anglo-Irish and the ambivalence about them provoked by that corruption do not point to the costs of conquest or the results of inequity; rather they measure the distance between the Anglo-Irish aristocracy and an ideal aristocracy that would benefit the nation as a whole. Thus while Edmund Burke was a sharp critic of the Ascendancy, and was among the first Irish writers to use the term, he recommended that the Ascendancy be replaced by a "true aristocracy."[7] Maria Edgeworth's *The Absentee* takes a similar view and ends with Lord Colambre returning to his Irish estate where "he will long diffuse happiness through the wide circle, which is peculiarly subject to the influence and example of a great resident Irish proprietor."[8] Thomas Carlyle's 1849 tour through famine-ravaged Ireland merely impressed upon him the slothful character of the peasantry and the need for a true aristocracy. "Alas," he exclaimed, "*when* will there any real aristocracy arise (here or elsewhere) to need a Capitol for residing in!"[9] As John Kelly has pointed out, despite Yeats's praise of Burke, Carlyle is even more his political precursor than Burke.[10] Robert Lynd characterized the landed Irish gentry as "one of the most worthless aristocracies in history."[11] Standish O'Grady's famous description of the aristocracy "rotting from the land in the most dismal farce-tragedy ever seen, without one brave deed, one brave word,"[12] was nothing new, nor was his insistence that in saving themselves the Anglo-Irish could also save Ireland.

Yeats once claimed that he used the phrase "middle class" to denote "an attitude of mind more than an accident of birth" (*UPII*, 241), and some critics have made similar assertions about his notions of "aristocracy."[13] Such interpretations focus on the virtues Yeats associated with the aristocracy, arguing that his aristocracy was metaphorical or aesthetic rather than material. It is true that for Yeats the most important meanings of "aristocracy" involved particular kinds of cultural continuity, artistic value, intellectual integrity, individual autonomy and political leadership, and that he claimed that other people, such as artists and the Irish peasantry, could also possess these qualities. It is equally true, however, that for the most part he based his ideal aristocracy firmly in a material one; his works insist again and again that such virtues flourish most readily under the conditions provided by wealth, privilege and leisure. In fact, his determination to base his ideal aristocracy in a material one was one of the driving forces behind his selective construction of Anglo-Irish culture and history. He over-estimated both the literary productiveness of the Irish aristocracy and the aristocratic status of the Ascendancy, conflating the terms "Ascendancy" and "aristocracy."[14] In his memoirs he observed: "In spite of myself my mind dwells more and more on ideas of class. Ireland has grown sterile, because power has passed to men who lack the training which requires a certain amount of wealth to ensure continuity from generation to generation, and to free the mind in part from other tasks" (*Mem*, 178). His autobiography claims that "intellectual freedom and social equality are incompatible" (*AY*, 154) and that "Leisure, wealth, privilege were created to be a soil for the most living" (*AY*, 348). In 1923 he told the Irish senate: "it is most important that we should keep in this country a certain leisured class" (*SS*, 38–9). The material aspects of Yeats's aristocracy were not merely metaphors for ideal ones; he consistently described wealth and privilege as necessary, though not sufficient, conditions for his true aristocracy of the mind. Like the Celtic writings examined in chapter 1, Yeats's Anglo-Irish writings imagined the cultural uniqueness of a "class" of the Irish people in part by meditating on the cultural productivity of a particular set of material conditions. His claims that a rich national culture and vigorous political leadership required social inequality are less the misguided means to a desirable end than the hallmarks of an impoverished political imagination that insisted on labelling such virtues "aristocratic" and refused to separate them from hierarchical politics in any sustained manner.

Yeats's ambivalent characterizations of the Anglo-Irish as an aristocracy revolved around their distance from a true aristocracy and around acknowledging the costs to individuals of establishing and maintaining such an aristocracy. Neither approach constitutes a conventional political critique of the Anglo-Irish. Both, however, organize themselves around constructions of family, gender and genealogy that shatter the natural and essential status of these concepts. In doing so, they suggest another kind of ambivalence, and a different kind of political critique. These poems examine the ideological work done by ordinary conceptions of gender and sexuality in national discourses – the work of naturalization.

"If I Were Four-and-Twenty," first published in the *Irish Statesman* in 1919, illustrates the structures of ambivalence in Yeats's Anglo-Irish nationality and the constructions of family, sexuality and genealogy that embody and support them. Earlier writers, from Burke to Edgeworth to O'Grady, presented their meditations on the Anglo-Irish as an aristocracy as responses, not merely to Anglo-Irish decline, but to more general problems in Ireland as well. Similarly, Yeats's essay offers its versions of family and genealogy in the context of the turbulent political scenes of 1919, both Irish and international. The essay recommends unity to the Irish nation – cultural, emotional, logical, religious – but the solutions it offers constantly reinscribe division and defeat. This ambivalent structure corresponds to the double perspective suggested by the title, and to the essay's presentation of two contradictory views of the family. Sexuality and the family, as Yeats constructs them here, represent principles of national community and traditional continuity that are also, irreducibly, principles of conflict and fragmentation.

The essay's main theme is Unity of Being, for the individual and for the nation, and it begins by introducing a theory of nationality that sees the individual and the nation as parallel formations. Its opening paragraph recalls Yeats's successful personal quest to "hammer" his thoughts into a unity and relate his major interests – an "interest in a form of literature, in a form of philosophy, and a belief in nationality" (*EX*, 263) – to one another. Yeats claims that "Now all three are, I think, one, or rather all three are a discrete expression of a single conviction" (*EX*, 263) and that he has become "a cultivated man" (*EX*, 263). His word choice points to the links between culture and cultivation, emphasizing that national culture does not simply "grow;" it must be nurtured and managed. The text then transfers this paradigm for achieving unity to the nation as a whole: "It is just the same with a nation – it is only a cultivated nation when it has related its main interests one to another" (*EX*, 263). The projects Yeats would pursue "if I were four-and-twenty" are designed to help the Irish nation achieve this unity, and are based on the notion that the individual and the nation are homologous, that "it is just the same with a nation." However, the ironic, discouraged perspective of the man of four-and-fifty acknowledges the impossibility of this project and the suspect nature of such parallelism. The essay ends:

if I were not four-and-fifty, with no settled habit but the writing of verse, rheumatic, indolent, discouraged, and about to move to the Far East, I would begin another epoch by recommending to the Nation a new doctrine, that of unity of being. (*EX*, 280)

Of course, on one level this joking compilation of things that prevent him from making such a recommendation clearly constitutes that recommendation. On another level, this and all the essay's other suggestions are constantly haunted and ironized by the authoritative negating voice of the older speaker.

This double perspective corresponds to the competing versions of the family offered in the essay. The text describes the family both as the emblem of harmonious national unity and as the site where individual interests and group needs clash. Although it also discusses political integration as a necessary part of constructing a cultured nation, the essay emphasizes specifically religious division, religious unity, as suggested by the claim "We are a religious nation" (*EX*, 263). This claim looks back to Yeats's early theories of the theatre, which saw religion and nationalism as analogous powerful mobilizing forces. In its attempt to find a basis for unity in the very ground that appears to separate the Irish from one another, it is also symptomatic of the essay's particular method. In rewriting religion into a basis for Irish unity rather than a source of Irish conflict, Yeats chooses the family as its central paradigm, suggesting a natural and universal Christianity as the foundation of a social order:

When I close my eyes and pronounce the word "Christianity" and await its unconscious suggestion, I do not see Christ crucified, or the Good Shepherd from the catacombs, but a father and mother and their children. (*EX*, 272)

The text offers kinship ties, the sexual relationship between man and woman and the genealogical relationship between generations, as the model and origin of a national community based on nonrational bonds: "I understand ... by 'family' all institutions, classes, orders, nations, that arise out of the family and are held together, not by a logical process, but by historical association" (*EX*, 273–4). Here family or kindred describes a principle of communal association which emphasizes emotional bonds and continuity over time figured as genealogical.

But these appeals to the family as the model for a harmoniously unified Irish nation do not assume that the family represents a natural, stable economy of affection and reproduction. This definition of the kindred relation asserts that individual sexual identities and desires are socially constructed, and that if they are to assume a form that will ensure the reproduction of the original, founding energies of a family/nation, they must be properly shaped and vigilantly regulated. Yeats's version of genealogy combined an essentialist insistence on genetic inheritance with an acute consciousness of the socially constructed nature of desire. He argues:

If, as these writers affirm, the family is the unit of social life, and the origin of civilisation which but exists to preserve it, and almost the sole cause of progress, it seems more natural than it did before that its ecstatic moment, the sexual choice of man and woman, should be the greater part of all poetry. A single wrong choice may destroy a family, dissipating its tradition or its biological force, and the great sculptors, painters, and poets are there that instinct may find its lamp. When a young man imagines the woman of his hope, shaped for all the uses of life, mother and mistress and yet fitted to carry a bow in the wilderness, how little of it all is mere instinct, how much has come from chisel and brush. Educationalists and statesmen, servants of the logical process, do their worst, but they are not the matchmakers who bring together the fathers and mothers of the generations nor shall the type they plan survive. (*EX*, 274–5)

Yeats's essay casts sexuality and familial relations as the very origins and building blocks of civilization and simultaneously deprives them of the "natural" status which myths of origin usually enjoy. Sex makes history, sex governs politics, and poetry that deals with sexual subjects is, in the most literal sense, historical and political. In Yeats's most extended attempt to elaborate a philosophy of history and a theory of politics, *A Vision*, he returned to the family as his central paradigm: "All these symbols can be thought of as the symbols of the relations of men and women and the birth of children" (*V*, 211). Sex itself, however, must be made and governed. Yeats does not simply assume compulsory reproductive heterosexuality; he theorizes the cultural mechanisms of its enforcement. The genealogical continuity of the generations conflates biological and cultural inheritance, and both are tenuous because they depend upon the potentially unreliable sexual choices of individuals. Individual desire is not a matter of "mere instinct," but must be shaped and managed by culture, in particular the creative imagination of the poet, giving a new twist to the notion that poets are the unacknowledged legislators of the world.

For this mood in the middle Yeats, the sexual relations and choices of individuals form the very foundations of civilization, and the family is the site where larger generational and civilizational imperatives are brought to bear on potentially uncooperative individual desires. Families and cultures struggle to organize individual desires around the reproductive imperatives of generational continuity. Most discourses of nationality deny any conflict between the individual and the community or code such conflict as the opportunity for the heroic self-sacrifice of the individual who is thereby merged with the national being. However, in Yeats's national community arising out of and modelled on the sexual and genealogical relationships of the family, the coherence and continuity of the group depend explicitly on the management and suppression of the individual. This nationality does not offer individuals the kind of mystic or emotional compensation for self-sacrifice or forced cooperation that other national discourses do. Accordingly, Yeats associated this construction of the family with thinkers who saw society as a struggle for survival of the fittest – Darwin, Nietzsche, and especially Balzac, of whom Yeats wrote:

his whole purpose was to expound the doctrine of his Church as it is displayed, not in decrees and manuals, but in the institutions of Christendom. Yet Nietzsche might have taken, and perhaps did take, his conception of the superman in history from his *Catherine de Medici*, and he has explained and proved, even more thoroughly than Darwin, the doctrine of the survival of the fittest species. Only, I think, when one has mastered his whole vast scheme can one understand clearly that his social order is the creation of two struggles, that of family with family, that of individual with individual, and that our politics depend upon which of the two struggles has most affected our imagination. If it has been most affected by the individual struggle, we insist upon equality of opportunity, "the career open to talent", and consider rank and wealth fortuitous and unjust; and if it is most affected by the struggles of families, we insist upon all that preserves what that struggle has earned, upon social privilege, upon the rights of property. (*EX*, 269–70)

Here, as often in this aspect of Yeats's work, "family" means an aristocratic, wealthy family, a dynasty. Each struggle, family and individual, implies a political system: aristocracy or democracy. The success of the individual struggle depends on the destruction of the conditions which allow families to flourish, and vice versa. This nation modelled on and arising out of the family is far from a safe and stable haven for individuals; it is a nation which by definition conflicts with the individual.

This is a version of the family/nation which can accommodate what Yeats called a vision of evil, and Balzac was the figure who exemplified it best for Yeats.[15] In "If I Were Four-And-Twenty" Yeats praises Balzac for being anti-utopian (*EX*, 269) and having just such a vision of evil (*EX*, 276–7).[16] He wrote to Maud Gonne in 1927, "You are right – I think – in saying I was once a republican, though like you yourself I would have been satisfied with Gladstone's bill. I wonder if I ever told you what changed all my political ideas. It was the reading through in 1903–4 of the entire works of Balzac" (*GY*, 434).[17] Later that same year he told Gonne, "The great political service that Balzac did me was that he made authoritative government (government which can, at need, be remorseless, as in his *Catherine De Medici*) interesting in my eyes" (*GY*, 437).

Yeats codified the conflict between the individual and the family, nation or "race" into a structural certainty in *A Vision*, which figures the opposition between antithetical and primary in part as an irreconcilable conflict between submission to the dictates of race and assertion of individuality. "It will be obvious," writes Yeats, "that self-sacrifice must be the typical virtue of phases where instinct or race is predominant" (*VA*, 26). In *A Vision*, as in "If I Were Four-and-Twenty," the dichotomy between individual and race, antithetical and primary, is also an opposition between aristocratic and democratic politics: "Primary means democratic. Antithetical means aristocratic" (*V*, 104). Phase 8 represents the turning point between the primary, feminine, self-sacrificing character of phases 1 through 7 and the antithetical, masculine, individual emphasis of phases 9 through 15. Along with its opposite, Phase 22, Phase 8 marks the stage where the two forces are most nearly equal and where the conflict between them is at its most intense: "Phase 8 and Phase 22 are phases of struggle and tragedy, the first a struggle to find personality, the second a struggle to lose it" (*V*, 83). From the earliest drafts of the automatic script onward,[18] Phase 8 represents the individual's efforts to escape the dictates of race and achieve an individual personality, and Yeats described the Will of this phase as "War between Individuality and Race" (*V*, 116).

Of course, there is some slippage here between the terms, "family," "nation" and "race;" "If I Were Four-and-Twenty" emphasizes national unity and familial continuity, while *A Vision* generally casts such unity and continuity in terms of race. Yeats often used "nation" and "race" more or less interchangeably, and he also alternated between two related meanings of "family" – simply a father, mother and children, and an aristocratic dynasty which encompassed a relation between past, present and future. All, however, function in this aspect of Yeats's work as exemplars of community and continuity based on bonds that were emotional, sexual and inherited in some sense. They also function as forces which demand the construction and regulation of individuals in ways that run counter to individual desires.

His conception of aristocracy, however, both demanded the subordination of the individual and provided the nurturing ground on which the individual could be free of all subordination. This aristocracy was actually based on a tension between two related aristocratic modes: a supportive, secluded atmosphere of gracious plenty and cultural continuity, and the individual creativity and autonomy which flourished in it.[19] The respective gender roles of men and women in the aristocratic family represented these two modes: Yeats consistently elaborated the distinction between them as a gender difference between a primary, feminine principle of continuity and an antithetical, masculine principle of originality. He wrote in his autobiography, "Surely the ideal of culture expressed by Pater can only create feminine souls. The soul becomes a mirror not a brazier ... Culture of this kind produces the most perfect flowers in a few highbred women" (*AY*, 323). This feminine culture produced individuals who were passive reflectors, submitting to the dictates of race, reproducing Anglo-Irish tradition from generation to generation, and providing the gracious, leisured foundation which brazier-like masculine culture both needed and defined itself against.

The feminine principle of continuity entailed loyalty to the "house," familial, material and cultural. A number of commentators have noted that Yeats's genealogical theory of tradition was indebted to the English country house tradition in literature. The basis of the country house tradition is generally assumed to be the correspondence between the aristocrats and their dwelling; architectural structure and moral order mirror each other.[20] Yeats's Big House poems pose such correspondence as a question rather than a given, and align it with the feminine principle of continuity. For Yeats, an aristocratic hostess was a woman who lived and embodied such correspondence, maintaining her house as a gracious nurturing atmosphere of tradition in which the individual talent might flourish. His autobiography records a growing conviction that for his intellectual projects he "needed a hostess more than a society" (*AY*, 155) and his disappointment at Maud Gonne's refusal to accept that role. When he abandoned the idea of an occult popular theatre in favor of an "unpopular theatre and an audience like a secret society," he predicted, "Instead of advertisements in the Press I need a hostess" (*EX*, 255). Yeats wrote to Edmund Dulac in 1924,

The psychological moment has come, for Dublin is reviving after the Civil War, and self-government is creating a little stir of excitement. People are trying to found a new society. It is quite amusing trying to create a society without hostesses, and without wealth. If you know a hostess of genius and great wealth, you might tell her that here is an opportunity worth living for, especially if she will search her ancestors till she finds an Irish one. (*L*, 702)

In all these instances, "hostess" signifies a set of social and political structures and commitments – the rule of the elite few rather than democracy, a gender hierarchy of male over female, the concentration of wealth in the hands of aristocratic families, the values of courtesy and custom – which made possible the cultural richness and freedom Yeats sought for himself and the new nation.

Yeats's descriptions of Lady Gregory consistently cast her as an exemplary aristocratic women whose loyalty to her tradition and her "house," both familial and material, was "a choice constantly renewed in solitude" (*AY*, 264). His description of her in his autobiography as "a friend and hostess, a centre of peace" (*AY*, 304), conflates the woman and her estate, which Yeats said he came to "love ... more than all other houses" (*AY*, 260). "Coole Park, 1929" meditates upon "an aged woman and her house" (*VP*, 488) as dual centers of traditional culture and supportive tranquility. Her connection with her house represented a commitment to the Anglo-Irish tradition/race; in *A Vision* he placed her in Phase 24, the phase where "Race is transformed into a moral conception" (*V*, 172). For Yeats, Lady Gregory embodied her house and sustained it; after her death he wrote in a letter that "when she died the great house died too" (*L*, 796).

If the feminine principle of continuity exemplified by Yeats's praise of hostesses and Lady Gregory provided the focal point for the coherence and continuity of an aristocratic Anglo-Irish nationality and tradition, it also provided the focal point for the crisis and disintegration of Big House culture. The major variety of ambivalence in these works is that the putative languages of continuity and community turn out to be the languages of fragmentation and alienation as well. Tradition is indeed kindred, but kindred is, ultimately, crisis. Yeats figured the continuity of Anglo-Irish nationality as a genealogy, but he also redefined genealogy as a crisis in reproduction, and with each generation this original crisis is re-enacted. He claimed that sexuality and the family were the bases of civilization, but he also asserted that they themselves required founding in the social construction of sexual identity and the education of desire. Sexuality, being unstable and malleable, recapitulates the war between individuality and race in each individual. He made a gendered distinction between the traditional continuity and gracious atmosphere of his aristocracy and the individual talent which could arise within it, but acknowledged that the alliance between femininity and commitment to tradition was open to disruption, resistance and decay.

In "A Prayer For My Daughter" (*VP*, 403–6), Yeats depicts the Anglo-Irish as a community constantly in crisis by representing them as a tradition whose continuity is both dependent on and threatened by female sexual choice. Yeats began the poem while staying at the tower during the Anglo-Irish war, two days after Anne's birth on February 26, 1919. It is clear that on a biographical level Yeats's prayer for his daughter is in part that she grow up to be like her mother rather than like Gonne and the other women in Yeats's life. More important, however, is the way the poem structures these two alternatives. Similarly, while it is certainly true that the poem's speaker offers an obviously sexist prescription for his daughter's future life and development, that observation alone leaves much about the text unexplained. We need to read his prescription with two other points in mind. First, the poem relentlessly casts questions about female social and sexual development as, simultaneously, political questions about the survival of the Anglo-Irish aristocracy. Second, while the text initially depicts the Big House as threatened by violent forces from without, it blurs the boundaries between these forces and the internal threat posed by the potentially turbulent desires of aristocratic women.

The poem's opening stanzas function as a framing device, calling attention to the violence and chaos of the turbulent political scene of

1919, both in Ireland and in Europe, embodied by the storm,[21] and indicating that the speaker's prescriptions for his daughter form part of his response to a larger set of political issues and dangers:

> ... There is no obstacle
> But Gregory's wood and one bare hill
> Whereby the haystack- and roof-levelling wind,
> Bred on the Atlantic, can be stayed.

These lines designate Anglo-Irish estates like Coole as crucial but tenuous sites of resistance to such chaos; the screaming wind, ironically "bred" on the Atlantic, can only be countered by those who have been bred to better things in the Big House. Yeats wrote "The Second Coming" (*VP*, 401–2) just before Anne's birth, and he placed that poem just before "A Prayer For My Daughter" in *Michael Robartes and the Dancer* to highlight the connections between the public apocalypse of the one and the private trauma of the other. Both are figured as crises of sexual reproduction. The "rough beast" that "slouches towards Bethlehem to be born" in "The Second Coming" embodies history as driven by divine (or demonic) sexual acts or annunciations. Like the ill-bred screaming wind, its monstrous birth figures destiny as the product of a kind of cosmic miscegenation.

A number of critics have pointed out that the speaker's prayer is actually a contradictory combination of two opposing prayers; the poem contains a tension between the speaker's wish that his daughter become an autonomous individual and his wish that she become a custodian of traditional sanctity and loveliness.[22] On one hand, the speaker wants her to be "self-delighting," on the other, he wants her to "choose right," and marry into an aristocratic house. The contrast between individual pleasure and properly educated desire corresponds to Yeats's two conflicting but inseparable aristocratic modes, and the conflict between them embodies reproduction (the sexual and social production of the next generation) as the repetition of an original crisis. The speaker's explicit prayer for his daughter is that she be granted the independent qualities which will enable her to be happy despite the chaos around her. However, several aspects of the poem emphasize that the outcome of her psycho-sexual development will determine whether she will counter or contribute to that chaos. As a woman, the speaker's daughter must ultimately be relegated to embodying the feminine principle of continuity.

Female sexual identity is a subject for fatherly concern and management because the continuity of traditional, aristocratic culture depends on women, who, left to their own devices, may betray it by making improper sexual choices. Venus, "Being fatherless could have her way," and chose poorly. The negative examples of beautiful women who made unwise sexual choices combine public consequences with personal cost. Helen is probably Western culture's prime example of the catastrophic social consequences of private obsession, and the poem's laconic observation that she "later had much trouble with a fool" merely underscores this by understating it so arrestingly. The "Horn of Plenty," the cultured feminine principle of continuity and reproduction symbolized by Coole, can be "undone" from within by the appetites of fine women: "It's certain that fine women eat / A crazy salad with their meat / Whereby the Horn of Plenty is undone." The horn of plenty refers not only to the gracious fecundity of individual women, but also to the material wealth and cultured fertility of the aristocratic setting. Maud Gonne is another such woman whose desires endanger the tradition that produced her and that depends upon her for its continued existence:

> Have I not seen the loveliest woman born
> Out of the mouth of Plenty's horn,
> Because of her opinionated mind
> Barter that horn and every good
> By quiet natures understood
> For an old bellows full of angry wind?

Gonne has betrayed, not merely (or even primarily) herself, but the horn of plenty which produced her and which she in turn must reproduce. She has sold away, not goods in her own eyes, but goods in the eyes of "quiet natures." The play on "goods" suggests that their sale might be more appropriate than the speaker wants to admit.

While an individual might find it natural and desirable to barter things intended for that purpose, following such inclinations threatens the continuity of the house or the nation/race. The poem reinforces the daughter's role as a potential danger to the very culture she is supposed to support by constructing a number of verbal parallels between the external threat of violent and commercial forces and the internal corruption of transgressive female desire. Does the screaming wind that threatens the horn of plenty originate, as the first stanza suggests, on the Atlantic, or in Gonne's choice of MacBride as a husband, "an old bellows full of angry wind?" The poem's last stanza claims that "arrogance and hatred are the wares / Peddled in the thoroughfares" outside the estate, but Gonne has fallen into commercial exchange and has "bartered" her rightful aristocratic existence. The speaker himself admits that his own mind has been choked with hatred; he knows "that to be choked with hate / May well be of all evil chances chief."[23] The external forces which threaten the Big House are mirrored by the dangerous desires of the women within it. The speaker's daughter can contribute to the resistance to the storm offered by the custom and ceremony of Coole, or she can succumb to those desires within her which ally her with the screaming wind.

The speaker ends by projecting his daughter's sexual maturity, a future in which she chooses the former course and embodies the correspondence between woman and house that illustrates the feminine principle of aristocratic continuity. The first line of the last stanza illustrates her passivity, in sharp contrast to the emphasis on autonomy in the previous stanza. The values of custom and cere-mony are first introduced as attributes of the house, and then transferred, not to the daughter herself, but to the symbols with which the poem associates her – the "rich horn" and "spreading laurel tree." The last stanza is dominated by the metonyms of aristocratic life and the adjectives the speaker associates with them, rather than by either the bride or the groom. In the original draft, Yeats did not even include the figure of a bridegroom, writing "and may she marry into some old house."[24]

In "A Prayer For My Daughter" the internal weaknesses of the Anglo-Irish are equivalent to the potentially "crazy" sexual identities and choices of "fine women." "Nineteen Hundred and Nineteen" (*VP*, 428–33) also aligns the corruption of the public and private virtues Yeats attributed to the Anglo-Irish with female sexual depravity. Yeats's Big House poems connect the laudable aspects of Anglo-Irishness with integrity in public life, strong political leader-ship, and a vigorous cultural tradition; "Nineteen Hundred and Nineteen" laments the decline of all these things during the Anglo-Irish War. The end of the poem embodies the political, moral and cultural decay it chronicles in Lady Kyteler's perverse desire for the succubus Robert Artisson, the rough beast whose coming heralds the beginning of a new and barbarous age:

> But now the wind drops, dust settles; thereupon
> There lurches past, his great eyes without thought
> Under the shadow of stupid straw-pale locks,
> That insolent fiend Robert Artisson
> To whom the love-lorn Lady Kyteler brought
> Bronzed peacock feathers, red combs of her cocks.

Like the corrupt erotic choices of the women in "A Prayer For My Daughter," Lady Kyteler's lust for the "insolent" fiend suggests a natural aristocrat's inappropriate desire for an unworthy and disrespectful inferior. In addition, the contrast between Artisson's lurching stupidity and lack of thought and Lady Kyteler's active and slightly pornographic gift-giving makes her appear as the real instigator of the historical rupture symbolized by Artisson, as does the fact that the poem ends with her.

"A Prayer For My Daughter" ends by projecting continuity rather than apocalyptic change. The poem's linking of female sexual development and the survival of the Anglo-Irish finds its corollary in the merging of woman and estate; in the final stanza, the speaker's daughter dissolves into the gracious house and atmosphere of the Anglo-Irish. The conflation of the daughter with her future house also constitutes the poem's acknowledgment that she can serve the communal goods of custom and ceremony only by surrendering herself as an individual. The poem constructs an Anglo-Irish community which maintains itself through victories over individual women. While one could read the poem's unresolved tension between autonomy and subordination for the daughter as a mark of incoherence, in the context of Yeats's definition of kindred as crisis, by refusing to resolve this tension the poem highlights the violence inherent in this conception of the family.

The ultimate embodiment of a kindred relation that involves coerced sexuality as the engine of history, familial or civilizational, is the rape of the daughter. "Leda and the Swan" (*VP*, 441) presents such a rape. The poem emphasizes the helplessness of the "staggering girl," with her "helpless breast" and "terrified vague fingers." It also emphasizes the power and savagery of her attacker in the mimetic force of the opening – "A sudden blow" – and the descriptions of the swan's "great wings" and "feathered glory." Contemporary critics accused Yeats of eroticizing rape and glorifying violence, but in relation to most previous poetic treatments of Leda and the swan Yeats had put the violence back into a scene that was frequently figured more as a seduction than a rape. While the poem insists on Leda's violent subjugation it does not simply imagine her going gently into the night of her own violation. Instead, it raises the question of her subaltern subjectivity: "How can those terrified vague fingers push / The feathered glory from her loosening thighs? / And how can body, laid in that white rush, / But feel the strange heart beating where it lies?" The final question also posits Leda's experience as important but inaccessible: "Did she put on his knowledge with his power / Before the indifferent beak could let her drop?" These lines introduce the question of the relationship between power and knowledge; what kind of knowledge accrues to the woman whose only power lies in the fact that she is a vessel through which some large impersonal force actualizes itself? In "A Prayer For My Daughter" that force is dynastic continuity, while in "Leda and the Swan" it is the historical rupture implied by the destruction of Troy and the death of Agamemnon. In both cases, knowledge and power are divided from each other. In "A Prayer For My Daughter" the daughter's support for Anglo-Irish tradition coincides with her "innocence" rather than her knowledge. The question of Leda's knowledge is more complicated: the poem holds out the possibility that she acquires Jove's knowledge and power, but it balances that possibility with the suggestion that Leda's knowledge is merely the inarticulable knowledge of her own subordination. Yeats's Anglo-Irish meditations and related poems like "Leda and the Swan" enact the subordination of women to the particular imperatives of kindred reproduction.

"Meditations in Time of Civil War" reveals many of the same family and sexual structures that "A Prayer For My Daughter" employs to construct the Anglo-Irish as a nationality and a tradition founded in crisis. While the title of the series suggests a meditation on the threat posed to the aristocracy by the violence of the civil war and the burnings of estates,[25] the series enacts a recognition of internal corruption and fragmentation, structured as a crisis of reproductive sexuality, as the more threatening danger. The title also suggests attention to the issue of horizontal division or unity; instead, like "A Prayer For My Daughter," much of the series focuses on the kind of generational community and fragmentation characteristic of Yeats's Anglo-Irish aristocracy.

The sequence also aligns itself with the tension between the individual and the race as Yeats was developing it for *A Vision*. The possessive emphasis of many of the sequence's titles, "My House," "My Descendants," "My Table," "The Road at my Door," and "The Stare's Nest by my Window," is unique in Yeats's work.[26] It invokes Yeats's description of the Body of Fate of Phase 8 as "'Discovery of Strength,' its embodiment in sensuality" (*V*, 85). Yeats explains that the individual has rejected service of the race but has not yet achieved an individual personality: "The imitation that held it to the enforced Mask, the norm of the race now a hated convention, has ceased and its own norm has not begun. Primary and antithetical are equal and fight for mastery" (*V*, 85). Embodiment in sensuality means the assumption of an individual, possessive attitude toward the world: "The automatic script defines 'sensuous' in an unexpected way. An object is sensuous if I relate it to myself, 'my fire, my chair, my sensation'" (*V*, 87). The sequence is, among other things, the speaker's meditations on his relation to his "race," figured as family genealogy, and elaborated under the assumption that this relation is problematic and conflictual. Tradition is kindred, but this is far from comforting.

Yeats's comments on Lady Gregory and the final stanza of "A Prayer For My Daughter" illustrate the feminine principle of continuity in his aristocratic meditations by imagining the merging of woman and estate. "Ancestral Houses" (*VP*, 417–18), the first poem in "Meditations," contains no actual woman to embody this principle, but the description of the gracious and cultured house and grounds suggests the kind of feminine, reflective culture that Yeats claimed "produces the finest flowers in a few highbred women" in the "rich man's flowering lawns," the feminine "rustle of his planted hills," the "delicate" feet of the peacock, and the presence of the goddess Juno.[27] The estate itself embodies an originary natural energy and the principle of continuity through which it may be sustained. The poem examines several possible relations between this gracious setting and the inhabitants and culture within.

First the speaker proposes a fountain as an emblem of the aristocratic culture available among a rich man's flowering lawns. The fountain, reminiscent of the self-delighting autonomy the speaker of "A Prayer For My Daughter" wants for his child, embodies an ideal relation between the masculine and feminine aristocratic modes.[28] Dependent on the fecund setting – such fountains flourish among a rich man's wealth – it is also self-sufficient and self-sustaining; it "mounts more dizzy high the more

it rains" and need "never stoop to a mechanical / Or servile shape,
at others' beck and call." The fountain is organic rather than
"mechanical," the description of the aristocrat's riches conflates
wealth with the natural plenitude of the landscape, and the relation
between the two is constructed as a self-reproducing natural order.
Here the autonomous individual and the nurturing principle of
continuity exist in organic harmony with one another, and reproduction assumes the reassuring mask of natural fecundity and self-
perpetuation.

The speaker spends the rest of the poem tearing down this ideal
organic order as an impossible and deluded fantasy. He rejects the
image of the fountain as "mere dreams" (while using the reference to
Homer to insist on its continued validity, however) and substitutes
another:

> ... now it seems
> As if some marvelous empty sea-shell flung
> Out of the obscure dark of the rich streams,
> And not a fountain, were the symbol which
> Shadows the inherited glory of the rich.

The shell is "empty," dead, and elaborate, the hollow structure of
former glory, the horn of plenty undone. It has become separated
from its origins in the "rich streams" and the "inherited glory of the
rich" now represents a falling off, a second-hand glory that is a mere
shadow of the original nobility. Now inheritance brings not abun-
dance but degeneration, as stanza 3 makes explicit: "But when the
master's buried mice can play, / And maybe the great-grandson of
that house, / For all its bronze and marble, 's but a mouse." The
degenerate descendent of the initial aristocrat leaves the house,
despite its beautiful and lasting structure, empty like the marvelous
shell. The original vitality of the Big House is no longer reproduced
in subsequent generations as part of a self-perpetuating natural
order; family genealogy has assumed the mode of crisis.

Another way of putting this is to say that the original vitality of the
house also contains an original impulse towards crisis and disintegration. The shell is an appropriate metaphor for the aristocratic culture
and beauty Yeats associated with the charms of highbred women.
Both had their origins in crime, violence and barbarism. *The Only
Jealousy of Emer* (1919) begins with a prologue about the nature of a
woman's beauty, which the speaker characterizes as

> A strange, unserviceable thing,
> A fragile, exquisite, pale shell,
> That the vast troubled waters bring
> To the loud sands before day has broken.   (*VPI*, 531)

Like the gracious beauty of the aristocracy, this beauty's origins lie in its savage and cruel antithesis, and the prologue asks:

> What death? what discipline?
> . . .
> What pursuing or fleeing,
> What wounds, what bloody press,
> Dragged into being
> This loveliness?   (*VPI*, 531)

In much of Yeats's work, civilization is based on barbarism, beauty on violence and cruelty.[29] For Yeats, as for Ernest Renan, tenable constructions of nationality, cultural tradition and, by extension, artistic beauty, depend for their stability and acceptability on an act of repression. This is because their origins are barbarous and forced rather than natural – natural in the sense of being given and natural in the sense of being continuous with their later manifestations. In "What is a Nation?" Renan argued:

Forgetting, I would even go so far as to say historical error, is a crucial factor in the creation of a nation, which is why progress in historical studies often constitutes a danger for [the principle of] nationality. Indeed, historical enquiry brings to light deeds of violence which took place at the origin of all political formations, even of those whose consequences have been altogether beneficial. Unity is always effected by means of brutality.[30]

In his memoirs, Yeats records a debate with Augustine Birrell, who asserted that " 'Wealth has very little power, it can really do very little' " (*Mem*, 145–6). Yeats replied, " 'Yet every now and then one meets some charming person who likes all fine things and is quite delightful and who would not have had these qualities if some great-grandfather had not sold his country for gold' " (*Mem*, 146). As chapter 2 pointed out, in many Irish nationalist discourses, selling one's country for gold represented the ultimate political betrayal. In 1907 he wrote, "I think that all noble things are the result of warfare; great nations and classes, of warfare in the visible world, great poetry and philosophy, of invisible warfare, the division of a mind within itself" (*EI*, 321). In "If I Were Four-and-Twenty," Yeats compared Balzac's "founder or renovator" of a "house" with "some obscure toiler or notorious speculator," and observed, "often as not the beginning of it all has been some stroke of lawless rapacity" (*EX*, 271).

"Ancestral Houses" first figures this cruel and contradictory origin for the cultured beauty of the aristocracy as the relationship between the "violent" and "bitter" men who founded it and the "sweetness" and "gentleness" of the house they create:

> Some violent bitter man, some powerful man
> Called architect and artist in, that they,
> Bitter and violent men, might rear in stone
> The sweetness that all longed for night and day,
> The gentleness none there had ever known.

The questions of the final stanzas reject this neat antithetical formulation, which divides violence and gentleness into separate spheres, asking, "what if levelled lawns and graveled ways ... But take our greatness with our violence?" There are two possible readings of these lines, the ambiguity of which turns on the word "take." Reading "take" as "take away" emphasizes what the founding men lose through their creation of the house, while reading "take" as "take on" emphasizes the suggestion that the beauty of the house is infected by the violence of its creators. Both readings accord with Yeats's representation of the Anglo-Irish as a nation in crisis. The first illustrates a national culture or community that suppresses and impoverishes the individual; the second suggests the corruption of the very foundations of the Big House. Both readings indicate the inseparability of greatness and violence, culture and crime, beauty and cruelty, and the speaker's linguistic movement from "a rich man's flowering lawns" to "our" greatness, bitterness, and violence implicates himself and his whole community. This movement completes the rejection of the poem's earlier "dreams": ancestral houses are not self-perpetuating elements in the self-regulating economy of nature; their very foundations and original energies are corrupt, and they are part of a different economy of crisis and depletion.

The next poem in the sequence, "My House," presents a different version of the relationship between nature, generational continuity and ancestral houses. Daniel Harris has analyzed the systematic ways in which the poem offers, point for point, an alternative to the kind of house in "Ancestral Houses."[31] The natural setting is resolutely unlike the rich man's fecund flowering lawns; it is an "acre of stony ground" in which the symbolic rose will "break in flower," suggesting simultaneously flourishing and death. The act of founding does not institute a self-sustaining genealogy; two men have founded here. Neither one will leave behind a tradition that perpetuates itself. The previous occupant founds there only to dwindle away, and the speaker will leave to his "bodily heirs" emblems of adversity, the knowledge that this tradition is sustained only in crisis. The harshness of the poem's landscape and its revision of the relationship between the founding moment and energy and subsequent genealogical continuity go together as part of the text's effort to separate "genealogy" from "nature" and natural (sexual) reproduction. What the speaker's children inherit is isolation and adversity.

"My Table" also arrives at a version of genealogy that separates it from natural reproduction by designating "inheritance" as the repetition of an original crisis. The sword's most important quality is that it is "changeless" or "unchanging"; the poem revolves around these words. The poem makes a series of comparisons between the kind of continuity or genealogy represented by the sword and other versions of genealogy. The poem begins by comparing the objects on the speaker's table – the sword, pen and paper. The speaker's opening sentiment is the hope that the "changeless" character of the sword will inspire him to take up pen and paper and produce an equally changeless artifact:

> Two heavy trestles, and a board
> Where Sato's gift, a changeless sword,
> By pen and paper lies,
> That it may moralise
> My days out of their aimlessness.

The first complication occurs in the lines comparing the sword to a new moon, a comparison the speaker retracts because although the sword has lain unchanged for five hundred years, "Yet if no change appears / No moon; only an aching heart / Conceives a changeless work of art." The moon and the sword are not comparable objects; they embody different kinds of continuity. The moon embodies the continuity-in-change of nature, while the sword embodies the changelessness of a man-made artifact. Such continuity does not occur in nature but must be the product of an aching human heart.

The next comparison offered and then modified is a comparison

between the sword's changelessness and the genealogical continuity
of artistic accomplishment in the culture that produced it:

> Our learned men have urged
> That when and where 'twas forged
> A marvellous accomplishment,
> In painting or in pottery, went
> From father unto son
> And through the centuries ran
> And seemed unchanging like the sword.

The flowing syntax of these lines suggests an easy continuity from
line to line, from generation to generation; in the original version of
the poem they did not even contain the two commas which now
provide the only breaks in that fluidity (*VP*, 421). But "learned men"
are usually wrong, or at least not entirely right, in Yeats's poems,
and of course the key word here is "seemed." The next lines go on to
explain why individual talents appear to have taken on the unchanged traditions of their fathers. Because such men dedicated
themselves to the soul's unchanging beauty they and "their business"
borrowed its "unchanging look." The appearance of continuity and
of genealogy as unchanging inheritance proves to be an illusion: even
the "most rich inheritor" does not inherit his artistic skill; instead, he
achieves it through the suffering of his "aching heart" and the
sharpness of his "waking wits." The poem ends with the scream of
Juno's peacock. Instead of embodying a feminine cultured setting
which nurtures the rich inheritor and provides the ground for his
artistic autonomy, Juno's peacock shatters this image with a cry
signifying the struggle, isolation and pain involved in the production
of cultural artifacts.

According to "My Table," marvelous artistic accomplishments do
not pass unchanging from generation to generation; each generation
must go through the painful process of acquiring them for itself.
What appears to be changeless, inherited continuity turns out to be
repetition of an original crisis, a moment of founding or self-
fashioning. As in "My House," what is inherited is isolation and
adversity, the burden of responsibility for recreating the accomplishments of the past on one's own, and that very burden forms the
genealogical link with past generations who also bore it.

"My Descendants" (*VP*, 422–3) also moves from one kind of
genealogy to another; from natural, biological inheritance to a

version of genealogy that separates it from nature and continuity and aligns it with isolation and adversity instead. The speaker begins by citing an inheritance from his ancestors that demands its own repetition in a similar legacy for his children: "Having inherited a vigorous mind / From my old fathers, I must nourish dreams / And leave a woman and a man behind / As vigorous of mind ..." Inheritance, figured as genealogical continuity, dictates that an original energy or quality, here vigor of mind, must be passed down unchanged and undiminished. But the rest of the poem wrestles with the difficulties involved in this project and the unlikelihood of its success: "and yet it seems / Life scarce can cast a fragrance on the wind, / Scarce spread a glory to the morning beams, / But the torn petals strew the garden plot; / And there's but common greenness after that." Here, as in "Ancestral Houses," the fortunes of the people are initially bound up with and represented by the fortunes of the "natural" landscape of the estate itself: both the speaker's descendants and the garden are in danger of declining from glorious flowers to "common greenness." The second stanza continues this association by asking that the tower become a "roofless ruin" housing the desolate owl to mirror the decline of the speaker's descendants.

The final stanza rejects this parallelism, however. While the owls are part of the same cosmic plan as the human world – "The Primum Mobile that fashioned us / Has made the very owls in circles move" – this does not mean that the natural landscape or the structure of the house should mirror the state of the inhabitants. The last lines separate the fate of the family from the flourishing and declining of the rest of the natural world and indicate that the stones will remain merely a monument to the speaker and his family: "And know whatever flourish and decline / These stones remain their monument and mine." The stones will signify the family without representing them or reproducing their original essence.

At the same time the speaker moves from a consideration of his ancestors and his descendants to a meditation on affectionate familial relationships which are not subordinated to and valued for their reproductive capacities. Now "love and friendship are enough." Several interdependent constructions break down or are discarded simultaneously – a conventional definition of genealogy as biological continuity, a conception of human sexuality organized around and subordinated to reproduction, a representational imperative that the

natural landscape and house mirror the state of the human inhabitants, and a definition of the continuity of (national) tradition as the
transmission of an unchanging originary essence from generation to
generation.

Many of the sequence's early poems begin with genealogy as
natural reproduction and end with genealogy as corruption and
crisis. "The Stare's Nest by My Window" (*VP*, 424–5) begins with a
Big House under threat from external forces and ends with internal
corruption, again figured as a crisis of reproduction. The first stanza
introduces three related levels or sites of emptiness and deterioration:
the speaker, the "empty house of the stare" and the tower:

> The bees build in the crevices
> Of loosening masonry, and there
> The mother birds bring grubs and flies.
> My wall is loosening; honey-bees,
> Come build in the empty house of the stare.

These three sites are all intertwined. "My wall is loosening" refers
equally to the speaker and his dwelling, and the empty house of the
stare obviously suggests an analogy with the tower whose masonry is
loosening. But the stare's nest is both inhabited *and* empty, for the
mother birds bring food to their young. The mother birds who
occupy the deserted house of the stare serve two functions in the
poem. As the paradoxical denizens of an empty nest, they parallel
the Anglo-Irish occupants of the tower, reproducing themselves
feebly in a setting rendered empty by their degeneration, and
indicate that the crisis in the tower is a crisis of sexual reproduction
and genealogical continuity.

As mothers who are in fact reproducing, however, the stares
contrast the inhabitants of the house. As Michael North has observed, during this period Yeats often used a bird's innate knowledge
of nest-building as an image of the individual motivated by racial
intuition.[32] The automatic script declared that "racial intuition is
'same as immigration of birds' – that is, instinctive,"[33] and in his
autobiography he claimed that "revelation is from the self, but from
that age-long memoried self, that ... teaches the birds to make their
nest" (*AY*, 164). Birds were among his favorite emblems associated
with kindred aristocracies. In his memoirs, Yeats records a half-line
he wanted to use in *The Player Queen*: "Kinship that fierce feathery
thing" (*Mem*, 232). Both "Upon a House Shaken by the Land

Agitation" and "To a Wealthy Man who promised a Second Subscription to the Dublin Municipal Gallery if it were proved the People wanted Pictures" use an eagle's nest to represent this kind of historical memory. Section III of "The Tower" contains a similar image of a mother bird whose racial instincts will lead her to "warm her wild nest" (*VP*, 415) and provide a model of the feminine principle of continuity which the poem's human world lacks. The stares illustrate racial consciousness and emphasize the absence of such consciousness in the human inhabitants.

"The Stare's Nest by My Window" reinforces the suggestion, illustrated by the birds, that the crisis here is a reproductive and genealogical one by staging a movement from external threat to internal guilt. The second stanza describes the house as surrounded by the violence of the civil war:

> We are closed in, and the key is turned
> On our uncertainty; somewhere
> A man is killed, or a house burned,
> Yet no clear fact to be discerned:
> Come build in the empty house of the stare.

The violence surrounding the house is mysterious; because "we" can't tell where it is, it is everywhere, and constrains us, closes us in. The emphatic passive construction of every verb in the stanza except the imperative invocation of the honey-bees, even to the awkward phrasing of "no clear fact to be discerned" when "no clear fact can be discerned" would be a much more natural choice, indicates that questions of agency inform the poem. The violence in this poem has no clear source and no clear target; the agents and victims of destruction remain equally unidentified throughout. This uncertainty continues in the next stanza, with "That dead young soldier in his blood."

Like "A Prayer For My Daughter" and "Ancestral Houses," "The Stare's Nest by My Window" suggests the identity of outer threat and inner weakness. The last stanza suddenly implicates the threatened and apparently innocent "we" of the first three stanzas as directly responsible for the violence; "we" are no longer the occupants of the tower, disconnected from and threatened by a bloodshed we had no part in causing. Now "we" are to blame because:

> We had fed the heart on fantasies,
> The heart's grown brutal from the fare;

More substance in our enmities
Than in our love.

This is the only causal relationship presented or even implied by the poem; because we fed the heart on fantasies, it grew brutal. Whether "we" refers to the occupants of the house alone, to the Anglo-Irish generally, or to the whole Irish nation, the poem's major movement shatters its illusions and takes that "we" from innocence to guilt, from claiming external dangers to acknowledging internal responsibility, and from ignorance and uncertainty to knowledge of cause and effect. "More substance in our enmities / Than in our love" has two inseparable referents: the civil war, a public crisis, and the private sexual and genealogical crisis suggested by the stares.

Yeats's works which claim that "tradition is kindred" do not construct a version of Anglo-Irish nationality which seeks to borrow the organic status, security and harmony that we generally associate with family and kinship. The relationship between gender, sexuality and nationality presented in these works offers an argument about foundations, about the myths of essence and origin which usually play such an important role in discourses of nationality. It gives an ambivalent or double structure to gender, sexuality, genealogy and family. They are all designated as exemplars and guarantees of naturalness, stability, continuity and coherence – as foundations. However, they also reveal themselves to be unfounded. Individual sexual identities and desires are socially constructed and regulated, genealogy means the reproduction of an original crisis, the family struggles against the interests of the individual. The major ambivalence in Yeats's Anglo-Irish poems is not a liberal ambivalence about aristocracy, as opposed to democracy, nor is it a humanist ambivalence about a civilization that is based on barbarism, as opposed to a civilization that is not. It is an ambivalence about foundations and essences, repeatedly enacting their desirability, necessity, and functions only to confront their chimerical nature. It is the ambivalence particular to a version of nationality that is splendidly vulnerable, that refuses to pose as natural and continuous, and that flaunts its origins in arbitrary acts of will, constant crises and the political degeneration of the class that embodies it.

CHAPTER 5

Desiring women: feminine sexuality and Irish nationality in "A Woman Young and Old"

The realm of sacred things is composed of the pure and of the impure. Christianity rejected impurity.

Georges Bataille[1]

To-day the man who finds belief in God, in the soul, in immortality, growing and clarifying, is blasphemous and paradoxical.

(*EX*, 334)

Yeats's aristocratic meditations and kindred politics offered Anglo-Irish nationality as a willful, arbitrary, imaginative response to the political and economic marginalization of the Anglo-Irish. In the years following the Anglo-Irish war, Yeats also engaged with a version of Irish nationality he associated with the newly hegemonic Catholic middle classes. The "Irishness" of the post-revolutionary Irish Free State was the subject of much debate and anxiety among members of the government, the Catholic church and society at large. During this period the version of postcolonial Irish nationality that emerged as dominant enforced Catholic social teachings and placed a heavy emphasis on gender roles and sexuality as important indicators of and potential threats to national identity. This chapter reads Yeats's representations of female personae and feminine sexuality in "A Woman Young and Old" as his response.

It may seem perverse to argue that "A Woman Young and Old" is, on some level, "about" Irish nationality; unlike Yeats's theatrical theories or Anglo-Irish poems, the sequence does not thematize the question of nationality explicitly. It is customary in Yeats criticism to contrast *The Tower*'s embittered engagement with politics and *The Winding Stair*'s rejection of politics in favor of sensual pleasure and an all-accepting joy.[2] Critics also commonly argue that Yeats's preoccupation with sex and female personae represents a rejection of his earlier idealized notions of womanhood and a withering into the naked truths of femininity and sexuality.[3] I will argue, however, that the difference between the two volumes does not lie in the presence or absence of Irish politics but in the version of nationality each one examines and the methods employed. I will also argue that rather than achieve a greater realism or frankness, Yeats's representations of female personae and explicit sexuality follow a complex set of conventions governed by his critique of the Free State's postcolonial Irishness. What exactly does Yeats turn to when he investigates "femininity?" What construction of "feminine sexuality" does he celebrate, and for what purpose? To answer these questions is to describe the shape, strengths and limitations of Yeats's critique.

Yeats's desiring women employ a combination of mimicry and transgression in their engagement with hegemonic Irish nationality. Both are forms of resistance that emphasize their dependence upon that which they oppose. Instead of undermining the stability of foundations, like Yeats's Anglo-Irish poems, they appropriate them and shore them up. Rather than advocating a liberal, secular nation, "A Woman Young and Old" sacralizes sexuality and sin and offers an alternative theology. Elizabeth Cullingford has argued convincingly that the sequence responds to the Free State's social and sexual conservatism by writing the female body.[4] What I would like to emphasize here is that in writing the female body Yeats was more preoccupied with *embodiment* than with the sheer materialities and pleasures of bodies.

Post-revolutionary Irish government and society were preoccupied with their "Irishness." Any postcolonial state is likely to pursue national self-definition vigorously, and the degree and shape of Ireland's independence made the pressure to do so especially acute in the Free State. Ireland remained in the British commonwealth, the island was partitioned, and tension between the Free State government and republicans who rejected the treaty erupted into civil war. Even after the war's end in 1923 republican resistance and general lawlessness continued throughout the 1920s. During its first decade, the Cosgrave government faced a serious crisis of legitimation. It had to assert the new state's political and cultural integrity in the face of partition, the ambiguity of Ireland's "independence," armed republican resistance, and the competing narratives of national self-definition offered by republicans. A further factor was the paucity of visible change wrought by independence. In its economic structures, civil service, legal system, and lack of social welfare, postcolonial Ireland looked uncomfortably like colonial Ireland.[5]

Clifford Geertz has suggested that most new states pursue national self-definition through some combination of essentialism, which stresses abstract notions of the indigenous way of life, and epochalism, which emphasizes equally abstract conceptions of the spirit of the age.[6] The Free State's construction of Irish nationality was heavily essentialist, and, though it failed to ward them off, in general it set itself against the modernizing trends of the period. Its purist conception of the indigenous way of life was heavily identified with Catholicism. Church and state were never synonymous in Ireland, and the Church was not always able to influence the government as it would have liked. In addition, the Irish Catholic Church itself was not a political monolith and there was at least some disagreement among the clergy on most of the important questions of the time.[7] The 1922 constitution had also carefully guaranteed the rights of religious minorities. However, a number of factors combined to render the legislative and social enforcement of Catholic moral codes attractive and possible to an unusual degree in the Free State. Irish popular nationalism and Catholicism had always been closely, if not entirely comfortably, allied, and partition and post-revolutionary Protestant flight made the Catholic majority even more overwhelming than it had been in the past. The Church also had a unique and virtually unquestioned monopoly on Irish education, both before and after independence.[8] The hierarchy was not blind to the advantages of appropriating Irishness; its language often reflected the assumption that Catholicism and nationalism were synonymous.[9] During and after the civil war the Church, fearing social anarchy and anxious to reassert its moral leadership of the nation,[10] sided with the Cosgrave government against the republicans. The government in turn was composed of Catholic men who were sympathetic to Catholic teachings and sensitive to the dangers of giving the opposing party the opportunity to accuse them of being too secular. Church and state occasionally conflicted, but more often were at least tacitly allied. This alliance furthered national self-definition in a way that accorded with the Free State's famous social and economic conservatism; it generated no class antagonisms, altered no social structures, and marked a clearly visible difference from Britain, creating numerous opportunities for resurrecting revolutionary rhetoric that characterized England as the major threat to the integrity of Irish national character.

This last point is particularly important. Irish nationalism had been structured around antitheses between Ireland and England, and Free State government and culture modified such antitheses rather than discarding them. As Margaret O'Callaghan observes, "a nation that had defined itself in terms of an external enemy no sooner lost that enemy than she created a substitute within herself. In Ireland that internal enemy was immorality."[11] Immorality in this context meant, above all, sexual immorality. While the Church had always policed the sexual morality of the faithful, this period saw an increased emphasis on such policing at the expense of other areas where the Church might have exerted its authority. Before World War I, for example, the Church had been more concerned over the Irish rate of alcoholism than over sexual immorality. Alcoholism remained a serious problem in Ireland; in 1925, a government study revealed that Ireland maintained, in proportion to its population, twice as many licensed houses as England.[12] In that statistic lies one likely reason why sex eclipsed drink as the nation's chief evil. While this degree of alcohol abuse was apparently an indigenous Irish problem, most of the "obscene" literature (mostly periodicals), new dances, and "immodest" fashions which brought immorality to Ireland did come from England, a fact that virtually all commentators warning against them were careful to point out.[13] After 1923 the hierarchy fulminated most consistently and vitriolicly against sexual immorality, not merely as wrong, but, increasingly during the 1920s, as a threat to the Irishness of the Irish nation.[14]

The Free State's preoccupation with immorality burdened women with particularly heavy and over-determined surveillance and regulation. There is some debate among scholars about whether this represented the legacy of Ireland's history of Catholic piety and rural traditionalism or the colonial vestiges of Victorian prudery.[15] Whatever its origin, Ireland's sexual conservatism was closely bound up with the influence of the Catholic Church. The Church's regulation of sexuality and the Irish body had targeted women in particular since the early nineteenth century,[16] and a striking rise in clerical power during that century had enabled the Church to assume more effective control than ever of its adherents just when it was focusing increasingly on controlling women and sexuality.[17] These developments also coincided with an enormous increase in the number of nuns in Ireland,[18] which meant that by the turn of the century, nuns, whose most important social role was education, provided virtually ubiquitous examples of a cultured, middle-class Catholic femininity that was pious, chaste and submissive. Despite its vexed and frequently antagonistic relationship with Irish feminism,[19] Irish revolutionary nationalism had given some women limited opportunities for becoming involved in national politics, and had to some extent fostered a new atmosphere of freedom and equality between the sexes in Ireland during the Anglo-Irish war. However, the civil war and its aftermath entailed a return to a more repressive sexual and social order, and the Irish feminist movement became weakened and fragmented.[20]

During its first fifteen years, the Free State passed a series of legislative measures to enforce Catholic moral codes. The Censorship of Films Act (1923) provided for the censorship of films, nearly all of which were, of course, foreign. The Censorship of Publications Act (1929) extended government censorship to printed matter and made it an offense to publish, sell or distribute literature advocating birth control. The Criminal Law Amendment Act (1935) later made it illegal to import or sell contraceptives. While the 1925 bill to prohibit divorce was dropped, the 1937 constitution forbade the enactment of a law to grant divorce. Ireland's sluggish economy, the Free State's cautious, ultra-stable economic policies and a slight rise in women's share of the work force,[21] all led to efforts to protect the male work force from the incursions of women workers. The 1935 Conditions of Employment Bill set a limit on the number of women workers in industry, and married women were banned from most jobs. Eamon DeValera's 1937 constitution combined a republican political agenda with a Catholic moral tone. The most important difference between the two documents was that while the 1922 constitution made Ireland a dominion of the Crown, the 1937 constitution made no reference to any outside ties. But DeValera's constitution also recognized the "special place" of the majority church in the nation's spiritual life,[22] and designated the home as women's special and proper sphere.[23] While there had been no popular agitation for such a change beforehand, in many ways the new constitution was not really an innovative document; it merely reflected the legislative impulses and popular sentiments that characterized the first decades of Irish independence.

Of course, such Irish puritanism was not a completely isolated phenomenon; J. H. Whyte argues that it was an extreme example of social and legislative trends in many countries during the years after World War I.[24] The important point here is that the trend's severity and its relation to the postcolonial pursuit of national self-definition meant that moral and sexual issues were more explicitly and more intimately bound up with actual or potential crises of national integrity and identity than elsewhere: government, Church and cultural observers all discussed Irish sexual identity and morality as things that distinguished the Irish from other nationalities.

Another aspect of Ireland's sexual conservatism that sets it apart from contemporary developments in other nations was its relationship to several unusual and much-discussed Irish demographic and social patterns. Comments on these trends persistently outlined other anxiety-producing relationships between Irish sexual behavior and national character. The anthropologists Conrad Arensberg and Solon Kimball used the term "familism" to describe the ways in which the economic imperatives of post-famine rural life structured cultural norms about such phenomena as aging, parent-child relationships, group social events, and, most important, gender boundaries, matchmaking and marriage.[25] Under familism, farmers did not subdivide their already small plots of land among their children; instead they left the farm to one son and dowered one daughter. Other siblings had to learn a trade, enter the Church or emigrate. In addition, a son could not marry until his parents retired and turned the farm over to him, but this often did not happen until he was in his 40s or older. These social structures helped make the Irish world-famous for their high rates of celibacy and emigration. By the early 1920s, 43 percent of Irish-born men and women were living abroad.[26] Fertility rates within marriage were high, especially in rural areas. However, while there is currently some debate among historians about just how great a change in marriage practices the famine occasioned,[27] there is general agreement that from the late nineteenth to the mid-twentieth century, the Irish were the most celibate nation of any country that kept such records.[28] The burgeoning Irish diaspora and high rates of celibacy at home fostered several fears about the potential decline of the nation. Some commentators feared that the Irish were in danger of vanishing as a distinct ethnic group, and therefore as a true nation. Others lamented the dispersal of the nation into far-flung, atomized groups who could no longer live the intimate connection with the land and the local community that was so important to many Irish national discourses.

Yeats wrote in "Sailing to Byzantium" (1926) that Ireland was "no country for old men" (*VP*, 407), but the more striking feature of its distinct national culture was that Ireland was a place that young unmarried women wanted to leave. During the late nineteenth and early twentieth centuries, Ireland was the only European country from which more women emigrated than men, and emigration actually increased under DeValera.[29] Moreover, this period was unique in that the women who emigrated were overwhelmingly single; while previous female immigrants had often been members of emigrating families, now 90 percent of all female emigrants aged fifteen to thirty-five were single women.[30] The Free State's definition of Irish identity demanded that women, with few exceptions, fill the domestic role of wife and mother. The Irish rate of celibacy rendered this ideal unavailable to roughly one quarter of the female population. While women who did not marry lacked the job opportunities open to their male counterparts, many also appear to have rejected the often harsh life that rural marriage offered them. The droves of women who left Ireland did not necessarily do so seeking husbands; many sought better economic opportunities, a higher standard of living, or greater social and sexual freedom.[31]

Thus sexual and gender questions were embedded in discussions of Irish nationality in contradictory ways. Catholic social teachings mandated celibacy outside marriage but demanded fertile procreation within it. While many sexual discourses cast chastity and sexual morality as national characteristics that indicated Irish difference and superiority, especially in relation to England, others treated the "excessive" celibacy of the Irish and the emigration it encouraged as a recipe for national suicide. Fears that the Irish were race-suicidal encouraged a cult of maternity, already strong in Ireland's Catholic culture. This cult insisted that women could best embody and safeguard the national character by staying home and becoming mothers, and in this context female emigration, women working outside the home, and resistance to traditional gender roles were all linked as threats to the national being. Irish sexual and familial behavior was a crucial, but ambiguous, indicator of national character, making the unmentionable topic of sex the subject of frequent discussion.[32] Most national discourses defined femininity through the twin images of chaste virgin and prolific mother, excluding female sexuality organized around pleasure rather than child-bearing and casting female desires and female bodies as primary threats to true Catholic femininity.

There were other ways in which the Free State tried to assert the national independence and identity of Ireland, for example the government's ambitious project to revive the Irish language and, later, its carefully crafted neutral stance in international affairs. Neither of these projects had as wide-ranging effects or aroused Yeats's resistance as the enforcement of Catholic social teachings did. Yeats was ambivalent about compulsory Gaelic; he told the senate he wanted to see Ireland Irish speaking (*SS*, 58), but he objected to the compulsory element in the government's program.[33] Although Yeats's ideal for Irish culture was an international, cosmopolitan one that would be open to the best traditions of Europe, politically he appears to have agreed with the Free State's isolationism: in 1923 he objected to Ireland's joining the League of Nations.[34] But Yeats had a long history of attacking the sexual and political timidity of the Catholic middle classes, and he fought consistently, though ineffectually, against Ireland's sexual conservatism.[35]

Many of the controversies in which Yeats involved himself between 1923 and 1929 illustrated the intimate links between gender, sexuality and nationality that structured the postcolonial quest for national self-definition. State censorship (the debate over the Irish copyright bill was cast in part as a debate about a potential means of censorship as well) was mainly directed at sexually "immoral" literature and literature advocating, advertizing or explaining birth control.[36] Other nations were engaging in similar censorship,[37] but in Ireland some calls for censorship used the phrase "race-suicide literature" to denote "birth control literature,"[38] suggesting that anxieties about Ireland's uniquely low marriage rates and high emigration rates made the lapse of Catholic morality represented by birth control a particularly immediate and serious threat to the national integrity in the eyes of many observers. As Beckett remarked dryly, "France may commit race suicide, Erin will never. And should she be found at any time deficient in Cuchulains, at least it shall never be said that they were contraceived."[39] Obviously, the question of divorce also foregrounded the relationship between sexual and national identity.

Culturally, as well as legislatively, debates about the definition of the new state's Irishness often invoked sexual and gender standards. The Catholic press continued to accuse Yeats of paganism and sexual immorality,[40] and most Irish citizens, while not openly hostile, were not in sympathy with him. Many Irish writers fell foul of official and unofficial censorship. When Lennox Robinson's "The Madonna of Slieve Dun," a story about a young girl who is raped by a tramp and imagines herself to be another Madonna, was published in the new magazine *To-morrow* in 1924 it provoked Catholic outrage and led to Robinson's dismissal from his position as Secretary and Treasurer of the Carnegie Libraries' Trust's Advisory Committee and to the suspension of the entire committee. Yeats published the first version of "Leda and the Swan" in the same issue and was vilified by the Catholic press.[41] Sean O'Casey's *The Plough and the Stars* was first staged in February of 1926, and the ensuing riots were due in part to his representation of Rosie Redmond, a Dublin prostitute.[42] The Municipal Gallery Yeats later revisited was not the same; by 1930 all the nudes had been removed from it.[43]

During the 1920s Yeats spoke in the senate and/or published essays on censorship, the copyright bill, and divorce, and he scolded O'Casey's audiences and Robinson's detractors in print. His comments on these controversies displayed an acute awareness that for postcolonial Ireland questions of morality and sexuality were explicitly national questions about what definition of Irishness the country would embrace. In his infamous speech on divorce, he focused less on individual sexual freedom than on the bill's role in the construction of a national identity that he saw as oppressive and politically counter-productive. He told the senate: "If you show that this country, Southern Ireland, is going to be governed by Catholic ideas and by Catholic ideas alone, you will never get the north" (SS, 92). He made a similar argument in the version of the speech published in the *Irish Statesman*.[44]

Yeats also understood that the Free State's hegemonic definition of Irishness often placed its heaviest demands on women and feminine sexuality. In 1926 the Abbey Theatre produced a comedy by Brinsely Macnamara, *Look at the Heffernans!*. The play pokes fun at the excessive celibacy of two brothers, wealthy farmers, one a "withered widower" and the other an "unrepentant bachelor,"[45] and at the monetary conflicts and confusions, based on the familistic structure of Irish rural life, that beset the widower's children when

they want to marry. Yeats hated Macnamara's play, writing to Olivia
Shakespear:

I sat it out in misery and had two furious interviews with the author by
phone. Every country likes good art till it produces its own form of vulgarity
and after that will have nothing else. The theme is young women throwing
themselves at the heads of horrible old men for marriage' sake. I phoned to
the author "We did your play that you might judge it for yourself. Do you
think the degradation of youth a theme for comedy – the comedy of the
newspapers? To me it is a theme for satire or tragedy." I have given orders
that all the young women are to tousle their heads that we may not mistake
them for whole women, but know them for cattle. (*L*, 713)

For Yeats, Ireland was developing an identifiable national culture –
but a vulgar and oppressive one that demanded a maimed version of
femininity. Women whose only options were marriage or emigration
were forced to sell themselves like livestock, degrading their youth
and bodies by organizing their sexuality around economic and
practical concerns rather than around romance and pleasure.

   Yeats's battle against the new vulgar forms of Irish nationality was
in large part a battle against what he perceived as the vulgarities of
the Irish Catholic Church. Yeats linked Catholicism to the other
aspects of modern Ireland he disliked: democracy, materialism,
journalism and popular amusements: "What devout man can read
the Pastorals of our Hierarchy without horror at a style rancid,
course [sic] and vague, like that of the daily papers?" (*UPII*, 438). In
his senate speech on divorce he contrasted the Church of Ireland's
lack of influence in politics with the Catholic Church's power over
the senators. During the 1928 debate over censorship he charged that
the Christian Brothers had protested against "The Cherry-Tree
Carol" because they did not believe in the Incarnation and the
Second Coming. He repeatedly invoked "the philosophy of St.
Thomas, the official philosophy of the Catholic Church," (*UPII*, 477)
in order to argue that Catholic proponents of censorship were
violating their own religious philosophy. Maud Gonne wrote to him
in 1927, "You hate the Catholic Church with the hate of the Daemon
condemned by the old monk of the Mariotic Sea & when you take
your stand on certain papal Encyclicals you always remind me of
Satan rebuking Sin" (*GY*, 442). Yeats enjoyed his adversarial relationship with the Catholic papers, writing in a 1928 letter, "the Catholic
press is calling me all the names it can think of. I am in the highest

spirits" (*L*, 747). As late as 1936, he told Ethel Mannin, "an ignorant form of Catholicism is my enemy" (*L*, 873).

Yeats's interest in Irish education also brought him into conflict with the Church, which guarded its control over the educational system jealously. In 1925 and 1926 Yeats visited primary schools as a government representative and reported to the senate that many of them were not fit places for children because of poor sanitary, heating and structural conditions (*SS*, 106–12). He proposed that the schools be improved before compulsory education went into force, anticipated hierarchy resistance, and tried to forestall it: "No one proposes to interfere with the present manager's right to appoint and dismiss teachers. That right is cherished by the clergy of all denominations, but the ablest managers would, I believe, welcome popular control if confined to heating, housing, clothing, cleaning, etc" (*UPII*, 456). He was wrong; beginning in 1926 the Irish National Teachers' Organization waged an intermittent campaign, which Yeats read about in the *Irish Times* and praised in the senate (*SS*, 114), to get responsibility for cleaning, heating and sanitation of primary schools transferred to local authorities. The hierarchy resisted successfully and in 1952 formally requested that they stop trying.[46]

Yeats's criticisms of the alliance between Church and state were anti-clerical but not anti-theological. On the contrary, during this period he was deeply involved in his own theological project. During the early 1920s Yeats was working to finish the first version of *A Vision*, and formulated his system in contrast to other available theologies. His increasingly explicit emphasis on sexuality at this time constituted a crucial aspect of the metaphysical speculations inscribed in *A Vision*. Whereas Irish Catholicism viewed the desires of the body as threats to the soul, for Yeats the two were interdependent. As he wrote in "The Phases of the Moon," whose title is taken from *A Vision*, "All dreams of the soul / End in a beautiful man's or woman's body" (*VP*, 374). He linked sex and spiritual vision in the 1925 edition of *A Vision*, lamenting, "I have not even dealt with the whole of the subject, perhaps not even with what is most important, writing nothing about the Beatific Vision, little of sexual love" (*VA*, xii). In one version of his senate speech on divorce he denied that marriage was a sacrament but insisted that "the love of man and woman, and the inseparable physical desire, are sacred" (*UPII*, 451). He wrote in a 1926 letter, "One feels at moments as if one could with a touch convey a vision – that the mystic way and sexual love use the same means – opposed yet parallel existences" (*L*, 715), and in 1927 he described "sexual torture" and "spiritual excitement" as "somehow inseparable" (*L*, 731).[47] He found in some of the Eastern literature and philosophy he read a doctrine of spiritual life through physical life that opposed the asceticism of Western Christianity and recognized the interdependence of sexual and divine knowledge,[48] and in Nietzsche the idea that "we must not believe in the moral or intellectual beauty which does not sooner or later impress itself upon physical things" (*EI*, 389). Yeats did not merely insist on the beauty or importance of desire, sexuality and material bodies, he sacralized them.

All the poems in the series "A Woman Young and Old" were written between 1926 and 1929.[49] During this time Yeats was serving in the senate (he retired a few weeks before his term ended in 1928) and was involved in a number of Irish controversies that highlighted the relationship between gender, sexuality and nationality. He was also lamenting the vulgarity of hegemonic Irish culture. He was focusing increasingly specifically on the Catholic nature of this vulgarity, particularly on its Platonizing tendencies to oppose body and soul and to denigrate the former as a threat to the latter, and he was formulating his alternative in *A Vision*.[50] "A Woman Young and Old" represents a continuation of these projects rather than a departure from the bitterness of politics.

A comparison between "A Woman Young and Old" and its companion series, "A Man Young and Old," which was written in 1926 and 1927,[51] and published in *The Tower*, will highlight the preoccupations and strategies particular to Yeats's critique of the Free State's nationality as it appears in his female personae. Both series feature speakers who take up various, even contradictory positions. Both are concerned primarily with the sexual life of the speakers, both stress the pain that accompanies or even outweighs the pleasures of love, and both emphasize the inevitable physical and emotional losses that come with old age. Each speaker confronts this decay with defiant self-assertion at times. But there are revealing differences between the sequences as well.

The supernatural functions differently in each series. The first three poems in "A Man Young and Old" recall conventional love lyrics which typically figure an abject lover and a beautiful and heartless beloved. They also echo some of Yeats's earlier love poems.

"First Love" (*VP*, 451) and "Human Dignity" (*VP*, 452) present a woman whose beauty is supernatural and allied with the moon, and whose cruelty is equally unearthly or, literally, inhuman. In "First Love" the speaker has erred in thinking his beloved has "A heart of flesh and blood" when in fact she has "a heart of stone." In "Human Dignity" the woman's kindness is inhuman because it is "like the moon" and "has no comprehension in it." In "The Mermaid" (*VP*, 452–3) the femme fatale's "cruel happiness" is literally fatal. In all three poems, the inhuman or supernatural is a quality of the beloved which makes her all the more dangerous to the speaker. The speaker himself has no supernatural power, knowledge or experience. "His Wildness" (*VP*, 458–9) expresses a wish to "mount and sail up there / Amid the cloudy wrack" to escape the deterioration of the material world. But this impulse does not participate in the metaphysical world; it springs from the "natural" state of an old man: "For that is natural to a man / That lives in memory."

In "A Woman Young and Old," in contrast, the supernatural is a metaphysical truth or moment possessed, sought or embodied by the speaker, and is inseparably intertwined with her sexuality, rather than with the status of her beloved. In addition, "A Woman Young and Old" takes up a number of Yeats's favorite metaphysical questions or paradoxes – eternal beauty, the relationship between body and soul, the interdependence of sexual love and spiritual hate, and the soul's union with God after death. In general, "A Man Young and Old" does not address such issues directly. The female sequence is part of Yeats's critique of Irish Catholicism's vulgarity and his effort to formulate an alternative metaphysics in which the mystic way and sexual love use the same means.

Each sequence interrogates and resists some conventional attitudes or poses for lovers. But while the speaker of "A Man Young and Old" is often involved in a quarrel with himself, the speaker of "A Woman Young and Old" frequently challenges the criticisms and directives of an actual or implied listener. In "The Death of the Hare" (*VP*, 453) the speaker examines his complicity in the conventions of love-making that dictate that the man must pursue the woman. His successful courtship reminds him of a victorious and violent hunt – the "death of the hare" – and he laments the "wildness lost" in his beloved through the enforcement of such standards.[52] The poem's first stanza suggests the pressure of romantic convention upon the speaker who responds to the chase "as lover should;" but he resists his own internalization of the law rather than its imposition from some external authority.

In contrast, many of the poems of "A Woman Young and Old" are dialogues, or contain self-justifying questions directed at an implied and hostile listener. "Father and Child" is spoken in the voice of the disapproving father, "Parting" is a dialogue between "he" and "she," "Her Triumph" is addressed to the speaker's male rescuer, and "Meeting" presents a hostile confrontation between the speaker and an old man that looks ahead to the Crazy Jane poems. The titles of "A First Confession" and "A Last Confession" invoke and ironize sexual guilt and the confessional regime which, as Foucault argues, enables Western civilization's production of the "truth" of sex.[53] "Before the World Was Made," "A First Confession," "Consolation," and "A Last Confession" all employ questions which, whether we read them as rhetorical or not, suggest the presence of an interlocutor. They also suggest that the speaker is usually under surveillance by some force or person external to her. None of the poems in "A Man Young and Old" contains a single question mark. Throughout "A Woman Young and Old," the standards of the father, society, the conventional constructions of femininity and the symbolic role of women in national discourses, retain a ghostly presence that must be answered or resisted. No such presence haunts "A Man Young and Old." Yeats's female personae, in other words, are emphatically oppositional voices whose explicit purpose is transgression of the very discourses that constitute them.

Both speakers confront their aging bodies and lost loves defiantly. But while in "A Man Young and Old" the speaker often turns to memory as a source of self-knowledge and a ground for self-assertion, the speaker of "A Woman Young and Old" draws on a paradoxical physical/metaphysical wisdom. Memory is a powerful theme in the poems of a man old. In "His Memories" (*VP*, 454–5) the speaker acknowledges his current decrepitude and counters it by remembering past passion and beauty. In "The Friends of His Youth" (*VP*, 455–6) the speaker's defiant laughter in the face of madness and barrenness is empowered by memory: "And then I laugh till tears run down / And the heart thumps at my side, / Remembering that her shriek was love / And that he shrieks from pride." In "The Secrets of the Old" (*VP*, 457–8) the speaker's special knowledge is cast as a set of memories no longer available to others in the living present: "For none alive to-day / Can know the stories that we know

/ Or say the things we say." These are memories of earthly loves: "How such a man pleased women most / Of all that are gone, / How such a pair loved many years / And such a pair but one." "His Wildness" asserts that the speaker is a man who "lives in memory," and, appropriately, "From 'Oedipus At Colonus,'" (*VP*, 459) in which the speaker bravely accepts his own death, counsels, "Cease to remember the delights of youth, travel-wearied aged man."

"A Woman Young and Old" does not thematize memory in this way; indeed, although the speaker does refer to past events, the sequence never mentions memory as such, except perhaps in "Her Vision in the Wood." The strengths of Yeats's woman young and old depend on a version of knowledge and power that is intensely physical and sexual and at the same time transcendent and metaphysical. Neither level coincides with the individual subjectivity and private consciousness of personal memory. In "A Woman Young and Old" supernatural knowledge or status belongs to the speaking woman rather than the object of her desire, and this, rather than individual memory, provides the ground for her defiant self-assertion.

These differences – "A Woman Young and Old"'s preoccupation with transgression and its persistent linking of feminine sexuality and the sacred – indicate the sequence's project to extend Yeats's critique of postcolonial Catholic Irishness. The series defines femininity and feminine sexuality through precisely those things that the Free State's hegemonic version of nationality depended on excluding from them. Unlike the speakers of "A Man Young and Old," the speakers of the female sequence are usually embattled with a social and symbolic order that seeks to confine them – a disapproving father, a censorious society, a hostile listener, or a conventional "feminine" role. At the same time, rather than replacing the Free State's insistence on chastity and maternity with a feminine sexuality organized around personal pleasure and the private and subjective dramas of romance, "A Woman Young and Old" offers feminine desires whose significance is not confined to or even primarily involved in the personal. Feminine sexuality, which Free State nationality cast as a major threat to metaphysical knowledge and status (salvation), is the very vehicle through which these poems formulate a version of religious truth. Feminine sexuality is the mark of rebellion against conventional social and symbolic structures and simultaneously the embodiment of a divine/profane metaphysics.

To alter Georges Bataille's terms slightly, Yeats's feminine sexuality is a sacred erotic transgression, sacred precisely because it is a transgression.[54] For Bataille, eroticism, including and especially what he calls religious eroticism, is based on transgression, which "suspends a taboo without suppressing it,"[55] and the impure, rather than being divorced from the sacred, is an intimate and necessary part of it. In his 1930 diary Yeats wrote, "to-day the man who finds belief in God, in the soul, in immortality, growing and clarifying, is blasphemous and paradoxical" (*EX*, 334). Bataille claims that "what paganism regarded as unclean was customarily regarded as sacred at the same time," and he argues that modern Christianity suppressed the sacred character of transgression and banished impure sacredness to the realm of the profane.[56] Sexuality was relegated to the profane world, and eroticism depended on the transgression of taboos against it. Foucault's reading of Bataille in "A Preface to Transgression" begins by contrasting profane and sacred sexuality:

We like to believe that sexuality has regained, in contemporary experience, its full truth as a process of nature, a truth which has been lingering in the shadows and hiding under various disguises – until now, that is, when our positive awareness allows us to decipher it so that it may at last emerge in the clear light of language. Yet, never did sexuality enjoy a more immediately natural understanding and never did it know a greater "felicity of expression" than in the Christian world of fallen bodies and of sin. The proof is its whole tradition of mysticism and spirituality which was incapable of dividing the continuous forms of desire, of rapture, of penetration, of ecstasy, of that outpouring which leaves us spent: all of these experiences seemed to lead, without interruption or limit, right to the heart of a divine love of which they were both the outpouring and the source returning upon itself. What characterizes modern sexuality from Sade to Freud is not its having found the language of its logic or of its natural process, but rather, through the violence done by such languages, its having been "denatured" – cast into an empty zone where it achieves whatever meager form is bestowed upon it by the establishment of its limits. Sexuality points to nothing beyond itself, no prolongation, except in a frenzy which disrupts it. We have not in the least liberated sexuality, though we have, to be exact, carried it to its limits: the limit of consciousness, because it ultimately dictates the only possible reading of our unconscious; the limit of the law, since it seems the sole substance of universal taboos; the limit of language, since it traces that line of foam showing just how far speech may advance upon the sands of silence.[57]

Yeats's female personae embody a sacred sexuality that has affinities with Bataille's eroticism. Yeats's sexual frankness in "A Woman

Young and Old" is not the secular, naturalizing, limiting conception
Foucault associates with modern discourses of sexuality. It is much
closer to a sexual mysticism that cannot separate the erotic and the
divine and that values transgression as the foundation and limit of
the law. Sexuality in these poems constantly points beyond itself.
Yeats's female personae emphatically oppose society and the law, but
the larger significance of this oppositional relation lies in their status
as windows on the sacred. Non-reproductive feminine sexuality and
desiring female bodies are defiantly asserted, and asserted specifically
as transgressions, because they are precisely what is forbidden. At the
same time, however, many of these assertions are structured so that
they value feminine sexuality and desire less "for their own sake"
than for the philosophical and theological aporias they generate or
embody.

The opening poem, "Father and Child" (*VP*, 531), pits paternal
and clerical authority against the daughter's desire. Like the anxious
father of "A Prayer For My Daughter," the speaker wants his
daughter to make an appropriate sexual choice. The poem looks to a
wider social context; the father's disapproval is mirrored by community disapprobation, and "ban" and "father" suggest a clerical
prohibition:

> She hears me strike the board and say
> That she is under ban
> Of all good men and women
> Being mentioned with a man
> That has the worst of all bad names.

The poem's focus on hearing, speaking, gossip, and naming emphasizes the linguistic and contingent construction of the community's
ethical judgments. One of the most salient features of the daughter's
object of desire is his oppositional relation to society and its standards
of respectable behavior, as indicated by the neat contrast between
the extremes of "all good men and women" and "the worst of all
bad names." This opposition is formal insofar as its content remains
unspecified, except in the linguistic coupling of "all good men and
women," which suggests a sexual transgression. On the other hand,
the daughter appeals to aesthetic and erotic criteria that make the
man's bad reputation irrelevant rather than refuting it: "his hair is
beautiful, / Cold as the March wind his eyes." Individual desire
operates according to two different logics: one that functions directly,

formally in opposition to the law that binds communities together on the basis of common vocabularies and judgments, and another, which operates without any reference to it and embodies an alternative law.

On one level, then, the poem pits the imaginative and sexual energies of the individual woman against the repressive imperatives and sexual timidity of the community. But attending to the poem's source reveals that the daughter's desire has divine rather than merely personal sanction. In Herbert's "The Collar" it is the rebellious child/speaker who strikes the board; here it is the angry parent. "The Collar" ends with the speaker's submission to the Lord's authority; "Father and Child" closes with the daughter's unanswerable and victorious retort. The father in Yeats's poem parallels the child in Herbert's.[58] Yeats's revision of Herbert reverses the positions of father and child in the poem whose title now takes on an added meaning: father and child in Yeats's poem play very unfatherly and unchildlike roles. The daughter represents not merely transgressive feminine sexuality, but feminine eroticism: transgressive feminine sexuality elevated to a divine principle, which gives her beloved the beauty of the natural elements themselves, and to which the rebellious child/father must submit. Her transgression is the linchpin of an alternative theology that needs and sacralizes bodies and the forbidden, rather than simply issuing or defying edicts against them.

In keeping with the sequence's persistent linking of bodies and embodiment, several poems take up the relationship between individual women and their symbolic functions. "Before the World Was Made" (*VP*, 531–2) examines the Yeatsian convention of figuring eternal beauty as a woman. The poem looks back to such poems as "The Rose of the World," "The Song of the Wandering Aengus," "He Remembers Forgotten Beauty," "He Gives His Beloved Certain Rhymes," "He Tells of Perfect Beauty" and "The Secret Rose"; in "The Rose of the World," for example, eternal beauty pre-exists everything in heaven and earth except God, who "made the world to be a grassy road / Before her wandering feet" (*VP*, 112). "Before the World Was Made" maps an individual woman's appropriative and critical relation to the symbolic role such poems assign her. Rather than simply accept or reject it, the speaker mimics this role for her own purposes and reveals some of its contradictions: her social and sexual transgressions are generated out of this mimicry.

Her association with eternal beauty, "the face I had / Before the world was made," is a symbolic convention the speaker appropriates and uses against the society who criticizes her vanity and the lover who laments her heartlessness. The speaker argues that such behaviors arise directly out of the symbolic role they assign her. Since her beauty exemplifies eternal beauty, her efforts to improve her looks artificially should be considered attempts to reach eternal beauty rather than personal vanity: "No vanity's displayed: / I'm looking for the face I had / Before the world was made." Rather than reject the conventional notion that she is for "display," she pushes it to its logical conclusion.

Similarly, in the second verse she uses her association with eternal beauty to defend herself against the charge of cruelty:

> What if I look upon a man
> As though on my beloved,
> And my blood be cold the while
> And my heart unmoved?
> Why should he think me cruel
> Or that he is betrayed?
> I'd have him love the thing that was
> Before the world was made.

This is both an injunction to the lover to seek eternal beauty in his earthly love and a suggestion that the "thing that was / Before the world was made" is, for the human lover, no substitute for the real woman. Her status as an avatar of eternal beauty is equivalent, on a personal and social level, to her narcissism. Her symbolic role becomes a weapon against the very discourses that constructed it; those discourses cast her as a "thing," an object of display and an entity to which standards of individual responsibility, honesty and love do not apply. What she resists is the contradictory demand that she become both a thing and a person, both an icon of eternal beauty and an autonomous ethical subject. Her mimicry reveals the ambivalence or split at the heart of a discourse that is both idealizing and regulatory and allows her to disrupt it.[59]

"A First Confession" (*VP*, 532–3) also uses a form of mimicry. It rewrites the theme Yeats saw in *Look at the Heffernans!*: the constriction of women's options to the narrow and competitive confines of the marriage market. In this case, the speaker experiences the coercive force of a cliched feminine pose rather than actively appropriating it:

> I long for truth, and yet
> I cannot stay from that
> My better self disowns,
> For a man's attention
> Brings such satisfaction
> To the craving in my bones.

The woman's desires force her into a social realm where she must play the dissembling coquette. Her behavior is determined not by her own will but by the fact that such deceit is the commodity demanded of her in the romance market. Part of her "disowns" her stake in this market, emphasizing the economic metaphor, but her body's desires betray her and impel her to it. In contrast to the works examined in chapter 4, which figured sexual desire as shaped by education and culture, this poem represents desire as an inherent, bodily force, a craving in the bones. When he saw *Look at the Heffernans!* Yeats thought the plight of Irish women on the marriage market a theme for tragedy rather than comedy because they had to throw themselves at undesirable old men for the sake of marriage. Instead of the economic and cultural imperatives of rural familism or urban patriarchy, however, the poem abandons history and social determination and figures a naturalized desire as the force that separates the speaker from her better self.

This naturalized desire is also supernatural, however. The last stanza is notoriously ambiguous, but it is clear that it constructs a homology between the speaker's body and the cosmos. The craving in the speaker's bones becomes inscribed on a celestial scale:

> Brightness that I pull back
> From the Zodiac,
> Why those questioning eyes
> That are fixed upon me?
> What can they do but shun me
> If empty night replies?

Like many other speakers in the sequence, the speaker answers the interrogation or disapproval in the eyes of a listener, possibly her lover. She also documents her anxiety lest she fail to gain a man's attention and be ignored instead. Yeats glossed this stanza by referring to Macrobius, the "learned astrologer" of "Chosen," according to whom the soul exists as a perfect, non-human sphere before birth, and then is drawn downward into a cone and into life.[60] This may or may not be helpful; what I want to emphasize here is

that the natural and personal form of the speaker's desire is inseparable from its supernatural and impersonal form: the "empty night" is
the opposite of the "Brightness that I pull back / From the Zodiac,"
but it also represents her nights without a man's attention. Although
she longs for the conventional truth that would come with honesty,
she embodies a more profound truth about the interpenetration of
physical and metaphysical worlds.

"Her Triumph" (*VP*, 533–4) employs a traditional gendered
narrative of female captivity and male rescue to reject another
conventional construction of femininity: the pose of the coquette for
whom love is a "casual improvisation, or a settled game." In contrast
to the previous poem, in which the speaker practiced feminine deceit
to gain a man's attention, here a man's attention rescues her from
the role of the femme fatale and brings her a more worthwhile love
relationship. While in "A First Confession," the speaker is caught
between two forces equally out of her control – her body's desires
and the confessional regime – "Her Triumph" emphasizes that the
speaker's "chain," her shallow and conventional construction of
femininity, has its source in a powerful external force that imprisons
her, literally in this case. Although the speaker admits that initially
she "mocked" the rescuing lover, he masters "it," – the dragon of
social and romantic convention – rather than her, to stress this point.

The poem also looks back to "Michael Robartes and the Dancer"
(*VP*, 385–7), in which the pompous, Latin text-toting Robartes tries
to rescue the unwilling maiden from her intellect and deliver her to
the composite blessedness of absorption in her own carnal beauty.
The poem is, as Elizabeth Cullingford has suggested, "the portrait of
an attitude rather than a portrait of the artist."[61] Robartes' elaborately pedantic attempts to compel the dancer's assent are deflated
by her terse, ironic replies, and the last word belongs to the dancer.
"Her Triumph" returns to the same story, St. George/Perseus and
the dragon, to delineate a different kind of rescue, one that refuses
the opposition between the carnal and intellectual which motivates
"Michael Robartes and the Dancer."

In the first draft of the poem, Yeats invoked this opposition; the
knight originally rescued the lady from the very pleasures of the
body to which Robartes tries to chain his dancer.[62] When Yeats
revised, however, he abandoned this distinction. The speaker's
rescue is both intellectually and sexually liberating. Her chain is
apparently an ankle chain, suggesting both imprisonment and

chastity, like the ankle chains of "oriental" women in works like Flaubert's *Salammbo*. The liberated love is a radically alien force, symbolized by the sea and the "miraculous strange bird," and the sexual freedom suggested by the broken ankle chain indicates that it is physical as well as metaphysical. Like the previous poem, "Her Triumph" combines a critique of a socially constructed and limiting version of femininity with a less self-reflexive engagement with female desire, figured simultaneously as a natural good and a supernatural force or realm.

"Consolation" (*VP*, 534), emphasizes the fallen, "criminal" nature of earthly existence, a criminality represented, ultimately, by sex. Instead of the traditional divine consolation for the fallen status of the physical world that the "wisdom" of the sages would provide, however, the speaker offers a consolation that is both physical and metaphysical:

> O but there is wisdom
> In what the sages said;
> But stretch that body for a while
> And lay down that head
> Till I have told the sages
> Where man is comforted.

In contrast to Christian doctrine, which would cast the soul's reunion with God as the consolation for original sin and the fallen state of the world, the poem claims an opposite consolation: the way to forget original sin is to repeat it: "But where the crime's committed / The crime can be forgot."

The poem embodies a conception of sex that equates it with sin; indeed, as in Bataille's eroticism, the intensity of passion and pleasure depend on their association with crime: "How could passion run so deep / Had I never thought / That the crime of being born / Blackens all our lot?" But it uses this conception as the basis for an alternative theology which refuses the traditional opposition between earthly sin and divine consolation; here the "divine" consolation offered is only available through sex, the very thing that produces the need for consolation. Instead of an opposition between body and soul, the poem presents a kind of infinite loop in which the degradation of the body finds temporary resolution in itself. Rather than challenging the equation of sex with sin and filth that prevailed in the Free State, the poem mimics this conception of sex and casts it as the foundation of a new metaphysics, a version of the sacred that sacralizes the impure and profane.

"Chosen" (*VP*, 534–5) also presents a sexual moment, in this case post-coital tranquility, that participates in a metaphysical reality. Yeats glossed this poem and "Parting" (*VP*, 535–6) (they were originally part of the same poem) by writing "I have symbolized a woman's love as the struggle of the darkness to keep the sun from rising from its earthly bed" (*VP*, 830). Which is to say that a woman's love conducts a doomed struggle to prevent the inevitable departure of its object. Love, by definition, is transient and must confront "the horror of daybreak." The speaker is both woman and cosmic force; she compares post-coital tranquility to the moment of Neoplatonic transcendence in Macrobius' astrology where "the Zodiac is changed into a sphere." "Chosen" emphasizes the painful and changeable nature of earthly love, and insists that this love is inextricably linked to a metaphysical or cosmic realm usually defined by wholeness and permanence. As in "Consolation" a traditional definition of love or sexuality is aligned with eroticism and designated the path to the divine rather than its opposite; simultaneously, this reversal refigures and enlarges the realm of the sacred.

"Before the World Was Made" exploits a symbolic feminine role in order to critique its work as a mechanism for regulating the activities of individual women. "Her Vision in the Wood" (*VP*, 536–7) also examines the gap between the symbolic and the individual subject, this time from the perspective of a speaker who tries unsuccessfully to bridge that gap in order to escape the human pain and decay of age. The poem, an ironic reworking of the myth of Venus and Adonis, begins by introducing a discrepancy between the scene's rich mythic potential and the woman's lack of it:

> Dry timber under that rich foliage,
> At wine-dark midnight in the sacred wood,
> Too old for a man's love I stood in rage
> Imagining men . . .

"Wine-dark midnight" and "sacred wood" invoke ancient religious rituals, but beneath the mythic trappings suggesting fertility rites, access to the sacred, and renewal, "that rich foliage," the woman herself is only "dry timber," and enters the poem belatedly in the third line.

The rest of the poem revolves around variations on this discrepancy. The speaker is physically too old for love, but, enraged by her body's decay and tortured by memories of love, imagines men. The act of remembering sensual pleasure leads her to tear the body that has betrayed her:

> Imagining men. Imagining that I could
> A greater with a lesser pang assuage
> Or but to find if withered vein ran blood,
> I tore my body that its wine might cover
> Whatever could recall the lip of lover.

She tries to blot out, with a literal covering of blood and the intoxication of wine, the pain of remembered pleasure. The occurrence of "Imagining" twice in one line, capitalized both times, emphasizes the speaker's imaginative effort to create a correspondence between the literal (blood) and the figurative (wine), between meaningless self-wounding and meaningful self-sacrifice. Her self-mutilation is a violent erotic transgression designed to transport her profane, aging body into the realm of the sacred. The confluence of blood and wine suggests both ritual sacrifice (Bataille observes that "in the etymological sense of the word, sacrifice is nothing other than the production of *sacred* things,"[63]) and an ironic, because unfulfilled, promise of renewal or transfiguration.

The speaker also gives an alternative motive for her self-wounding: "Or but to find if withered vein ran blood." She mutilates her body to reassure herself that it still has the properties of flesh and blood, that it is still a body. The act, then, springs from opposing desires, to obliterate memories of the material body by transmuting it into a mythic embodiment, and to demonstrate the continuing presence of the material body. Her attempt to give her self-sacrifice a mythic significance fails, and she learns only that her withered veins do still run blood. As she holds up her hands, in triumph over her bleeding body or in supplication to divine regenerative forces, her blood stubbornly refuses to maintain its metaphorical identity with wine:

> And after that I held my fingers up,
> Stared at the wine-dark nail, or dark that ran
> Down every withered finger from the top;
> But the dark changed to red . . .

The transition from dark to red here indicates that her blood is just blood. Her self-mutilation does not obliterate her memories of love, her violent pagan sacrifice does not give her body the status of a sacred profane object and lead to regeneration. The natural and supernatural remain painfully separated.

At this point the procession who seem to have succeeded where the speaker failed enters. The mourning women and wounded Adonis figure appear to participate in a mythic ritual, as the torches, music, and stately movement suggest. The old woman's decrepit body is all too real to her, while the bodies of the mourners are emphatically products of the artistic imagination, "a Quattrocento painter's throng, / A thoughtless image of Mantegna's thought," and "bodies from a picture or a coin." The women in the procession are "drunken with singing as with wine;" they have attained the oblivious intoxication the speaker sought from her body's "wine." They are part of a mythic rite of death and rebirth, but the mutilation they mourn is not their own; it is displaced onto the wounded man. Yeats based the scene on the pagan rites in Flaubert's *Temptation of St. Anthony*, and could have found in Frazer's *Golden Bough* an account of the myth and rituals of Adonis which claimed that they had originated in human recognition of the seasonal cycle of birth, death and regeneration, especially that of vegetable life.[64] The man's death is part of a coherent symbolic system, as the emphasis on art, song and ritual indicates, and the mourners' thoughtless oblivion is a function of their ability to grasp his place in that system. His sacrifice has a sacred public meaning, a mythic significance.

In contrast, the old woman is unable to perceive the man's death as a ritual sacrifice. Instead, she experiences it as the intensely personal loss of her own lover: "they had brought no fabulous symbol there / But my heart's victim and its torturer." She is unable to transform her own sacrifice or her lover's into anything more or less than intense personal suffering that achieves no purpose. The mourners who inhabit a world of mythic representation experience sacrifice as sacred and meaningful and are therefore immune to its horror. The speaker's experience of sacrifice is an ambiguous compound of memory and desire: "love's bitter-sweet had all come back." While other poems in the series insist on linking the individual and the mythic, the earthly and the supernatural, the speaker of "Her Vision in the Wood" fails to do so. In either case, the link itself is at stake.

"A Last Confession" (*VP*, 538) rings changes on the Christian tradition of representing the soul's reunion with God after death as sexual union or marriage. The poem begins by accepting the opposition between body and soul and comparing two kinds of love: a love of the body, which produces "great pleasure," and a love of the soul, which brings "misery": "I answer that I gave my soul / And loved in misery, / But had great pleasure with a lad / That I loved bodily." The confession of the title is that the speaker revelled in the bodily love which was no more meaningful than the coupling of animals: "beast gave beast as much."

The speaker also predicts, in contrast, her soul's perfect union with God after death, "when this soul, its body off, / Naked to naked goes." But this perfect union oddly replicates rather than resolves the contradictions of earthly love. The poem ends:

> And though it loved in misery
> Cling so close and tight
> There's not a bird of day that dare
> Extinguish that delight.

Like the earthly soul-love this union will be a combination of misery and delight. In addition, nothing indicates explicitly that God is the soul's lover after death. Yeats wrote to Olivia Shakespear: "Do you think it would be less shocking if I put a capital to 'he' in the last stanza?" (*L*, 716).[65] Although "A Last Confession" appears to be structured around a contrast between earthly loves and divine ones, the poem describes the soul's union with God in terms that refuse an absolute distinction between it and earthly love. The difference between this love and earthly love is that the love of God is eternal, unlike the transient love on earth which passes, like the love in "Chosen" and "Parting," as night passes into day. The poem takes up Irish Catholicism's separation of body and soul and transgresses it without rejecting it.

"Meeting" (*VP*, 539) also de-stabilizes the opposition between body and soul, this time in the context of Blake's notion that sexual love is based on spiritual hate. The poem organizes itself around a series of oppositions – the old man versus the old woman, external appearance versus internal reality, love versus hate. But it renders the content of those oppositions thoroughly ambiguous. The speaker begins with an opposition between the characters' aging bodies and an unspecified reality underneath: they are "Hidden by old age a while / In masker's cloak and hood." The end of the poem returns to this opposition:

But such as he for such as me –
Could we both discard
This beggarly habiliment –
Had found a sweeter word.

It is never clear whether the opposing state beneath the mask of old age is a soul, as the poem's proximity to "A Last Confession" might suggest, or a younger and more beautiful body, as the possibility, raised in the second stanza, that the two were "lover[s] in the past" might indicate. Does the speaker wish to discard the beggarly habiliment of the body and achieve a union in soul, or does she wish to exchange her aged body for a youthful one and enjoy the pleasures of the flesh? As in "Consolation," the opposition between body and soul threatens to metamorphose into or be supplanted by an opposition between body and body.

This ambiguity continues in the poem's repetition of "such" (the word appears six times in the text). Each use of "such" gestures towards a characterization of one speaker or the other, as in, " 'that I have met with such,' he said, / 'Bodes me little good.' " But instead of delivering information about them, the word conceals their qualities by standing in for them. The substitution of "such" for specific characterizations emphasizes the fact that the positions of the two speakers are only meaningful in relation to each other: "Each hating what the other loved." The poem empties the differences between them of content; each term depends entirely upon and consists of its opposition to the other. Like the "mask" of the aging body, the repetition of "such" suggests an opposition but refuses to specify it. Even the opposition between love and hate is structured around the speakers' antithetical relationship – "Each hating what the other loved" – rather than differences between the particular qualities or effects of the two emotions.

The striking contrast between the oppositional structure of the poem, a dialogue between two speakers who stand "face to face," and the categorical emptiness of their opposition indicates the poem's two major impulses. First, the poem is strictly, rigorously oppositional; as the refusal to specify the content of various oppositions indicates, what is important here is the structure of opposition itself. Although "Meeting," like the other poems in the sequence, emphasizes its oppositional purpose, its other major impulse is to subject the construction of such oppositions to scrutiny. Yeats's critique of Irish Catholic theology rejected its "Platonizing theology" involving an opposition between body and soul and substituted a conception of the divine that made the two inextricable. Sometimes he formulated this inextricability in terms calculated to shock; other times he insisted on its Christian, even its Catholic orthodoxy, invoking St. Thomas Aquinas's doctrine that "the soul is wholly present in the whole body and in all its parts" (*UPII*, 478). Yeats, who praised and needed perennial conflict but hated negation, here conducts a simultaneous critique of the body/soul opposition and of the kind of "oppositional" discourse produced by his female personae.

The series began with a stern father criticizing his rebellious daughter. It ends with a poet figure celebrating the archetypal disobedient daughter, Antigone, in "From the 'Antigone'" (*VP*, 540). As in "Father and Child," the poem celebrates feminine sexuality and desire; it is a Chorus hymn to Eros, that powerful "bitter sweetness" that inhabits "the soft cheek of a girl." As in "Father and Child," the poem assigns this force divine rather than merely individual significance; like the daughter in the sequence's opening poem, Antigone answers to a higher principle than her antagonist. But Cullingford has acutely pointed out that in the *Antigone* the heroine rebels against Eros; her transgression is not a sexual one, but an act of civil disobedience in the name of family loyalty; Haemon is the character motivated by erotic love.[66] As in "A First Confession," other social and political structures are subsumed into a version of desire, gendered female because it inhabits her cheek, that is both natural and supernatural.

"From the 'Antigone'" emphasizes the cosmic disruptive power of Eros, a power which defies an exclusively male symbolic and social order: "The rich man and his affairs," "Mariners, rough harvesters," and creates a destructive force so great that the speaker calls on it to "hurl / Heaven and Earth out of their places." The result of Eros overcoming the ordinary order of things will be conflict: "Brother and brother, friend and friend, / Family and family, / City and city may contend." On one level, this suggests civil war. On another level it suggests that once again Yeats has replaced the binary oppositions of Catholic thought with the contradictory dual existence for the same object which characterizes his alternate theology. Finally, by suggesting the breakdown of identity between the literal and figurative planes of meaning, these lines ally the poem with others in the sequence that expose discrepancies between the symbolic status assigned to objects or categories and the material situation of individual subjects.

The distinguishing structures, gestures and subject matter of "A Woman Young and Old" coincide with the terms of Yeats's explicit critique of the Free State's version of Irishness. On one hand, it measures the cost of that Irishness by emphasizing social control and rebellious women, and it persistently inverts the symbolic formulations of gender and sexuality that structured Irish national discourses during the 1920s. On the other hand, the sequence's interest in female subjectivity repeatedly modulates into a conception of feminine sexuality as eroticism: a sacred transgressive force or principle. "A Woman Young and Old"'s construction of female desire in the service of Yeats's alternate theology brings together the body and soul, impure and pure, that Church and state had put asunder; Yeats's efforts to write the female body are often more precisely characterized as attempts to inscribe and examine the soul's embodiment. The sequence frequently meditates on its own oppositional nature and on the limits inherent in it; so much of its transgression explicitly relies on and shores up that which it resists, and so many of its oppositions are categorically empty. Stallybrass and White have pointed out that a "poetics" of transgression does not necessarily constitute a progressive politics,[67] and the virtues of Yeats's transgressions of Free State nationality lie in their critical function rather than in an ability to offer more desirable constructions of nationality. The intimacy and tension in these poems between feminine sexuality as oppositional in itself and feminine sexuality as a sacred transgression in the service of an oppositional theology point instead to a discourse that persistently attempts to escape a constraining nationality by emphasizing two sites or scales that conflict with it: on the one hand, the materialities and pleasures of individual bodies, and on the other hand, the cosmic realm of an alternative metaphysical system.

CHAPTER 6

The rule of kindred: eugenics, "Purgatory" and Yeats's race philosophy

What's equality? – Muck in the yard:
Historic Nations grow
From above to below.

(*VP*, 547)

In recent years there has been much debate and little agreement over Yeats's late politics, particularly their relationship to fascism. The question of "Yeats's fascism," however, does not generate the most revealing answers about his work and attitudes during the 1930s.[1] This chapter will argue that the most useful way to assess Yeats's late politics – and the conception of nationality they embody – is to approach them through the recognition that Yeats's central political philosophy during these years was, in his words, a "race philosophy" which accorded with European fascism in some respects and differed from it in others. This race philosophy, with, of course, some changes of structure and emphasis, provides a thread of consistency linking Yeats's construction of Anglo-Irishness in the 1920s, his increasing preoccupation with authority and public order in postcolonial Ireland, his interest in eugenics, his flirtation with fascism, and the harsh rhetoric of *On the Boiler* and *Purgatory*. The model of Irish nationality in Yeats's later works extended and refigured his Anglo-Irish meditations and his definition of kindred as both tradition and its crisis. Most of the elements of this nationality were in place by the time he became explicitly interested in the British eugenics movement, but his particular version of eugenic thinking was crucial to it throughout the 1930s.

When I say that the intellectual structures of Yeats's Anglo-Irish nationality in his later years were eugenic, I am not referring simply to the thematic preoccupation with degeneration, lineage and breeding that Paul Scott Stanfield has traced quite ably in Yeats's

160

work beginning as early as 1904.[2] I mean instead a particular conception of nationality whose founding assumptions and goals I have labelled eugenic, for reasons which I hope will become clear in what follows. This nationality was anti-democratic and anti-representational. It theorized the relationship between the individual and the nation or race as irreducibly conflictual and asserted that the interests of the group should take precedence. It was imagined as a response to a crisis of foundations and as a solution to a deteriorating national character. In contrast to the Anglo-Irish nationality examined in chapter 4, which was founded in part on the absence of political power, this nationality was enforced on the masses from above by an elite and was only possible if the power and institutions of the state supported it. Like Yeats's Anglo-Irish meditations, it revealed the emptiness of its own foundations by relying on conceptions of gender and sexuality that exposed it as contingent and constructed rather than naturalizing it. It focused on reproductive heterosexuality and femininity as the central guarantors of traditional continuity and national integrity. At the same time, it acknowledged that these guarantors, far from being natural and stable foundations, required careful construction and vigilant regulation.

In 1933 Yeats wrote down a set of propositions which he initially titled "Irish Philosophy."[3] In it, he offered Ireland a way of thinking about the individual, the family and the state that corrected the errors he saw in both communism and fascism. This alternative political philosophy was "A Race Philosophy," as he later retitled the document. Like "If I Were Four-and-Twenty," "A Race Philosophy" presented a vision of the nation in which the interests of the family, and, by extension, the nation, conflicted, by definition, with those of the individual and in which the contrast between the two also signified a contrast between opposing political systems or philosophies – authority or democracy:

Communism, Fascism, are inadequate because society is the struggle of two forces not transparent to reason – the family and the individual.
From the struggle of the individual to make and preserve himself comes intellectual initiative.
From the struggle to found and preserve the family come good taste and good habits.
Equality of opportunity, equality of rights, have been created to assist the individual in his struggle. Inherited wealth, privilege, precedence, have been created to preserve the family in its struggle.[4]

Yeats also associated this race philosophy with the philosophies of
thinkers who saw society as the product of constant and irreducible
struggle, such as Darwin and especially Balzac. In his 1934 essay on
Louis Lambert Yeats elaborated Balzac's race philosophy:

> In the Comedie Humaine society is seen as a struggle for survival, each
> character an expression of will, the struggle Darwin was to describe a few
> years later, without what our instinct repudiates, Darwin's exaltation of
> accidental variations. Privilege, pride, the rights of property, are seen
> preserving the family against individual man armed with Liberty, Equality,
> Fraternity; and because the French Revolution was recent, he seems to
> prefer that wing of the Historical Antinomy that best fosters fine manners,
> minds set too high for intrigue and fear. (*EI*, 444)

This antinomy was part of a larger series of antinomies which
structured Yeats's political and poetic judgments throughout his later
years. Michael Robartes formulates it concisely in *A Vision*: "After an
age of necessity, truth, goodness, mechanism, science, democracy,
abstraction, peace, comes an age of freedom, fiction, evil, kindred,
art, aristocracy, particularity, war" (*V*, 52). Did Yeats, like Balzac,
prefer the wing of the antinomy allied with aristocracy and family
authority? His attitudes towards democracy and authority, individual
and race, during this period are complex and require some sorting
out. Briefly, the most adequate answer to this question is: on most
levels, yes, on a few other levels, no.

   On a theoretical level that coincides with the grand historical scale
of *A Vision*, Yeats accepts both democracy and authority, individual
and race, equally, as the necessary and interdependent faces of an
important historical and political antinomy. Ethically, he was no less
committed to his own version of values like intellectual initiative and
individual liberty than he was to family strength and inherited
wealth. Like the good Blakean that he was, Yeats affirmed that each
contrary was no less true because its opposite was also true. Accordingly, "A Race Philosophy" refuses to take sides, claiming "the
business of Government is not to abate either struggle but to see that
individual and family triumph by adding to Spiritual and Material
wealth." The document ends "It must not be forgotten that Race,
which has for its flower the family and the individual, is wiser than
Government, and that it is the source of all initiative."[5] This level of
thinking is profoundly inimical to practical decision-making; it is the
level at which the course of human events is determined by immense
and obscure forces beyond human understanding and control – the

historical movement of the gyres and the mysterious machinations of racial imperatives.

As a Free State senator from 1922 to 1928, however, Yeats was constantly confronted with the necessity of making and defending political choices that could have immediate material consequences. Yeats took his responsibilities in the senate quite seriously; he had a better than average attendance record, and composed his speeches carefully in advance and dictated them to his wife.[6] His performance in the senate reveals a general preference for authority and elitist government punctuated by occasional defenses of individual liberty and minority rights. On the whole, Yeats supported the Cosgrave government's often harsh stance against the disaffected republicans, and placed a high priority on establishing and maintaining social and political order. He admired Kevin O'Higgins, who was responsible for the execution of seventy-seven republicans, for his inflexibility and determination. There were, however, some exceptions to this pattern. Yeats opposed a clause in the Enforcement of Law Bill (1923) which would make bailiffs immune to prosecution for wrongful entry (*SS*, 34), he insisted that officials who inspected prison conditions for incarcerated republicans should be independent rather than government appointees (*SS*, 55, 60), and, most famously, he attacked the Free State's attempt to outlaw divorce.

Michael North has argued convincingly that Yeats's alternation between defense of individual liberty and praise of authority arises from the ideological contradictions of his project to make a small minority, the aristocracy, representative of the nation. In Yeats, he claims, "the aristocracy represents the conjuncture of two different political theories: the cultural nationalism of the 1890s and the liberalism that emerges as Yeats confronts his own nationalism rampant against him."[7] North's argument does not register the distinctions between Yeats's construction of Irishness in different periods and moods that this books seeks to describe. However, his central point offers an important corrective to critics who have read in Yeats's work a reconciliation, synthesis or balance of individual liberty and community needs. Yeats's formulation of the conflict between individual and race in his aristocratic model of kindred and his race philosophy explicitly refuses to claim such resolution. "A Race Philosophy" begins with the stark assertion: "The antinomies cannot be solved."[8] *A Vision* symbolizes their resolution while insisting on its impossibility, asserting that marriage is "a symbol of that eternal instant where the antinomy is resolved. It is not that resolution itself" (*V*, 214). Yeats's late works set up Hegel's dialectic as the opposite of the formulation in his race philosophy, constructing Hegel as a thinker who emphasized synthesis rather than conflict and for whom negation meant refutation.[9] While this is not a necessary or even a particularly compelling reading of Hegel, it illustrates the important features of Yeats's dialectic: an emphasis on the unending nature of conflict and an insistence that contraries were equally true and did not refute or resolve each other.

From 1922 on, Yeats's comments on the shape and direction of the Free State consistently predict, with varying degrees of enthusiasm ranging from the neutrality of the historian to the explicit endorsement of the partisan, that democracy in Ireland will collapse and give birth to its opposite – some form of authoritarian rule based on kindred. This became increasingly true as his support for Cosgrave suffered shocks over the issues of divorce and censorship, and even more so after DeValera's election in 1932.[10] He wrote in a 1922 letter that "out of all this murder and rapine will come not a demagogic but an authoritative government" (*L*, 682). In "From Democracy to Authority: Paul Claudel and Mussolini – A New School of Thought," a 1924 interview with *The Irish Times*, Yeats asserted that "Authoritative government is certainly coming" (*UPII*, 435) in Ireland and elsewhere and predicted that he would be a very old man before it might become "capable of taking up the tasks for which I care and of which I dream" (*UPII*, 435). He also crafted a carefully neutral position on Mussolini himself and distanced himself from the practical politics of the other Italian thinkers whose organicist conception of the state he admired.[11] In 1933, at the height of his enthusiasm for the Irish proto-fascist group known as the Blueshirts,[12] he took a more partisan stance, writing "A Fascist opposition [to DeValera] is forming behind the scenes to be ready should some tragic situation develop. I find myself constantly urging the despotic rule of the educated classes as the only end to our troubles" (*L*, 811–12). In the note to the marching songs he wrote for the Blueshirts and published in the *Spectator* he asserted, "In politics I have one passion and one thought, rancour against all who, except under the most dire necessity, disturb public order, a conviction that public order cannot persist without the rule of educated and able men" (*VP*, 543).

"Kindred" remained a crucial word for describing the antithetical, authoritarian conception of the nation he thought was approaching through the movement of the gyres, a politics he recognized as brutal but which, in its ideal form, he also thought capable of recreating the Irish nation. In the introduction to *The Words Upon the Window-pane* Yeats equated kindred relations with a shared national mythology, claiming "Thought seems more true, emotion more deep, spoken by someone who touches my pride, who seems to claim me of his kindred, who seems to make me a part of some national mythology" (*EX*, 345). In the last paragraph of "A General Introduction For My Work" (1937), he intimated his desire for the coming antithetical government but claimed he was ignorant of its precise nature. He recorded the hatred that the modern "heterogeneity" of Dublin inspired in him, and predicted

I am certain that wherever in Europe there are minds strong enough to lead others the same vague hatred rises; in four or five or in less generations this hatred will have issued in violence and imposed some kind of rule of kindred. I cannot know the nature of that rule, for its opposite fills the light; all I can do to bring it nearer is to intensify my hatred. (*EI*, 526)

In the 1937 version of *A Vision*, Yeats has the bloodthirsty Robartes praise war as necessary for a "nation or a kindred" to achieve greatness (*V*, 52) and claim "When a kindred discovers through apparition and horror that the perfect cannot perish nor even the imperfect long be interrupted, who can withstand that kindred?" (*V*, 53). Owen Aherne, Robartes's counterpoint, objects to Robartes's praise of war, but his words have none of the deliberate Yeatsian rhetorical force of Robartes's speech.[13] Yeats quoted a related passage from that speech in *On the Boiler*.[14]

Whatever stance Yeats assumed at a particular moment, several things remain constant during these years. First, whenever he diagnosed the ills of modern Ireland or DeValera, or even of fascism once he had become disenchanted with it,[15] the faults he pointed to were invariably those associated with the wing of the antinomy that favors the individual – democracy, degeneration and equality, which Yeats took to mean a homogenizing loss of individuality. Second, the vast majority of his praise during these years was reserved for the opposing wing of the antinomy. Third, when he was not openly advocating authoritarian government, he was predicting its coming as a historical inevitability. In short, notwithstanding the complexities of Yeats's political thinking during this period, authoritarian government organized around the kindred principles of his race philosophy represented both necessity and desire for Yeats. He wrote the epigraph to this chapter in February 1934, and had replaced those lines with less strident phrasing by December, but this moderated his tone rather than changed his general views. Whereas at one point he thought fascism might accord with his race philosophy, by 1933 he was using his race philosophy to point out what was wrong with fascism. Yeats's construction of eugenics was highly selective and idiosyncratic.[16] But long before he joined the London Eugenics Society, his thinking about nationality as kindred formed a crucial feature of his meditations on democracy, authority, Irish politics, the senate, and historical change. In eugenics, Yeats found an intellectual movement that seemed to gather together and confirm many important aspects of his race philosophy.

Yeats's kindred politics and eugenics shared a concept of the nation that was explicitly normative and anti-representational. For the science-oriented part of the eugenics movement, particularly the biometric wing which emphasized the statistical study of large populations rather than the study of individual variations or sports, a nation was simply a population or a set of statistical parameters.[17] But to the social and political reformers who were interested in "national efficiency"[18] and saw in eugenics a "scientific" solution to such social problems as crime, poverty, and alcoholism,[19] the nation meant a great deal more. A nation was not a mere collection of individuals, the "soul" of the folk, or an intersubjective state. It was a norm, an ideal, which recognized individual deviation and theorized about how to minimize or even eliminate it. Eugenics sought to safeguard the integrity of the national character by regulating sexual activity to alter the shape of the population in accordance with an abstract concept of the true "nation." Revolutionary nationalism was also normative in the sense that it deemed some characteristics or behaviors truly Irish and others not, but eugenics was explicit about the fact that nationality needed to be shaped, rather than merely expressed, that norms required explicit enforcement, and that the only entity with that power of enforcement was the state.

Like eugenics, Yeats's race philosophy sought to create an Irish nationality that would be disseminated and enforced "from above to below." It was concerned with the health of the population as a whole, and judged that health in relation to a standard embodied, not by the majority of the nation, but by a superior minority who shaped the people rather than representing them. In 1926 he reversed revolutionary nationalism's conception of itself, arguing:

Of one thing we may be quite certain: at no time, neither in the beginning nor in its final maturity, does an intellectual movement express a whole people, or anybody but those who are built into it, as a victim long ago was built into the foundation of a bridge. Sometimes if those few people are great enough, if there is amongst them a Sophocles or a Shakespeare, or even some lesser genius who has the sincerity of the Great Masters, they give their character to the people. (*UPII*, 470)

w>Such men expressed, and could perhaps impart to the masses, a national being deeper and more significant than transitory popular characteristics or opinion – what Swift, in a phrase Yeats quoted repeatedly, had called the "bent and current" of a people. Yeats copied the passage from Swift in which this phrase occurs into his 1930 diary,[20] discussed it at some length in his introduction to *The Words Upon the Window-pane*, and said of DeValera in his 1933 journal: "If we must have an autocrat let him express what Swift called the 'bent & current' of a people not a momentary majority."[21]

The political corollary to locating the bent and current of the national spirit in an elite minority was the theory that the political power of the state should be vested in that elite. In contrast to Celticism, revolutionary nationalism and Anglo-Irish nationality, Yeats imagined this kindred nationality as necessarily a state nationalism. Not only would this aristocracy of able men shape the masses of the nation, their character would also give rise to an appropriate political system. Yeats repeatedly predicted and called for a government composed, not of representative men, but of an educated and able elite. In "From Democracy to Authority" he claimed that Ireland and Europe were witnessing "a steady movement towards the creation of a nation controlled by highly trained intellectuals" (*UPII*, 435). He wanted to think of the Irish senate as such a governing body (half of the original senators, including Yeats, had been appointed by the government rather than elected), and offered this view to the senate in several of his speeches.[22] In *On the Boiler* Yeats claimed that the new nation should be molded around its able few: "Do not try to pour Ireland into any political system. Think first how many able men with public minds this country has ... and mould your system upon those men ... These men, whether six or six thousand, are the core of Ireland, are Ireland itself" (*EX*, 414).

Like Yeats, eugenists thought it crucial that the class which embodied the standard for the nation also be granted the political power to enforce it. This was particularly true of Raymond B. Cattell, whose *The Fight For Our National Intelligence* (1937)[23] provided Yeats with many of his ideas about the eugenics movement. Yeats's library contained several other books on eugenics,[24] and, as a member of the London Eugenics Society, which he joined in 1936, he would have received quarterly issues of the *Eugenics Review*. But he found Cattell's book particularly congenial to his way of thinking, and recommended it to his readers in the section of *On the Boiler* entitled "Tomorrow's Revolution" (*EX*, 423). Cattell was not a mainstream eugenist; his political language and attitudes were more reactionary, alarmist and coercive than those of most eugenists, and they drew criticisms from his fellow eugenists. For example, Cattell admired Germany's 1933 Eugenic Sterilization Law, something most eugenists disapproved of. The publication of his book caused considerable controversy within the eugenics movement and outside it.[25] Like Yeats, Cattell associated the current ills of democracy with the multiplication and degeneration of the masses and predicted a shift to more authoritarian government: "certainly the notion and practice of democracy, of government responsive to intelligent public opinion must give way to less happy forms of authority if the landslide of intelligence continues. For democracy is only just practicable at the level of intelligence we now possess."[26] Cattell's solution to the eugenic problem involved the embrace of aristocratic values and the resuscitation of family pride for the upper classes: "Education must carry the slogan, 'Every family a dynasty,'"[27] and he claimed that the mentally deficient need "a benevolent dictatorship, a tradition, and simple, binding rules of conduct."[28] Cattell's authoritarian political language and his praise for family dynasties allowed Yeats to fit him securely into his race philosophy of national government by kindred aristocracy. In addition, neither one was squeamish about the coercive exercise of state power.

Yeats shared with eugenics, especially the British movement, a biological and political preoccupation with classes. The eugenics movement by and large treated classes as biological phenomena.[29] It assumed that social problems like poverty were hereditary, and that intelligence was directly proportional to income and social class. Because the poor were reproducing faster than the rich, eugenists concluded that the nation's intelligence was deteriorating. Yeats's elite was not merely a state of mind; it was (among other things) a class: Yeats continued to insist that wealth, leisure and travel were necessary (though not sufficient) for the production of such men. While he had long rejected the notion that "the great are but the rich" (*EX*, 246), the aristocratic autonomy such men enjoyed included freedom from material subservience and financial necessity as important contributors to intellectual freedom. He saw in eugenics a confirmation of his convictions that the protection of an aristocratic leisured class of "the best born of the best" was a crucial necessity for Ireland.

But though they were both interested in classes, Yeats and eugenics were interested in different classes. For most eugenists, the most desirable classes were the professional middle classes; the movement as a whole was resoundingly middle class, in membership and in outlook.[30] Most eugenists, including Cattell, had mixed or even negative feelings about the landed aristocracy, and viewed them as a group that was originally eugenically superior, but also suspected that natural selection had ceased to operate in that class and that luxury was debilitating, in short, that the aristocracy was decaying.[31] Yeats wrote to the Eugenics Society several times in 1937 and 1938 to ask about the intelligence quotients of "people living upon inherited money" and predicted "One would expect it to be pretty high."[32] He was told that no such data existed, another indication of the Society's lack of interest in Yeatsian aristocracies,[33] and Yeats lamented the absence of this information in a footnote to *On The Boiler* (*EX*, 421).

Both eugenics and Yeats's race philosophy were imagined as responses to crises. The eugenics movement in Britain originated amidst fears that the nation was deteriorating and that national integrity would soon be compromised to the point of crisis.[34] This is one reason why nearly all the eugenic measures proposed or passed in England and America during the first half of the twentieth century were negative ones designed to check the multiplication of the "unfit," rather than positive eugenics, which encouraged the superior to have more children.[35] Of course, another reason for this was that negative eugenic measures targeted the members of society least able to organize in their own defense against them. Cattell attributed the falls of Greece and Rome to eugenic declines like the one England was experiencing.[36] Similarly, from the civil war on, Yeats imagined his kindred nationality as arising out of crisis, both the immediate

crises of Irish politics and the larger apocalypse he claimed was
approaching through the movement of the gyres. His conviction that
"civilisation has reached a crisis" (*EX*, 424), appeared in an
increasing number of poems and essays as he grew older.

For the eugenics movement, as for Yeats's Anglo-Irish meditations discussed in chapter 4, sexuality was both foundational and
unfounded. David Bradshaw has observed that by the mid-1930s
many sectors of the eugenics movement were becoming less hereditarian, and "an orientation towards environment was fast super-
seding an exclusively hereditarian approach to social welfare."[37]
Yeats's views were closer to the more reactionary, hereditarian wing
of the eugenics movement.[38] Eugenic thought was generally anti-
Lamarckian and drew much of its inspiration from the turn of the
century rediscovery of Mendelian genetics, and in that respect could
be said to represent a strict biologism – nature over nurture.
However, in another sense, even the more hereditarian eugenic
thinking was, by definition, a combination of hereditarian and
environmentalist thought. The determining operations of nature
must be guided and nurtured by humanity. As Sir Francis Galton,
who was generally acknowledged as the movement's founder, wrote,
"What nature does blindly, slowly, and ruthlessly, man may do
providently, quickly, and kindly."[39] While sexual reproduction was
the natural mechanism through which individuals acquired their
most important features, sex was not to be left to "nature." It was to
be managed, whether through environment, education or coercion.
Thus the foundations of eugenic theory were also its contingent
objects of management. The combination of biologism and construc-
tivism that critics have observed in Yeats's kindred thought[40] places
him in the eugenic tradition rather than apart from it.

Yeats's Anglo-Irish meditations had cast femininity as a supposed
principle of continuity which was also a source of crisis and
fragmentation. In Yeats's writings thematizing degeneration, sexual
selection, and the role of poets as educators of desire, they retained
this function. He tended to focus on two exemplary figures: a woman
who was the agent of sexual selection and whose choice determined
the status and lineage of her offspring, and a (male) poet, whose
creative powers could influence the desires of others, especially
women. Yeats's race philosophy imagines as the sexual pair for
eugenically sound reproduction, not a mother and father who choose
each other, but a woman, in whose hands lies the responsibility of

mate selection, and a poet, whose creative imagination shapes that selection. The woman is allied with the biologistic aspect of Yeats's kindred politics, the poet with the constructivist. The woman's role in reproduction should be foundational; the responsibilities of the poet reveal that foundation to be empty.

While his critique of the Free State's postcolonial Irishness had explicitly refused to conceptualize feminine sexuality in relation to maternity, Yeats's race philosophy theorized about women in terms of their reproductive capacities. In his memoirs Yeats castigated Catholic women for refusing to marry Protestants and thereby improve their bloodlines.[41] In *The King's Threshold* the poets' influence on mothers is the crucial factor which determines their sexual choices and the character of children.[42] In "Under Ben Bulben," the poets, sculptors and painters, explicitly gendered male, must do as their "great forefathers did" and create images that will shape the desire of the "globe-trotting madam" (*VP*, 638). And in *Purgatory* a woman's sexual choice leads to the downfall of an honored house. In *Letters on Poetry* Dorothy Wellesley recorded:

Speaking to W. B. Yeats of the difficulties confronting women who were creative artists, I said: "No women of genius should be expected to bear and bring up children." He, raising his hand and speaking like the prophets of old, replied: "No, we urgently need the children of women of genius!"[43]

For Yeats, it was women, the agents of sexual selection, whose desires required education and management; they were the sources of continuity who could also become the causes of fragmentation and degeneration.

Eugenics, like Yeats, was particularly concerned with maternity and the management of women in the pursuit of a healthy population. Many eugenists complained that the women who should have large families – cultured and intelligent women – seemed unwilling or unable to do so. The eugenic problems accompanying the advancement of women, while not a central preoccupation of the movement, was a theme found in a good bit of eugenic literature. Galton wrote disapprovingly in 1901, "There is unquestionably a tendency among cultured women to delay or even to abstain from marriage; they dislike the sacrifice of freedom and leisure of opportunities for study and of cultured companionship."[44] At the Second International Congress of Eugenics, held in 1921, one speaker complained of "the newer celibacy that is more distressing" than

old-fashioned priestly celibacy: "that evidenced by the low marriage
rate of many superior women."[45] Cattell also blamed the low birth
rate among the educated classes on the modern miseducation of
women. "It is the attitude of the wife which is most responsible for
deficient birth rates today," he declared.[46] Intelligent women, Cattell
argues, are having careers, marrying too late or not at all, and
having restricted families.[47]

The gender politics of the mainstream eugenics movement combined a liberal, middle-class belief in individual freedom and enrich-
ment with a more reactionary set of convictions about the
paramount and inalterable procreative responsibilities of women.
This combination, contradictory though it was in some respects,
echoes the combination of liberal and authoritarian political thought
which commentators like Cullingford and North (though they draw
very different conclusions about this combination) have outlined in
Yeats. In a 1921 essay on "The Higher Education of Women and
Race Betterment," Louis I. Dublin argued that

> As liberal persons, we must surely rejoice over the growing emancipation of
> women and their greater opportunities for personal enlightenment and
> social usefulness which education has made possible. As eugenists, however,
> we are not satisfied with the improvement of individuals alone, but must
> look for the effect of broad movements upon the race as expressed in terms
> of national tendencies. From this point of view, we cannot fail to be
> alarmed over the simple fact, now generally known, that educated women
> are being largely eliminated from parenthood.[48]

The contradictions in Dublin's formulations bear a family resem-
blance to those in Yeats's race philosophy. Like Yeats, Dublin
acknowledges the legitimacy and even the desirability of the ad-
vances women have struggled to achieve as individuals. But, like
Yeats, he cites a competing struggle that takes precedence over that
of the individual: the struggle of the race to better itself. While he
approved of cultured women, he worried that they would undo the
horn of plenty through poor marriage choices. Their warnings about
the low birth rate of educated women did not necessarily mean
eugenists advocated a barefoot and pregnant return to the home for
women; on the contrary, many (though not all) argued with Louis
Dublin that "we must educate public opinion to look with favor
upon the continuation of married women in the many positions of
responsibility they are now filling so capably"[49] and that "a woman
should no longer be confronted with a choice of either matrimony or

a career."[50] This attitude was in keeping with the generally progressive attitude of most eugenists, and was congenial to Yeats as well; in the 1925 Senate he had spoken critically of a proposed measure which discriminated against women in certain civil service appointments on the grounds that they were likely to get married and leave the service.[51]

When Yeats wrote *On the Boiler* in 1938, he incorporated his discovery of the British eugenics movement into a further consideration of the kindred issues which had been part of his thinking about Irishness for years. Critics have often claimed that in *On the Boiler* Yeats was deliberately courting the shock and outrage of his readers,[52] and his explanation of the essay's title also suggests that he wanted to flaunt his "Anglo-Irish solitude" (*EX*, 308, 325) and his thoroughgoing contempt for the pieties of the Free State. Yeats took the title from a "mad ship's carpenter" in Sligo who, during his working months, "broke off from time to time to read the Scriptures and denounce his neighbours" (*EX*, 407) from the top of an old boiler. Yeats continues, "Then I saw him at a Rosses Point regatta alone in a boat; sculling it in whenever he saw a crowd, then, bow to seaward, denouncing the general wickedness, then sculling it out amid a shower of stones" (*EX*, 407). This gives some indication of the response Yeats not only expected but wanted. The essay is deliberately provocative, casting its propositions in the most uncompromising terms available.

Its propositions, however, are those of the race philosophy Yeats developed out of his earlier meditations on Anglo-Irish nationality as kindred. The essay insists that what Yeats says here is what he really thinks, as opposed to the "patter" (*EX*, 417, 418, 434) he learned when he was young in order to hide the fact that "There was no dominant opinion I could accept" (*EX*, 417). Yeats adopts the stance of a closet "fanatic" (*EX*, 417) who will now reveal his true opinions and accept the stones they will provoke his readers to cast. He wrote to Maud Gonne in June of 1938, "For the first time I am saying what I believe about Irish and European politics. I wonder how many friends I will have left" (*GY*, 451).[53] While we should not underestimate the deliberate nature of this pose, the opinions *On The Boiler* offers represent an extension of his eugenic model of nationality as kindred rather than a deviation from it. If *On The Boiler* has a virtue, it is that the essay trumpets the authoritarian implications of this version of nationality clearly and uncompromisingly rather than softening or erasing them.

On the Boiler continues the late Yeats's critique of modern democracy: "Our representative system has given Ireland to the incompetent" (*EX*, 412). The first section of "Preliminaries" affirms the rule of the educated classes rather than representative politicians: "the whole State should be so constructed that the people should think it their duty to grow popular with King and Lord Mayor instead of King and Lord Mayor growing popular with them" (*EX*, 410). This passage restates, in exaggerated and inflammatory form, Yeats's doctrine that the masses should assimilate themselves to the elite minority who represented the deeper bent and current of the people, rather than the elite courting favor with or representing the masses. Later in the essay Yeats returns to the claim that the core of the nation is embodied not in its masses but in a few exceptional individuals: "Berkeley, Swift, Burke, Grattan, Parnell, Augusta Gregory, Synge, Kevin O'Higgins, are the true Irish people, and there is nothing too hard for such as these. If the Catholic names are few history will soon fill the gap" (*EX*, 442).

As before, Yeats connects the able and educated few with the Irish senate, claiming that the nominated element was the most able and that when it began to die out "the Senate declined in ability and prestige" (*EX*, 413). (When DeValera came to power he abolished the senate in its original form and substituted a body with more limited powers.) Although Yeats acknowledges that he felt alienated from them, he compared them favorably to the "typical elected man" (*EX*, 413), and characterized them as the elite who would govern Ireland in the future: "neither Gogarty nor I, with our habit of outrageous conversation, could get near those men. Yet their descendants, if they grow rich enough for the travel and leisure that make a finished man, will constitute our ruling class, and date their origin from the Post Office as American families date theirs from the *Mayflower*" (*EX*, 413).[54] These men will be a kindred aristocracy: "They have already intermarried, able stocks have begun to appear, and recent statistics have shown that men of talent everywhere are much linked through marriage and descent" (*EX*, 413).

Much of the section entitled "Tomorrow's Revolution" is devoted to Yeats's explicitly eugenic concerns, and relates them to his aristocratic kindred politics. This section takes up the arguments of "A Race Philosophy" and uses them to critique the two major contemporary alternatives to democracy: fascism and communism. Yeats linked fascism and communism as modes of government that had the potential ability to halt eugenic decline (unlike democracy), but encouraged it instead:

The Fascist countries know that civilisation has reached a crisis, and found their eloquence upon that knowledge, but from dread of attack or because they must feed their uneducatable masses, put quantity before quality; any hale man can dig or march. They offer bounties for the seventh, eighth, or ninth baby, and accelerate degeneration. In Russia, where the most intelligent families restrict their numbers as elsewhere, the stupidest man can earn a bounty by going to bed. Government there has the necessary authority, but ... thinks the social problem economic and not eugenic and ethnic. (*EX*, 424)

As most commentators point out, by 1938 Yeats no longer imagined that fascism represented the solution to the problems he thought afflicted Ireland and the rest of Europe. What I want to emphasize here is that not only is Yeats, as usual, rejecting economics (and therefore materialism) as the basis for a theory or a state; he substitutes another mode of analysis and frame of reference: the "eugenic and ethnic."

Much of "Tomorrow's Revolution" is devoted to just such an analysis. Yeats asserts that the "principal European nations are degenerating in body and in mind" (*EX*, 420), and that intelligence is directly proportional to social class (*EX*, 421–2). Yeats predicts that the educated classes will be driven to assume control of the masses and speculates that a "civil war" between the skilled and the degenerate may ensue. Such a war was to be desired because it could establish the supremacy of the educated and inaugurate a new historical phase: "The danger is that there will be no war, that the skilled will attempt nothing, that the European civilisation, like those older civilisations that saw the triumph of their gangrel stocks, will accept decay" (*EX*, 425). This is particularly bloodthirsty, but the late Yeats did not lack a vision of evil; he believed in the inevitability and the desirability of constant conflict and even of periodic violence. His race philosophy imagined society as organized around two kinds of conflict: family and individual, and he saw the state as necessarily embodying violence. After the Cosgrave government's execution of seventy-seven republican prisoners, Yeats commented "The Government of the Free State has been proved legitimate by the only effective test; it has been permitted to take life" (*UPII*, 487).[55] *On the*

Boiler restates this idea: "If human violence is not embodied in our
institutions the young will not give them their affection, nor the
young and old their loyalty. A government is legitimate because
some instinct has compelled us to give it the right to take life in
defence of its laws and its shores" (*EX*, 441). To be sure, violence was
not all the state embodied, but Yeats was comfortable with various
violences on a literal as well as a metaphoric level in a way that many
contemporary commentators are not.

On the other hand, Yeats also offers the kind of mundane practical
proposition which had characterized his senatorial work. The section
of "Tomorrow's Revolution" that follows his praise of war and its
horror observes matter of factly: "Sooner or later we must limit the
families of the unintelligent classes, and if our Government cannot
send them doctor and clinic it must, till it gets tired of it, send monk
and confession-box" (*EX*, 426). Once again, while it is hard to pin
Yeats down on the question of whether the Irish should really
"Desire some just war" (*EX*, 441) to facilitate national unity, what
remains constant, whether the language is apocalyptic or resignedly
practical, are the principles of his race philosophy.

Purgatory, which was first published in *On the Boiler*, represents the
culmination of Yeats's eugenic theory of nationality as kindred, not
simply because it offers an argument about how the stable continuity
of aristocratic tradition depends upon the sexual choices of women,
but, more significantly, because it both offers and undercuts that
argument. Commentators usually point to the play's overt eugenic
theme, in which the play indicts an aristocratic woman for a poor
sexual choice. The lady of the house marries a drunken, lowly groom
who ruins the estate and the family bloodline. A few days after the
play's first performance on August 10, 1938, Yeats commented on it
in an interview with a reporter from the *Irish Independent*. Yeats's
explanation emphasizes this theme by casting the erring woman as
the center of the play and her sexual misalliance as the exemplary act
of betrayal:

In my play, a spirit suffers because of its share, when alive, in the
destruction of an honoured house; that destruction is taking place all over
Ireland to-day. Sometimes it is the result of poverty, but more often
because a new individualistic generation has lost interest in the ancient
sanctities ... In some few cases a house has been destroyed by a
mesalliance. I have founded my play on this exceptional case, partly
because of my interest in certain problems of eugenics, partly because it

enables me to depict more vividly than would otherwise be possible the tragedy of the house.[56]

Yeats's comments emphasize the eugenic theme's relevance to contemporary Ireland, inviting comparison with *On the Boiler*'s "eugenic and ethnic" critique of modern Ireland and contemporary political systems. The drafts of the play had been even more explicit about this connection. Yeats originally wrote "He married her in the village church."[57] The village church would of course be Catholic, making the mixed marriage a transgression of Irish sectarian as well as class boundaries, and invoking more directly Ascendancy fears of racial degeneration.

Many of the things the old man says accord with Yeats's kindred politics on this thematic level, such as his assertion that "to kill a house / Where great men grew up, married, died, / I here declare a capital offence" (*VPI*, 1044). However, as W. J. McCormack has argued in his excellent discussion of *Purgatory*, the old man represents the foolish, nostalgic idealization of an irresponsible landlord class rather than a tragic lament for a noble aristocratic civilization.[58] As McCormack points out, Yeats had used the old man's description of the Ascendancy, "Magistrates, colonels, members of Parliament, Captains and Governors," who "came from London every spring / To look at the may-blossom in the park" (*VPI*, 1043–4) as an example of Ascendancy limitations, irresponsibility and decline in "Commentary on 'A Parnellite at Parnell's Funeral'" in 1935.[59] The old man does not merely diagnose the degradation his mother's sexual transgression has brought to the family, his method of confronting that degradation is a symptom of it as well. This is appropriate for a character who is the product of a degenerative union.

The play opens by emptying out the two major symbols of Yeats's kindred nation in the form of a hereditary aristocracy, an ancestral house and a Burkean tree. Politically, both the aristocratic house and the tree suggested natural hierarchies. Yeats wrote in "Blood and the Moon," of

> haughtier-headed Burke that proved the State a tree,
> That this unconquerable labyrinth of the birds, century after
> century,
> Cast but dead leaves to mathematical equality.   (*VP*, 481)

Yeats theorized such natural hierarchies as providing the ground on which individuality flourished. He equated hierarchy with difference and believed that democracy robbed men of their "uniqueness," a word he usually reserved to denote a positive kind of individuality, as opposed to the meaningless, decadent individuality of modern democracy. He wrote in *On the Boiler*: "Man has made mathematics, but God reality. Instead of hierarchical society, where all men are different, came democracy" (*EX*, 435). While Yeats was aware of the potentially threatening nature of such a hierarchy, writing in a 1921 letter, "In many ways a great state kills all under its shadow like a horse chestnut" (*L*, 666), he thought that democracy, by rendering all citizens the same and therefore interchangeable, displayed a deadly lack of respect for the individual human life, claiming:

No educated man to-day accepts the objective matter and space of popular science, and yet deductions made by those who believed in both dominate the world, make possible the stimulation and condonation of revolutionary massacre and the multiplication of murderous weapons by substituting for the old humanity with its unique irreplaceable individuals something that can be chopped and measured like a piece of cheese. (*EX*, 435–6)

Throughout his career, Yeats used the "great-rooted blossomer" as an emblem of an organic unity whose different parts were organized into an integrated, hierarchical whole. A wall poster for the 1932 Third International Eugenics Congress in New York City pictured a large tree, labelled "Eugenics," with diverse roots representing its constituent disciplines, areas of inquiry and issues. Yeats probably never saw the poster, but its caption, "Like a tree eugenics draws its materials from many sources and gives them organic unity and purpose,"[60] indicates that Yeats and the eugenics movement shared common metaphors as well as convictions.

Houses and trees often appear together to illustrate this set of political values in Yeats's poems of the 1920s and 1930s. *Purgatory* invites comparison by specifying the scene as "a ruined house and a bare tree in the background" (*VPI*, 1041). From *The Tower* on, Yeatsian speakers often confront ruined houses and bare trees. Most of them, however, do so much more successfully than *Purgatory*'s nameless old man, and this difference provides an important clue to how we should read him. The other speakers grapple with the deterioration of their bodies, the death of friends, the destruction of dynasties, or the decay of great houses. But the process of contemplating these various ruins leads each speaker to some sort of affirmation. Sometimes he asserts the power of his imagination or of a willful creative act; sometimes he affirms the force of memory;

sometimes he lauds the continued nobility of the virtues embodied by those who are gone; sometimes he attests to the continuity of the soul or the community despite individual death.

In "The Tower," the speaker confronts the ruin of his own body and simultaneously ponders the remains of a house and a blackened tree: "I pace upon the battlements and stare / On the foundations of a house, or where / Tree, like a sooty finger, starts from the earth" (*VP*, 409–10). His imagination calls forth "Images and memories / From ruin or from ancient trees" (*VP*, 410) as he interrogates his past. From this interrogation emerges a series of affirmations. In the third section of the poem the speaker asserts the supremacy of the human imagination, claiming that "Death and life were not / Till man made up the whole" (*VP*, 415), a sentiment echoed in other poems, such as "Death."[61] He writes his will, projecting his legacy into the future: "I leave both faith and pride / To young upstanding men" (*VP*, 416). He resolves "Now shall I make my soul" (*VP*, 416), a process which will enable him to view the "wreck of body" (*VP*, 416) with which the poem began with a new equanimity. Such decay will

> Seem but the clouds of the sky
> When the horizon fades,
> Or a bird's sleepy cry
> Among the deepening shades.

– small accompaniments to a sunset, the demise of an individual day preceding the birth of another.

As I argued in chapter 4, in "My House," "My Table," and "My Descendants" the persistent separation of genealogy and nature and the repeated recognition that the speaker's true legacy is the necessity for the creative, autonomous act of foundation leads to the affirmation of that act. In "A Dialogue of Self and Soul" the soul summons the self to accept bodily decay and contemplate the other world. The "broken, crumbling battlement" (*VP*, 477) parallels the body of "a man / Long past his prime" (*VP*, 477) and forms the appropriate setting for such a summons. But the self has the last word. He refuses to capitulate to this parallel, casts out remorse and affirms the validity, even the blessedness, of the messy, painful, error-ridden business of living. In "Coole Park, 1929" the speaker contemplates a house, a tree and their ruin: "I meditate upon a swallow's flight, / Upon an aged woman and her house, / A sycamore and lime-tree lost in night" (*VP*, 488). The speaker concludes by projecting the future ruin of the house and the death of Lady Gregory and demanding that all future visitors remember them, acknowledging physical decay but countering it by affirming an act of memory.

In *Purgatory* the old man's injunction to "Study that house ... Study that tree" (*VPI*, 1041), leads to none of these affirmations. His memory fails him; he cannot remember the house's "jokes and stories" (*VPI*, 1041), and he closes off the possibility that someone else will remember after he is gone: "If I cannot, none living can" (*VPI*, 1041). He gestures towards a Yeatsian assertion of the creative will to impose meaning on the scene, claiming, "The moonlight falls upon the path, / The shadow of a cloud upon the house, / And that's symbolical" (*VPI*, 1041). But he fails to elaborate its symbolism, and the reader is left to surmise that the shadow of the cloud over the house symbolizes its destruction or the curse that hangs over it. In either case, the parallelism here – between landscape and the moral or physical state of the house – is precisely what the affirmative moments at the end of poems like "A Dialogue of Self and Soul" and "Coole Park, 1929" labor to reject.

This feeble gesture towards the imaginative appropriation of the landscape peters out after the old man's second injunction: "study that tree" (*VPI*, 1041). He asks the boy "What is it like?" and the boy's answer aligns the old man's decay with the tree's: "A silly old man" (*VPI*, 1041). At this point the old man gives up and asserts the irrelevance of the tree's metaphoric potential: "It's like – no matter what it's like" (*VPI*, 1042). Thus *Purgatory* begins by invoking two major symbols in Yeats's middle and late work, symbols which usually provide the occasion for some version of creative, antithetical affirmation on the part of the speaker. Here, however, the old man fails, elaborately, to do so. He has given up the poetic vocation of producing such moments: "It's like – no matter what it's like. / I saw it a year ago stripped bare as now, / So I chose a better trade" (*VPI*, 1042).

"So I chose a better trade" echoes a line in the poem Yeats originally included at the end of *On the Boiler*, "The Statesman's Holiday" (*VP*, 626–7). Yeats explained the genesis of the poem this way: "Here in Monte Carlo, where I am writing, somebody talked of a man with a monkey and some sort of stringed instrument, and it has pleased me to imagine him a great politician. I will make him sing to the sort of tune that goes well with my early sentimental poems" (*EX*, 452). Like *Purgatory*'s old man, this speaker also appears to be a combination of diagnosis and symptom. The first stanza laments the decline of aristocratic civilization: "I lived among great houses, / Riches drove out rank, / Base drove out the better blood / And mind and body shrank." The speaker seems to have salvaged what he could, albeit in fragmented form, of the intellectual tradition which characterized the old days: "But I'd a troop of friends / That knowing better talk had gone / Talked of odds and ends." At the end of the first stanza the speaker claims that this degeneration led him to give up being a statesman and turn to poetry instead: "So I have picked a better trade / And night and morning sing: / *Tall dames go walking in grass-green Avalon.*"

But in the second stanza, the speaker asks a series of questions that identify him, not with great statesmen, but with politicians and public figures for whom Yeats felt little besides scorn:

> Am I a great Lord Chancellor
> That slept upon the Sack?
> Commanding officer that tore
> The khaki from his back?
> Or am I De Valera,
> Or the King of Greece,
> Or the man that made the motors?
> Ach, call me what you please![62]

This stanza calls into question the speaker's identification with the traditions which existed before "riches drove out rank," and raises the possibility that he is to be allied with the new, degenerate forces rather than the old. Like *Purgatory*'s old man, the speaker of "The Statesman's Holiday" is both. The last stanza does little to clear up the confusion, just as *Purgatory* compels the reader's agreement with the old man's criticism of his family's degeneration while at the same time refusing to let the old man's narrative stand unopposed by competing narratives.

By the end of the play's first page, then, the attentive reader, especially the attentive reader of *On the Boiler* and Yeats's other middle and late works, is aware that the old man is not necessarily to be trusted, and almost certainly not to be admired, as an interpreter of events and meanings. Yeats went to some lengths to make the old man's unreliability clear as he revised *Purgatory*. Early drafts of the play depicted the old man as a shrewd and self-aware character; as Yeats revised, he created a gap between the old man's assessment of himself and his actions and the audience's evaluation, making the old man an increasingly unreliable commentator on events.[63]

Yeats's race philosophy also indicates that we should not merely dismiss the boy's counter-arguments which undercut the old man's position. The old man laments the failure of the family's struggle to preserve itself; the boy re-casts that failure as the narrative of a successful individual struggle. While the old man condemns his mother's transgressive sexual choice, the boy sides with the old man's opportunistic father: "What's right and what's wrong? / My grand-dad got the girl and the money" (*VPI*, 1043). The association of low class status with lust for sex and money is an important aspect of Yeats's characterization of such figures as beggars, swineherds, drunkards, and fools, from *Responsibilities* on.[64] The refrain sung by the condemned man in part III of "Three Marching Songs" speaks for all of them: "Money is good and a girl might be better" (*VP*, 616). The boy's characterization of his grandfather's marriage places him in distinguished if unattractive company in Yeats's works, for "wisdom comes of beggary" (*VP*, 487). Together the old man and the boy represent the irreducible antinomy of "A Race Philosophy."

The text's emphasis on the sexual consummation as the act of betrayal also opens the way to a critique of the old man's position. As I have argued, the structure of Yeats's genealogical model for the Anglo-Irish race and culture acknowledged a central conflict between individual sexual identity and desire and those demanded by the imperatives of racial strength and continuity. *Purgatory* main-tains this conflict by coupling the dead woman's remorse for the destruction of the house with her pleasure in the act of betrayal:

> Can she renew the sexual act
> And find no pleasure in it, and if not,
> If pleasure and remorse must both be there,
> Which is the greater?   (*VPI*, 1046)

The souls in Purgatory "Re-live / Their transgressions" so that they may "know at last / The consequences of those transgressions" (*VPI*, 1042). "Driven to it by remorse" (*VPI*, 1046), she relives her transgression, but each repetition re-establishes the claims of indivi-dual desire that motivated it. In the repetition of her betrayal, the individual struggle and the family struggle meet in an irresolvable infinite loop.

The old man does not understand this. He kills the boy, his son, to break the cycle of degeneration: "I killed the lad because had he grown up / He would have struck a woman's fancy, / Begot, and passed pollution on" (*VPI*, 1049). Once again, the old man's inadequate response to the situation goes hand in hand with the failure of his creative will. After he stabs the boy, he tries to sing, but abandons the effort:

> "Hush-a-bye baby, thy father's a knight,
> Thy mother a lady, lovely and bright."
> No, that is something that I read in a book,
> And if I sing it must be to my mother,
> And I lack rhyme.   (*VPI*, 1048–9)

The old man's attempt to assert his imaginative power and sing also involves an attempt to create a more acceptable genealogy for his dead son (the lullaby) and an effort to establish a supportive relationship to the tradition his mother represents. All three fail. Then the old man returns to his injunction to "study that tree" and this time he apparently succeeds in asserting a symbolic meaning for it:

> Study that tree.
> It stands there like a purified soul,
> All cold, sweet glistening light.
> Dear mother, the window is dark again,
> But you are in the light because
> I finished all that consequence.   (*VPI*, 1049)

According to the old man the tree now symbolizes his mother's purified soul, freed at last from remorse and repetition by the murder of her grandson. But the old man's imaginative appropriation of the tree and the resolution it embodies are false and empty. The old man hears the sound of hoof-beats again, and realizes that his mother's soul is still trapped in its purgatorial cycle of repetition, and that he is "twice a murderer and all for nothing" (*VPI*, 1049).

Donald Torchiana argues that the section of *On the Boiler* entitled "Other Matters" provides subtle hints about how to read the play, and characterizes the theory of *Purgatory* as the theory that "no tragedy is legitimate unless it leads some great character to his final joy" (*EX*, 448).[65] If this is the theory of *Purgatory*, the play illustrates it by embodying its failure. The old man is no great character, he achieves no final joy, and part of his tragedy is that he is incapable of the "will or energy" that Yeats claims makes tragedy noble and leads the tragic hero to joy (*EX*, 449). The play ends with the old man's

unanswered plea to God to release him and his mother from
repetition and conflict: "O God, / Release my mother's soul from
its dream! / Mankind can do no more. Appease / The misery of
the living and the remorse of the dead" (*VPI*, 1049). This ending
does not suggest the final joy of a great character in the way that
The Death of Cuchulain does, for example.[66] The old man's imaginative efforts fail, his attempt to understand and remedy his mother's
purgatorial state fails, the murder serves no purpose. For *Purgatory*'s
old man, kindred is an unmanageable crisis that repeats itself
despite his efforts.

In *Purgatory*, kindred relations are those of violence, discontinuity
and death. The cast of characters does not indicate that the old man
and the boy are father and son; the reader learns this several pages
into the play, indicating that the conventional relations between
fathers and sons – affection, Oedipal rivalry – are purely incidental
to their Yeatsian kindred relation. This version of family is the family
of eugenic thinking, of "If I Were Four-and-Twenty" and "A Race
Philosophy," a family founded on a vision of evil. In *Purgatory*, the
antinomies of Yeats's race philosophy encounter each other violently
and irresolvably. The mother's dream re-enacts the conflict between
the family/national imperatives which generate her remorse and the
individual desires which drove her to seek transgressive pleasure.
The old man represents the family struggle; the boy embodies the
individual struggle. No reconciliation is possible, and the temporary
triumph of one over the other does nothing to abate the crisis and
conflict which structure their existence.

Purgatory performs a eugenic critique of the old man and his
mother. The mother represents both the continuity of aristocratic
tradition and its betrayal. She owned the house and embodied its
virtues, and the old man reports that "some / Half-loved me for my
half of her" (*VPI*, 1044). On the other hand, the play focuses on her
sexual choice as the cause of degeneration. Similarly, the old man,
product of an aristocratic mother and a lowly father, embodies
kindred as both tradition and its crisis. While he claims kinship to his
mother, he also admits "I am my father's son" (*VPI*, 1045).

The old man stands for something else too – a particular
inadequate way of confronting this crisis-ridden model of nationality,
the way of nostalgia, self-pity and the utopian hope that such kindred
aristocracies are founded on anything besides constant violence and
struggle. This inadequacy makes the old man a degenerate symptom

as well as a eugenic critic. His existential squeamishness and his inability to appropriate the scene imaginatively lead him to desire a release from conflict and repetition; he wants the antinomies to be resolved and the struggle to cease. This leads him in turn to murder his own son. Yeats structured *Purgatory* so that the denial of perennial conflict leads to murder, precisely the shape of his critique of utopian thought, particularly Marxism,[67] and of his assertion that the rule of kindred, organized around his race philosophy, would create, in its way, a more humane and individualistic society than democracy.

Yeats's race philosophy and the eugenic model of nationality that went along with it were certainly not fascism. But they were hardly more compatible with liberal democracy than fascism. Politically, such a model of nationality has few attractions. Analytically, however, it has several uses. The major achievement of this strand in the middle and late Yeats is that it does what *Purgatory*'s old man cannot do: through acts of creative will, it teases out, examines and come to terms with all the things that most conceptions of nationality work hardest to deny. Instead of secure and natural foundations, harmonious relations between the individual and the nation, and synthesis, Yeats's eugenic nationality and kindred politics offer arbitrariness, violence, and irresolvable conflict. In other words, they present, in exaggerated and explicit form the things that often lurk behind the facades of more attractive versions of the nation. They expose, by re-figuring and refusing, the naturalizing work that conventional conceptions of gender, sexuality and the family often perform. Finally, they point to an important problem for contemporary scholarship on nationality and postcolonial theory: the need to find a way of confronting the crisis and potential violence that underlies all constructions of nationality without succumbing to the temptation to repeat the old man's murderous desire for synthesis, stasis and purity.

Notes

INTRODUCTION

1 Benedict Anderson, *Imagined Communities: Reflections on the Origin and Spread of Nationalism* (London: Verso, 1983), p. 15.

2 See Lauren Berlant's *The Anatomy of National Fantasy: Hawthorne, Utopia, and Everyday Life* (University of Chicago Press, 1991) for her definition of the National Symbolic: "We are bound together because we inhabit the *political* space of the nation, which is not merely juridical, territorial (*jus soli*), genetic (*jus sanguinis*), linguistic, or experiential, but some tangled cluster of these. I call this space the 'National Symbolic'" (pp. 4–5).

3 Eve Kosofsky Sedgwick, "Nationalisms and Sexualities in the Age of Wilde," *Nationalisms and Sexualities*, ed. Andrew Parker, Mary Russo, Doris Sommer, and Patricia Yaeger (New York: Routledge, 1992), pp. 235–45.

4 Gayle Rubin, "The Traffic in Women: Notes on the 'Political Economy' of Sex," *Women, Class, and the Feminist Imagination: A Socialist-Feminist Reader*, ed. Karen V. Hansen and Ilene J. Philipson (Philadelphia: Temple University Press, 1990), pp. 74–113.

5 Sedgwick, "Nationalisms and Sexualities," p. 239.

6 For a critique of this model of mediation, see Judith Butler, *Gender Trouble: Feminism and the Subversion of Identity* (New York: Routledge, 1990).

7 Anderson, *Imagined Communities*, p. 12.

8 For an excellent and concise outline of some of these debates, see Luke Gibbons's introduction to "Constructing the Canon: Versions of National Identity," *The Field Day Anthology of Irish Writing*, vol. II (New York: Norton, 1991), pp. 950–5.

9 See Homi Bhabha's *The Location of Culture* (New York and London: Routledge, 1994) and his "Introduction: Narrating the Nation" in *Nation and Narration*, ed. Homi Bhabha (New York: Routledge, 1990), pp. 1–7.

10 For a critique of Bhabha's use of the language model, see Benita Parry, "Signs of Our Times: Discussion of Homi Bhabha's *The Location of Culture*," *Third Text*, 28/29 (Autumn/Winter 1994), pp. 5–24.

11 Conor Cruise O'Brien, "Passion and Cunning: An Essay on the Politics of W. B. Yeats," *In Excited Reverie: A Centenary Tribute to W. B. Yeats 1865–1939*, ed. A. Norman Jeffares (New York: St. Martin's Press, 1965).

12 See Elizabeth Cullingford, *Yeats, Ireland and Fascism* (New York and London: New York University Press, 1981), Grattan Freyer, *W. B. Yeats and the Anti-Democratic Tradition* (Dublin: Gill and Macmillan, 1981), Bernard Krimm, *W. B. Yeats and the Emergence of the Irish Free State 1918–1939: Living in the Explosion* (Troy, NY: Whitston Publishing, 1981), and Paul Scott Stanfield, *Yeats and Politics in the Nineteen-Thirties* (London: Macmillan, 1988). Cullingford's intelligent and thorough work counters O'Brien's attack by defending Yeats as a nationalist and a liberal, while Krimm's much less successful effort also seeks to exonerate him as an Irish nationalist. Freyer takes up a mixed position that negotiates between those of Cullingford and O'Brien, both of whom he criticizes for partial and extreme arguments. Stanfield emphasizes the complex and "inassimilable" (p. 187) qualities of Yeats's political thinking and casts him as an individualist, but also generally charts his progress from Irish nationalist to Anglo-Irish reactionary.

13 Edward Said, "Yeats and Decolonization," *Nationalism, Colonialism and Literature*, ed. Seamus Deane (Minneapolis: University of Minnesota Press, 1990). The quote is from p. 84. The essay is reprinted in Said's *Culture and Imperialism* (New York: Alfred Knopf, 1993).

14 See Seamus Deane's "Yeats and the Idea of Revolution," *Celtic Revivals: Essays in Modern Irish Literature 1880–1980* (London and Boston: Faber and Faber, 1985), and his "Heroic Styles: The Tradition of an Idea," *Ireland's Field Day* (Notre Dame, IN: University of Notre Dame Press, 1985 [1984]). For Richard Kearney's treatment of Yeats, see his *Transitions: Narratives in Modern Irish Culture* (Manchester University Press, 1985), and "Myth and Motherland," *Ireland's Field Day* (Notre Dame, IN: University of Notre Dame Press, 1985).

15 Mario Praz, *The Romantic Agony* (Oxford University Press, 1970 [1933]), p. xv.

16 Elizabeth Cullingford, *Gender and History in Yeats's Love Poetry* (Cambridge University Press, 1993).

17 See, for example, Stella Revard, "Yeats, Mallarme and the Archetypal Feminine," *Papers on Language and Literature* (supplement, Fall 1972), Gloria C. Kline, *The Last Courtly Lover: Yeats and the Idea of Woman* (Ann Arbor: UMI Research Press, 1983), Andrew Parkin, "Women in the Plays of W. B. Yeats," *Woman in Irish Legend, Life and Literature*, ed. S. F. Gallagher (Gerrards Cross: Colin Smythe, 1983), pp. 38–57, Patrick J. Keane, *Terrible Beauty: Yeats, Joyce, Ireland, and the Myth of the Devouring Female* (Columbia: University of Missouri Press, 1988), and Cassandra Laity, "W. B. Yeats and Florence Farr: The Influence of the 'New Woman' Actress on W. B. Yeats's Changing Images of Women," *Modern Drama*, 28:4 (Dec. 1985).

18 For example, see Curtis Bradford, "Yeats and Maud Gonne," *Texas Studies in Literature and Language*, 3:4 (Winter 1962), pp. 452–74, John Harwood, "Olivia Shakespear and W. B. Yeats," *Yeats Annual*, 4 (1986), pp. 75–98, and Carolyn Holdsworth, "Shelley Plain: Yeats and Katharine Tynan," *Yeats: An Annual of Critical and Textual Studies*, 2 (1983), pp. 59–92.

19 "Introduction," *Nationalisms and Sexualities*, ed. Andrew Parker, Mary Russo, Doris Sommer, and Patricia Yaeger, p. 2. George Mosse has documented the nineteenth-century rise of a series of alliances between nationalism and sexuality in Germany and England (George Mosse, *Nationalism and Sexuality: Respectability and Abnormal Sexuality in Modern Europe* [New York: Howard Fertig, 1985]).

20 Two important histories of the rise of modern conceptions of nationality which follow this dating are Eric Hobsbawm's *Nations and Nationalism Since 1780: Programme, Myth, Reality* (Cambridge University Press, 1990) and Anderson's *Imagined Communities*.

21 Hobsbawm observes that "We cannot … read into the revolutionary 'nation' anything like the later nationalist programme of establishing nation-states for bodies defined in terms of the criteria so hotly debated by the nineteenth-century theorists, such as ethnicity, common language, religion, territory and common historical memories" (*Nations and Nationalism*, p. 20).

22 For accounts of the rise of cultural nationalism in Ireland, see George Boyce, *Nationalism in Ireland* (London: Croom Helm and Dublin: Gill and Macmillan, 1982), and John Hutchinson, *The Dynamics of Cultural Nationalism: The Gaelic Revival and the Creation of the Irish Nation State* (London: Allen and Unwin, 1987).

23 See Michel Foucault, *The History of Sexuality Volume I: An Introduction* (New York: Vintage Books, 1980 [1978]), and Jeffrey Weeks, *Sex, Politics and Society: The Regulation of Sexuality Since 1800* (London and New York: Longman, 1981).

24 Anderson, *Imagined Communities*, p. 14.

25 Clifford Geertz, "Primordial and Civic Ties," *Nationalism*, ed. John Hutchinson and Anthony D. Smith (Oxford University Press, 1994), pp. 29–33.

26 For example, Gayle Rubin suggests that critics stop subsuming theories of sexuality under feminism and begin analyzing sexuality without reference to the binarism of gender ("Thinking Sex: Notes For a Radical Theory of the Politics of Sexuality," *The Lesbian and Gay Studies Reader*, ed. Henry Abelove, Michele Barale and David Halperin [New York and London: Routledge, 1993], pp. 3–44).

27 See Ernest Renan's famous essay, "What is a Nation?" for a good example of a formulation of the nation that draws upon Enlightenment discourses of reason, civilization and human rights (in *Nation and Narration*, ed. Homi Bhabha [New York and London: Routledge, 1990], pp. 8–22).

28 Peter Stallybrass and Allon White, *The Politics and Poetics of Transgression* (Ithaca: Cornell University Press, 1986).

29 For example, see Monique Wittig's *The Straight Mind and Other Essays* (Boston: Beacon Press, 1992) and Terry Eagleton's "Nationalism: Irony and Commitment," *Nationalism, Colonialism, and Literature* (Minneapolis: University of Minnesota Press, 1990).

30 For a useful discussion of this issue, see Michael McKeon, "Historicizing Patriarchy: The Emergence of Gender Difference in England, 1660–1760," *Eighteenth-Century Studies* 28:3 (1995), pp. 305–7.

31 For a discussion of how gender is used to naturalize global capitalism in twentieth-century European mass culture, see Judith Williamson, "Woman is an Island: Femininity and Colonization," *Studies in Entertainment: Critical Approaches to Mass Culture*, ed. Tania Modleski (Bloomington: University of Indiana Press, 1986).

32 Anderson, *Imagined Communities*, p. 17.

33 Fredric Jameson, "Third-World Literature in the Era of Multinational Capitalism," *Social Text*, 15 (Fall 1986), p. 73. For a critique of Jameson, see Aijaz Ahmad's "Jameson's Rhetoric of Otherness and the 'National Allegory,'" *In Theory: Classes, Nations, Literatures* (New York and London: Verso, 1992).

34 Jameson, "Third-World Literature," p. 71.

35 *Ibid.*, p. 69.

36 *Ibid.*, p. 71.

37 *Ibid.*, p. 72.

38 *Ibid.*

39 *Ibid.*, p. 79.

40 See Elin Ap Hywel, "Elise and the Great Queens of Ireland: 'Femininity' as constructed by Sinn Fein and the Abbey Theatre, 1901–1907," *Gender in Irish Writing*, ed. Toni O'Brien Johnson and David Cairns (Milton Keynes and Philadelphia: Open University Press, 1991), pp. 23–39.

41 Anderson, *Imagined Communities*, p. 14.

42 For an influential argument about how and why these elements enable a progressive politics, see Donna Haraway, *Simians, Cyborgs, and Women: The Reinvention of Nature* (New York: Routledge, 1991).

43 Bill Ashcroft, Gareth Griffiths, and Helen Tiffin, eds., *The Empire Writes Back* (London and New York: Routledge, 1989), p. 33.

44 See, for example, *The Wretched of the Earth*, trans. Constance Farrington (New York: Grove Weidenfeld), 1963), especially "The Pitfalls of National Consciousness."

45 Said, "Yeats and Decolonization," p. 76.

46 *Ibid.*, p. 83.

47 *Ibid.*, p. 76.

I THAT SWEET INSINUATING FEMINIE VOICE

1 Sir Horace Plunkett, *The United Irishwomen: Their Place, Work, and Ideals* (Dublin, 1911) repr. in Pat Bolger, ed. *And See Her Beauty Shining There: The Story of the Irish Countrywomen* (Dublin: Irish Academic Press, 1986), p. 15.

2 "Sojourn in the Whale," *The Complete Poems of Marianne Moore* (Middlesex: Penguin, 1981), p. 90.

3 Ashis Nandy has discussed the deformations of Indian national and gender discourses, including "hyper-masculinity," caused by British imperialism in *The Intimate Enemy: Loss and Recovery of Self Under Colonialism* (Oxford University Press, 1983).

4 Anca Vlaspolos has examined the gendered critical language Yeats scholars often employ to characterize the superiority of the later Yeats over his early work ("Gender-Political Aesthetics and the Early and Later Yeats" [*Yeats: An Annual of Critical and Textual Studies*, 8 (1990), pp. 113–25]). For David Cairns and Shaun Richards, femininity provides an index to the degree to which various nationalist discourses in Ireland were complicit with imperialism. They observe that some Irish intellectuals embraced Celticism's definition of the national character through "femininity, emotionalism, material and political incapacity" and argue that acceptance of these traits indicates Anglo-Irish Celticism's complicity with imperialism and its project to re-inscribe Anglo-Irish domination (*Writing Ireland: Colonialism, Nationalism and Culture* [Manchester University Press, 1988], p. 50).

5 Edward Said observes that Orientalism has been an effective and long-lasting Western strategy for creating, structuring and controlling "the Orient," not because it is rigid, but because it is flexible; it "puts the Westerner in a whole series of possible relationships with the Orient without ever losing him the relative upper hand" (Edward Said, *Orientalism* (New York: Vintage, 1979), p. 7. David Spurr's *The Rhetoric of Empire: Colonial Discourse in Journalism, Travel Writing and Imperial Administration* (Durham and London: Duke University Press, 1993) also emphasizes the flexibility of colonial discourses. On the rise of race as a central category of investigation for nineteenth century science, see Nancy Stepan's *The Idea of Race in Science: Great Britain 1800–1960* (Hamden, Conn.: Archon Books, 1982). On the confluence of race, gender and health/illness, see Sander Gilman, *Difference and Pathology: Stereotypes of Sexuality, Race, and Madness* (Ithaca and London: Cornell University Press, 1985). On the late nineteenth-century introduction of racial terminology into the language of anti-Irish prejudice, see Richard Ned Lebow, *White Britain and Black Ireland: The Influence of Stereotypes on Colonial Policy* (Institute for the Study of Human Issues, 1976) and Lewis Perry Curtis, Jr., *Apes and Angels: The Irishman in Victorian Caricature* (Newton Abbott, Devon: David Charles Ltd., 1971) and *Anglo-*

Saxons and Celts: A Study of Anti-Irish Prejudice in Victorian England (Bridge-port, Connecticut: University of Bridgeport, 1968).

6 Franz Fanon, *Black Skin, White Masks* (New York: Grove Weidenfeld, 1967 [1952]), p. 112.

7 See Luke Gibbons, "Race Against Time: Racial Discourse and Irish History," *Oxford Literary Review*, 13 (Spring 1991).

8 See Patrick Brantlinger, *Rule of Darkness: British Literature and Imperialism, 1830–1914* (Ithaca: Cornell University Press, 1988), pp. 114–18.

9 *The Complete Prose Works of Matthew Arnold*, vol. xi, ed. R. H. Super (Ann Arbor, The University of Michigan Press, 1973), p. 242.

10 See Seamus Deane, "Arnold, Burke and the Celts," *Celtic Revivals: Essays in Modern Irish Literature 1880–1980* (London: Faber and Faber, 1985).

11 The years 1865–6 saw enthusiasm for the Fenian movement peak, both in Ireland and in the United States. In addition, the British government and media became increasingly concerned with the Fenian threat. Early in 1866 the English suspended habeas corpus in Ireland. Many Fenians were locked up, others fled, and the movement was thrown into general disarray. Fenian enthusiasm and frustration culminated in the abortive rising of 1867. In September of 1867 an unarmed policeman was shot dead during a Fenian rescue of two Irish prisoners in Manchester. Three men were tried and hanged for their part in the affair, and the creation of the "Manchester martyrs" became a media success for the Irish. In December another rescue attempt at Clerken-well jail caused a number of deaths. Finally, the Fenian threat coincided with a period of civil unrest in England over such issues as manhood suffrage and trade unionism, making the English middle and upper classes all the more concerned about various forms of rebellion and the English government all the more anxious to assert its authority and deal harshly with disturbers of the peace (R. V. Comerford, *The Fenians in Context: Irish Politics and Society 1848–82* [Dublin: Wolfhound Press, 1985], especially chapters 4 and 5).

12 On the relationship between hysteria and femininity, see Janet Beizer, *Ventriloquized Bodies: Narratives of Hysteria in Nineteenth-Century France* (Ithaca and London: Cornell University Press, 1994), and Elaine Showalter, *The Female Malady: Women, Madness, and English Culture 1830–1980* (New York: Pantheon Books, 1985), especially chapters 5–7.

13 On Renan's and Arnold's knowledge of Irish literature and their construction of the Celtic element in literature, see John V. Kelleher, "Matthew Arnold and the Celtic Revival," *Perspectives in Criticism*, ed. Harry Levin (Harvard Studies in Comparative Literature, vol. ii, p. 20 [Cambridge, MA: Harvard University Press, 1950]), Rachael Brom-wich, *Matthew Arnold and Celtic Literature* (Oxford: Clarendon Press, 1965), and Maurice Riordan, "Matthew Arnold and the Irish Revival," *Literary Interrelations: Ireland, England, and the World; volume iii: National*

Images and Stereotypes, ed. Wolfgang Zach and Heinz Kosok (Tubingen: Gunter Narr Verlag, 1987). For a discussion of Arnold's debts to Henri Martin, see Frederick Faverty, *Matthew Arnold the Ethnologist* (Evanston: Northwestern University Press, 1951).

14 See Robert Young, *Colonial Desire: Hybridity in Theory, Culture and Race* (New York: Routledge, 1995), p. 9.

15 Arnold, *Complete Prose Works*, vol. XI, p. 335.

16 See Robert Young, *Colonial Desire*, p. 71. David Lloyd offers a differently focused formulation of this tension in "Arnold, Ferguson, Schiller: Aesthetic Culture and the Politics of Aesthetics," *Cultural Critique*, 2 (Winter 1985–6), pp. 139–52.

17 Matthew Arnold, "From Easter To August," *The Nineteenth Century*, vol. XXII (September 1887), p. 321. Quoted in Faverty, p. 142.

18 Julian Moynahan, "Lawrence, Woman and the Celtic Fringe," *Lawrence and Women*, ed. Ann Smith (London: Vision, 1978), p. 127.

19 See Sigmund Freud and Josef Breuer, *Studies on Hysteria*, trans. and ed. James Strachey (New York: Basic Books, 1955 [1895]), pp. 100, 103–4, 141, 161–2, 180, 232, 240.

20 Arnold, *Complete Prose Works*, vol. III, pp. 343, 344, 370, 343, 345, 347, and 298.

21 *Ibid.*, p. 344.

22 *Ibid.*

23 Ernest Renan, *The Poetry of Celtic Races and Other Studies*, trans. and ed. William G. Hutchison (London: Walter Scott, 1896), p. 8.

24 Arnold, *Complete Prose Works*, vol. III, p. 347.

25 For example, an 1897 article on "The Celtic Mind," attributes the Celt's distinct identity to physical differences in nervous structure: "The psychological quality is no doubt correlated with a physiological quality, i.e., a high tension in the nervous structures, making them liable to explode on very slight stimulus. Thus it may be that our quick-witted Irishman is what he is because he differs from the Teuton in the very quality of his nerve structure" (Sophie Bryant, "The Celtic Mind," *Contemporary Review*, 72 [July–December 1897] [London: Isbister, 1897], p. 538). Bryant drew similar conclusions in *The Genius of the Gael: A Study in Celtic Psychology and Its Manifestations* (London: T. Fisher Unwin, 1913). T. S. Eliot's 1919 review of Yeats follows this tradition: "The difference between his world and ours is so complete as to seem almost a physiological variety, different nerves and senses. It is, there-fore, allowable to imagine that the difference is not only personal but national" ("A Foreign Mind," *The Athenaeum*, July 4, 1919, p. 552). As late as 1927, Havelock Ellis writes that "Quick sensibility, again, or rapid feminine response in harmony with, or in reaction against, external stimuli, is *of all qualities* that which we most readily attribute to the Celt" (Havelock Ellis, *A Study of British Genius*, new edition, revised and enlarged [London: Constable, 1927], p. 221). Ellis also implicitly

connects the Celt's femininity with disease by reproducing his characterization of the Celt as a description of the "feminine order of genius"
of "eminent consumptives" (p. 163).

26 Arnold, *Complete Prose Works*, vol. III, p. 382.
27 See Daniel Pick, *Faces of Degeneration: A European Disorder, c. 1848–c.1918*
(Cambridge University Press, 1989), especially chapters 1 and 7.
28 Edmund Burke, *Reflections on the Revolution in France*, ed. Thomas Mahoney
(Indianapolis and New York: Bobbs-Merrill, 1955 [1790]), p. 82.
29 Arnold, *Complete Prose Works*, vol. III, p. 347.
30 Writing to Engels in 1869, he said: "For a long time I believed that it
would be possible to overthrow the Irish regime by English working-
class ascendancy ... Deeper study has now convinced me of the
opposite. The English working class will *never accomplish anything* before it
has got rid of Ireland. The lever must be applied in Ireland" (Karl
Marx and Frederick Engels, *Ireland and the Irish Question*, ed. R. Dixon
[London: Lawrence and Wishart], pp. 397–8. See also pp. 253–5, 394,
407–8, 419, 449–50).
31 "The weather, like the inhabitants, has a more acute character, it
moves in sharper, more sudden contrasts; the sky is like an Irish
woman's face: here also rain and sunshine succeed each other suddenly
and unexpectedly and there is none of the grey English boredom"
(*Ibid.*, p. 276).
32 *Ibid.*, p. 401.
33 *Ibid.*, p. 52.
34 *Ibid.*, p. 407.
35 *Ibid.*, pp. 43–4.
36 See Bram Dijkstra, *Idols of Perversity: Fantasies of Feminine Evil in Fin-de-
Siecle Culture* (Oxford and New York: Oxford University Press, 1986)
and Elaine Showalter, *Sexual Anarchy: Gender and Culture at the Fin de Siecle*
(New York: Penguin, 1990).
37 See Linda Dowling, "The Decadent and the New Woman in the
1890s," *Nineteenth Century Fiction*, 33:4 (March 1979), pp. 434–53.
38 See Pick, *Faces of Degeneration*.
39 See Max Nordau, *Degeneration* (London: William Heineman, 1913; trans.
from the second edn. of the German), especially book 1, chapters 2 and
3, and book 3, chapter 3. Nordau described the degenerate as a
"compound of feverish restlessness and discouragement" (p. 2) who was
afflicted with an incapacity for action, a predilection for "inane
reverie," and a lack of control over the workings of the imagination (p.
21). Nordau claimed that the degenerate was potentially brilliant, but
unbalanced, and he listed "emotionalism," "excitability," "impression-
ability," and suggestibility among the "intellectual stigmata" of degen-
erates (pp. 19, 25–6).
40 Otto Weininger, *Sex and Character*, trans. from the 6th German edn.
(London: William Heineman, 1906), p. x.

41 The book went through twenty-five editions in twenty-two years (Eric Hobsbawm, *The Age of Empire 1875–1914* [New York: Vintage, 1989], p. 206), and was also translated into English. George L. Mosse has called *Sex and Character* "one of the most influential racial tracts of the twentieth century" (*Nationalism and Sexuality: Respectability and Abnormal Sexuality in Modern Europe* [New York: Howard Fertig, 1985], p. 145), and Sander Gilman writes that Weininger's book "had an unprecedented influence on the scientific discourse about Jews and women at the turn of the century." (*Difference and Pathology*, p. 188).

42 Weininger, *Sex and Character*, p. 313.

43 Although of course other voices helped shape the discourse of Celticism, the Anglo-Irish writers of the literary revival tended to reproduce Arnold's formula so faithfully that in his 1910 preface to *On The Study of Celtic Literature*, Alfred Nutt complained that Arnold's influence had become so pervasive that in recent essays on the subject of Celtic literature, "paper after paper was a mere amplification of Arnold's theses" (Matthew Arnold, *On The Study of Celtic Literatures*, ed. Alfred Nutt [Phoenix, Long Acre: David Nutt, 1910], p. vi).

44 See also *LNI*, 12.

45 Edward O'Shea, *A Descriptive Catalog of W. B. Yeats's Library* (New York and London: Garland, 1985), p. 223.

46 See David Lloyd, "Arnold, Ferguson, Schiller," especially pp. 152–61.

47 Another indicator of Yeats's anxiously negative attitude towards Arnold is his repeated insistence that poetry is not "a criticism of life" (*UPI*, 84). See also *UPI*, 187, *UPII*, 42, and *UPII*, 131.

48 Robert Young, *Colonial Desire*, p. 73.

49 Blanaid was a woman; the important point here is that she is included in a collective comradeship rather than a romantic pair.

50 *The Critical Writings of James Joyce*, ed. Ellsworth Mason and Richard Ellmann (London: Faber and Faber, 1959), p. 150.

51 *Ibid.*, p. 151.

52 Paul Elmer More, *The Drift of Romanticism*, Shelburne Essays, Eighth Series (Boston and New York: Houghton Mifflin, 1913), pp. 122, 123.

53 *Ibid.*, p. 135.

54 Paul Elmer More, *Shelburne Essays*, First Series (New York and London: G. P. Putnam's Sons, 1904), p. 178.

55 *Ibid.*, pp. 179–80.

56 For a good discussion of the imaginative construction of the Irish peasant, see Edward Hirsch, "The Imaginary Irish Peasant," *PMLA* 106:5 (October 1991), pp. 1116–33.

57 Franz Fanon, *The Wretched of the Earth*, trans. Constance Farrington (New York: Grove Weidenfeld, 1963), p. 238.

58 *The New Spirit of the Nation* (London: T. Fisher Unwin, 1894), p. 125.

59 *The Spirit of the Nation*, second edn., revised (Dublin: James Duffy, 1844), p. 25.

60 *The Spirit of the Nation, Part 2*, (Dublin: James Duffy, 1843), p. 17.

61 "The Slaves Bill," *The Spirit of the Nation, Part 2*, p. 31.

62 D. P. Moran, *The Philosophy of Irish Ireland* (Dublin: James Duffy and Co., 1905), p. 6.

63 *Ibid.*, p. 2.

64 *Ibid.*, p. 10.

65 See David Lloyd, *Nationalism and Minor Literature: James Clarence Mangan and the Emergence of Irish Cultural Nationalism* (Berkeley: University of California Press, 1987), especially chapter 2.

66 See also Yeats, *Prefaces and Introductions*, ed. William H. O'Donnell (London: Macmillan, 1988), p. 148.

67 In "Magic" he wrote: "We cannot doubt that barbaric peoples receive such influences more visibly and obviously, and in all likelihood more easily and fully than we do, for our life in cities, which deafens or kills the passive meditative life, and our education that enlarges the separated, self-moving mind, have made our souls less sensitive" (*EI*, 41).

68 See also *EI*, 157, *UPI*, 376, and *EX*, 5.

69 See *LNI*, 124, 132, 137, 153.

2 FAIR ERIN AS LANDLORD

1 "The Eighteenth Brumaire of Louis Bonaparte," in Karl Marx and Frederick Engels, *Selected Works* (New York: International Publishers, 1968), p. 101.

2 Standish O'Grady, *The Crisis in Ireland* (Dublin: E. Ponsonby, 1882 [London: Simpkin, Manshell and Co.]), p. 26.

3 For example, in his discussion of the ubiquitous political cartoons of the period which represented Ireland as a beautiful woman in distress, Lewis P. Curtis observes, "This sorrowful and irresistible paragon of Irish womanhood, who was always being threatened or abused by some monster, was the one symbol on which the cartoonists of London, Dublin, and New York were wholly agreed" (Lewis Perry Curtis, Jr., *Apes and Angels: The Irishman in Victorian Caricature* [Newton Abbott, Devon: David Charles, 1971], p. 65).

4 For a useful historical treatment of gender as a category, see Denise Riley, *Am I That Name? Feminism and the Category of "Woman" in History* (Minneapolis: University of Minnesota Press, 1988). Increasingly, there are some excellent and helpful exceptions to the old unwillingness in Irish studies to think critically about gender. For an analysis of how the figure of Ireland as a woman varied over time, see Elizabeth Cullingford, " 'Thinking of Her . . . as . . . Ireland': Yeats, Pearse and Heaney," *Textual Practice*, 4:1 (1990). For a discussion of psychohistorical differences between Irish and American representations of the female body see Cheryl Herr, "The Erotics of Irishness," *Critical Inquiry*, 17:1 (Autumn 1990).

5 For a summary of all the volumes in which the play appears, see A. Norman Jeffares and A. S. Knowland, *A Commentary on the Collected Plays of W. B. Yeats* (Stanford University Press, 1975). The fullest discussions of the revisions can be found in David R. Clark, "Vision and Revision: Yeats's The Countess Cathleen," *The World of W. B. Yeats*, ed. Robin Skelton and Ann Saddlemyer (Seattle: University of Washington Press, 1967 [1965]) and in Peter Ure, *Yeats the Playwright* (London: Routledge and Kegan Paul, 1963).

6 See Russell K. Alspach's introduction to the Variorum edition of the plays (London: Macmillan, 1966), pp. xii–xiii.

7 For example, see J. J. L. Cribb, "Yeats, Blake and *The Countess Kathleen*," *Irish University Review*, 11:2 (Fall 1981), pp. 165–78, and M. J. Sidnell, "Yeats's First Work For the Stage," D. E. S. Maxwell and S. Bushrui, eds., *W. B. Yeats 1865–1965: Centenary Essays on the Art of W. B. Yeats* (Nigeria: Ibadan University Press, 1965), pp. 167–88. A. S. Knowland faults the play's "uncertainty of the dramatic aim" (A. S. Knowland, *W. B. Yeats: Dramatist of Vision* [Totowa, NJ: Barnes and Noble, 1983], p. 10). Even James Flannery, whose treatment of the play is serious and careful in many respects, asserts that the "loose episodic action" of the play reflected Yeats's "amorphous thought and feeling throughout the nineties" (James Flannery, *W. B. Yeats and the Idea of a Theatre* [New Haven and London: Yale University Press, 1976], p. 294).

8 Although he had considered writing on the subject earlier, and had included the original tale in *Fairy and Folk Tales of the Irish Peasantry* (London: Walter Scott, 1888), Yeats's first meeting with Maud Gonne in January of 1889 provided the catalyst that prompted him to start work on the play the next month (see *KLI*, pp. 138, 142, 145).

9 Quoted in Lady Gregory, *Our Irish Theatre* (London and New York: G. P. Putnam's Sons, 1913), pp. 8–9.

10 F. Hugh O'Donnell, *Souls For Gold: Pseudo-Celtic Drama in Dublin* (London: Nassau, 1899).

11 *New Ireland Review*, vols. 10–11, p. 248.

12 *Ibid.*, p. 248.

13 Quoted in Robert Hogan and James Kilroy, *The Irish Literary Theatre 1899–1901* (Dublin: Dolmen, 1975), p. 42.

14 *Ibid.*, p. 45.

15 Grattan Freyer, *W. B. Yeats and the Anti-Democratic Tradition* (Dublin: Gill and Macmillan, 1981), p. 40.

16 For example, Adrian Frazier muses that "the play is now as insignificant a piece of drama as a press keeps in print" and concludes that "we have found little of what the original audience found, and nothing so exciting" (*Behind the Scenes: Yeats, Horniman, and the Struggle for the Abbey Theatre* [Berkeley: University of California Press, 1990], pp. 3–4), and Robert Hogan and James Kilroy remark, "reading *The Countess Cathleen*

today, one finds it difficult to understand its controversial nature" (*The Irish Literary Theatre 1899–1901*, p. 30).

17 "The Saxon Shilling," *The Spirit of the Nation*, vol. I, p. 45.

18 "The Leinster War-Song," *The Spirit of the Nation*, vol. I, p. 56.

19 "The Union," *The Spirit of the Nation*, vol. II, p. 21.

20 Maud Gonne, *Dawn*, in *Lost Plays of the Irish Renaissance*, ed. Robert Hogan and James Kilroy (Proscenium, 1970). In the play, a starving woman refuses to take money from her brother because he has become a British soldier, telling him, "I cannot take it. It is the price of your soul, poor Seamus" (p. 80). Vivian Mercier has noted the importance of this tradition for the play, writing:

> Only those who are aware of the history and mythology of souperism can grasp the full significance of the fact that Yeats' *The Countess Cathleen* was the very first play presented by the Irish Literary Theatre (8 May 1899). Only they, too, can appreciate the full irony of the fact that this play about devils buying Irish souls for gold should have been denounced as anti-Catholic (Vivian Mercier, "Victorian Evangelicalism and the Anglo-Irish Literary Revival," Peter Connolly, ed., *Literature and the Changing Ireland* [Totowa, NJ: Barnes and Noble, 1982] p. 74).

21 Flannery, *Idea of a Theatre*, p. 144.

22 Bert Cardullo recognizes this conflict and characterizes the play as representing the transition from a feudal-aristocratic system to a capitalist one: "Cathleen may be viewed as wanting to save the Peasants' souls for the aristocracy, as wanting to keep their bodies in service to the feudal nobility, and out of the hands of businessmen" (Bert Cardullo, "Notes Toward a Production of W. B. Yeats's *The Countess Cathleen*," *Canadian Journal of Irish Studies*, 11:2 [December 1985], p. 63). I agree, but would add that this conflict/transition is also, and crucially, a national one in which Irishness is aligned with the older feudal system.

23 Standish O'Grady, *The Crisis in Ireland*, p. 26.

24 Quoted in Sidnell, "First Work for the Stage," p. 175.

25 Frazier, *Behind the Scenes*, p. 463.

26 For example, Richard Taylor's *A Reader's Guide to the Plays of W. B. Yeats* tells us that "The countess is a personification of Ireland" ([New York: St. Martin's Press, 1984], p. 24).

27 His description of the play in *Beltaine* in 1904 adopts the same tone: "It is the soul of one that loves Ireland", I thought, "plunging into unrest, seeming to lose itself, to bargain itself away to the very wickedness of the world, and to surrender what is eternal for what is temporary" (*EX*, 142–3).

28 Peter Alderson Smith points out the conflict between Yeats's descriptions of Maud as both hate-enslaved and pity-crazed, and sees the "biographical element" as a major source of confusion in the text (*W. B. Yeats and the Tribes of Danu* [Gerrards Cross: Colin Smythe, 1987], p. 159). Peter Ure also makes the point that "none of the versions of *The*

Countess Cathleen offers us a protagonist whose selling of her soul can possibly be interpreted as self-destruction through fanaticism or hate; nor can the Countess's bargain, in its context, be easily read as a symbol of the loss of peace and fineness through political activity" (*Yeats the Playwright*, p. 17). He concludes that "there is little reason to suppose that the first version of Cathleen would have been any different had Yeats and Maud Gonne never met" but that Yeats introduced biographical material into later versions (pp. 20 and ff.). For Maud's own (and factually unreliable) description of her activities, see Maud Gonne MacBride, *A Servant of the Queen* (London: Victor Gollancz, 1938).

29   Cassandra Laity, "Yeats's Changing Images of Maud Gonne," *Eire-Ireland*, 22:2 (Summer 1987), pp. 56, 59.

30   W. B. Yeats, ed., *Beltaine* (London: At the Sign of the Unicorn; Dublin: At the "Daily Express" Office), no. 1 (1899–1900), pp. 10, 11.

31   Horatio Sheafe Krans, *William Butler Yeats and the Irish Literary Revival* (London and New York: McClure, Phillips and Co., 1904), p. 109.

32   *Ibid.*, p. 113.

33   *Ibid.*, pp. 114–5.

34   *Ibid.*, pp. 123–4.

35   Ernest Renan, *The Poetry of Celtic Races and Other Studies*, trans. and ed. William G. Hutchinson (London: Walter Scott, 1896), p. 15.

36   See Krans, *Irish Literary Revival*, p. 142, Ure, *Yeats the Playwright*, pp. 19, 26–7, and Knowland, *Dramatist of Vision*, p. 13. For an extensive list of critical views of the play as a "failed tragedy," nearly all of which hinge on the lack of an inner struggle in the character of the countess, see Cardullo, "Notes," pp. 50–2.

37   Flannery, *Idea of a Theatre*, p. 149.

38   See Sidnell, "First Work for the Stage."

39   See, for example, Sidnell, *ibid.*, who describes Aleel's role as "the representation of the poet so afflicted with love and pity for a woman weighed down with responsibility, that poetry itself seems futile: the poet, Yeats; the woman, Maud Gonne" (p. 185).

40   See for example, Thomas Parkinson, *W. B. Yeats: Self-Critic* (Berkeley: University of California Press, 1951), p. 54, A. Norman Jeffares, *A Commentary on the Collected Poems of W. B. Yeats* (Stanford: Stanford University Press, 1968), p. 3 and Knowland, *Dramatist of Vision*, p. 12.

41   See also *Mem*, 130.

3   WHEN THE MOB BECOME A PEOPLE

1   Theodor Adorno, *Minima Moralia: Reflections From Damaged Life*, trans. E. F. N. Jephcott (London: Verso, 1974 [1951]), p. 241.

2   See Conor Cruise O'Brien, "Passion and Cunning: An Essay on the Politics of W. B. Yeats," *In Excited Reverie: A Centenary Tribute to W. B.*

Yeats, 1865–1939, ed. A. Norman Jeffares and K. G. W. Cross (New York: St Martin's Press, 1965).

3 In "Plans and Methods" Yeats makes the same point: "Their writers will appeal to that limited public which gives understanding, and not to that unlimited public which gives wealth" (*UPII,* 159).

4 See George Mosse, *The Nationalization of the Masses: Political Symbolism and Mass Movements in Germany from the Napoleonic Wars Through the Third Reich* (New York: Howard Fertig, 1975) for a discussion of this process as the development of a "secular religion" (p. 16).

5 See James Flannery, *W. B. Yeats and the Idea of a Theatre* (New Haven and London: Yale University Press, 1976), chapter 3.

6 For a discussion of these influences, see Flannery, *ibid.,* chapter 5.

7 Andreas Huyssen, *After the Great Divide: Modernism, Mass Culture, Post-modernism* (Bloomington and Indianapolis: Indiana University Press, 1986).

8 Yeats did not use "unconscious" in a specifically Freudian sense. For him, the term was interchangeable with "subconscious," and denoted any realms of subjectivity outside the rational, conscious will and intellect. This included the inner depths of the psyche as well as the external reaches of the Great Memory.

9 James Flannery cites the three precepts from "Magic" and observes "The theatrical implications of these ideas were of immense significance to Yeats. From them he derived his concept of tragedy as a powerful medium for effecting a spiritual unity among men, paradoxically, by celebrating their individual uniqueness" (*Idea of a Theatre,* p. 55).

10 Yeats made this argument in "Ireland and the Arts" in 1901 (see *EI,* especially pp. 206–10) and he wrote in Samhain in 1904: "The modern theatre has died away to what it is because the writers have thought of their audiences instead of their subject" (*EX,* 164).

11 Maud Gonne, "Yeats and Ireland" Stephen Gwynn, ed., *Scattering Branches* (London: 1940), p. 24.

12 Unpublished draft of *Per Amica Silentia Lunae,* quoted in Richard Ellmann, *The Identity of Yeats* (London: Macmillan, 1954), p. 305.

13 See Flannery, *Idea of a Theatre,* especially chapter 3. Flannery remarks that "Yeats's idea of a theatre was itself a direct result of his occult pursuits" (p. 55) and observes, "In Yeats's view, the 'eleusinian Rite' of the Celtic Mysteries, far from being an escape from life, was a necessary step towards the creation of an ideal society ... The means for effecting this spiritual regeneration in the body public of Ireland was, as it had been for Pisistratus, the creation of a theatre" (p. 65). Virginia Moore's *The Unicorn* contains an extensive discussion of the Castle of the Heroes (chapter 3). She asserts that "the Irish theatre as conceived, led by, and contributed to by William Butler Yeats was his Castle of Heroes transposed and transformed" (*The Unicorn: William Butler Yeats' Search*

For Reality [New York: Macmillan, 1954], p. 82). Allen Grossman also observes, "Before 1900 Yeats sought to express his sense of the rising tide of emotion in relation to Ireland through the establishment of a cult of Irish Heroes, after 1900 through the establishment of an Irish theatre" (*Poetic Knowledge in the Early Yeats: A Study of the Wind Among the Reeds* [Charlottesville: The University Press of Virginia, 1969], p. 72. See also Steven Putzel, *Reconstructing Yeats: The Secret Rose and the Wind Among the Reeds* (Dublin: Gill and Macmillan; Totowa, NJ: Barnes and Noble, 1986), pp. 215–16.

14 In *Beltaine* Yeats said of *The Countess Cathleen*, "The chief endeavour with Mr. Yeats' play has been to get it spoken with some sense of rhythm" (*UPII*, 160).

15 See also UPII, 154.

16 See Flannery, *Idea of the Theatre*, chapter 10. Flannery observes that Yeats's interest in ritual sprang from the rituals of the Golden Dawn, and comments that "Yeats viewed the overall stage picture as a kind of magical charm – a charm which through the highly formalized and patterned interrelationship of shapes and colours became for the audience a symbol of infinite perfection" (p. 242). Yeats described the acting style of the Irish players in 1901 this way: "The actors moved about very little, they often did no more than pose in some statuesque way and speak; and there were moments when it seemed as if some painting upon a wall, some rhythmic procession along the walls of a temple had begun to move before me with a dim, magical life" (*UPII*, 285).

17 "Victor Hugo said somewhere: 'It is in the Theatre that the mob becomes a people'" (*UPII*, 286).

18 John P. Frayne and Colton Johnson claim that Yeats is referring to a passage from Hugo's *Post-Scriptum de Ma Vie* that says in "the theatre the poet and the multitude gaze into each other's eyes; sometimes they touch each other, sometimes they insult each other, sometimes they mix with one another: fecund mingling. On one side a crowd, on the other a soul. That something of a crowd which enters into a soul, that something of the soul which enters into the crowd is dramatic art in its completeness" (Lorenzo O'Rourke, ed. and trans., *Victor Hugo's Intellectual Autobiography* [London, 1907], pp. 369–70; quoted in *UPII*, p. 286).

19 See George Mosse, *Nationalism and Sexuality: Respectability and Abnormal Sexuality in Modern Europe* (New York: Howard Fertig, 1985). Freud argued that group formation depends on the creation of libidinal ties among members. While he claimed "There is scarcely any sense in asking whether the libido which keeps groups together is of a homosexual or of a heterosexual nature, for it is not differentiated according to the sexes (*Group Psychology and the Analysis of the Ego* [New York and London: Norton, 1989 (1959)], p. 94), he also remarked "It seems certain that homosexual love is far more compatible with group ties,

even when it takes the shape of uninhibited sexual impulsions – a remarkable fact, the explanation of which might carry us far" (p. 95).

20 See Mosse, who observes that "the male stereotype, along with its homoerotic overtones, is more difficult to find in Italy or in France" (*Nationalism and Sexuality*, p. 21) than in England or Germany.

21 See, for example, Richard Ellmann, *The Identity of Yeats*, pp. 71–6, and Steven Putzel, *Reconstructing Yeats*.

22 In his analysis of the fantasy structure of men in the German Freikorps between the wars, Klaus Theweleit makes a similar distinction between Oedipal conflicts which can be articulated using the language of object relations, incest and castration, and the ambivalence that structured the desires of the Freikorpsmen, which resembled psychosis and revolved around the dissolution of the body and the pre-Oedipal symbiosis with the mother (*Male Fantasies, Volume 1: Floods, Bodies History* [Minneapolis: University of Minnesota Press, 1987], especially pp. 183–215). I am not arguing that Yeats's ambivalence is the same as that of the Freikorpsmen. Far from it; in contrast to their explicit misogyny, Yeats's representations of sexual murder or the conjunction of sexuality and death usually depict male victims. In addition, while the Freikorpsmen focused on bodily dissolution, Yeats's ambivalence centered more around mental dissolution.

23 Yeats characterized it this way: "It is the perpetual struggle of the cause of Ireland and every other ideal cause against the private hopes and dreams, against all that we mean when we say the world" (*VPI*, 234).

24 Some critics have read this as an indication of play's literary weakness. For example, Grattan Freyer claims: "There is no development or revelation of character. The young man, Michael, listens to the old woman's story and is immediately carried off. He expresses no agony of choice between his bride and his country. In essence the play is a model of the 'patriotic' literature Yeats deplored in Davis and others" (*W. B. Yeats and the Anti-Democratic Tradition*, [Dublin: Gill and Macmillan, 1981], p. 43).

25 See Patrick J. Keane, *Terrible Beauty: Yeats, Joyce, Ireland, and the Myth of the Devouring Female* (Columbia: University of Missouri Press, 1988), chapter 1.

26 Gonne, "Yeats and Ireland," p. 27.

27 See also *GY*, pp. 212, 224, 231, 240–1.

28 See, for example, this 1892 description of Gonne: "Every speech has been a triumph, and every triumph greater than the one that went before it. Thousands who come to see this new wonder – a beautiful woman who makes speeches – remain to listen with delight to her sincere and simple eloquence. Last week at Bordeaux, an audience of twelve hundred persons rose to its feet, when she had finished, to applaud her with wild enthusiasm" (*LNI*, 61).

29 When Yeats revised for his autobiography, he downplayed his sur-

render to the crowd, writing "Presently I hear a sound of breaking glass, the crowd has begun to stone the windows of decorated houses, and when I try to speak that I may restore order, I discover that I have lost my voice through much speaking at the Convention. I can only whisper and gesticulate, and as I am thus freed from responsibility I share the emotion of the crowd, and perhaps even feel as they feel when the glass crashes" (*AY*, 244).

30 Eric Hobsbawm, "Mass-Producing Traditions: Europe 1870–1914," *The Invention of Tradition*, ed. Eric Hobsbawm and Terence Ranger (Cambridge University Press, 1983), pp. 268–9.

31 The best history of political thought about the crowd is J. S. McClelland's *The Crowd and the Mob: From Plato to Canetti* (London: Unwin Hyman, 1989). See also Serge Moscovici, *The Age of the Crowd: A Historical Treatise on Mass Psychology* (Cambridge University Press, 1985 [1981]; Jaap van Ginneken, *Crowds, Psychology, and Politics 1871–1899* (Cambridge University Press, 1992); and Robert E. Park, *The Crowd and the Public and Other Essays* (Chicago and London: University of Chicago Press, 1972 [1904]).

32 McClelland, *The Crowd*, p. 4.

33 McClelland's dates, *ibid.*, p. 3.

34 As McClelland puts it, "from that time onwards the crowd becomes central to social and political theorizing, or from that time onwards at least any exercise in social theory which did not make room for the crowd at its centre looked makeshift, mistaken or wilfully obtuse" (*ibid.*).

35 Robert A. Nye, *The Origins of Crowd Psychology: Gustave Le Bon and the Crisis of Mass Democracy in the Third Republic* (London and Beverly Hills: SAGE Publications, 1975), p. 3. On Le Bon, see also McClelland, *The Crowd*, chapter 7, van Ginneken, *Crowds*, chapter 4.

36 Elias Canetti, *Crowds and Power*, trans. Carol Stewart (New York: Farrar Straus Giroux, 1962 [1960]).

37 As the latest and most "scientific" version of imitation, suggestion and contagion, hypnotism became an important part of crowd theory after the early 1880s (McClelland, *The Crowd*, p. 169).

38 McClelland comments: "The hypnotist could recall to the surface things which were unconscious; he seemed to fascinate his subject; he seemed to be able to control the subject's own will, and to be able to make the subject do things which were 'out of character'. If the leader of a crowd could do all these things too, then the hypnotic model offered an explanation of how the relationship between crowds and their leaders worked" (*ibid.*, p. 28).

39 van Ginneken, *Crowds*, p. 181.

40 Gustave Le Bon, *The Crowd: A Study of the Popular Mind* (Dunwoody, Georgia: Norman S. Berg, 1895), p. 22.

41 *Ibid.*, p. 80.

42 *Ibid.*, p. 96.

43 *Ibid.*, p. 54.

44 McClelland, *The Crowd*, p. 207.

45 *Ibid.*, p. 218.

46 *Ibid.*, p. 157.

47 See, for example, Gustave Le Bon, *The Psychology of Peoples* (New York: Macmillan, 1898), p. xvi.

48 On the femininity of crowds, see McClelland, *The Crowd*, p. 192, van Ginneken, *Crowds*, p. 158, Moscovici, *Historical Treatise*, pp. 107–14, and Le Bon, *Psychology of Peoples*, chapter 2.

49 Sigmund Freud and Josef Breuer, *Studies on Hysteria*, trans. and ed. James Strachey (New York: Basic Books, 1955 [1895]).

50 McClelland, *The Crowd*, pp. 205–7, 220–3.

51 See Le Bon, *The Crowd*, especially pp. 216–19.

52 "Before Canetti," notes McClelland, "only Sighele and Hitler saw clearly that nationalism *is* the crowd's atavism" (McClelland, *The Crowd*, p. 306).

53 Sighele's *La Folla Delinquente* (1891), Le Bon's *Psychologie des Foules* (1895), Tarde's important essays in *Essais et Melanges Sociologiques* (1895) and *L'Opinion et la Foule* (1901), Fournial's *Essai sur la Psychologie des Foules* (1892). Taine's multi-volume *Les Origines de la France Contemporaine*, which appeared between 1875 and 1893, was also influential.

54 See van Ginneken, *Crowds*, pp. 185–6.

55 Freud devoted an entire chapter of his book to Le Bon's theory of the group mind. See *Group Psychology*, chapter 2.

56 See, for example, James Longenbach, who observes, "At Stone Cottage, an apparently apolitical discussion of symbolism nurtured the social attitudes of the secret society of modernism" (*Stone Cottage: Pound, Yeats and Modernism* [New York and Oxford: Oxford University Press, 1988], p. 77).

57 Richard Kearney observes that Yeats repudiated "the 'filthy modern tide' of contemporary reality in deference to the sacred mythologies of the Celtic Twilight" ("Myth and Motherland," *Ireland's Field Day* [Notre Dame IN: University of Notre Dame Press, 1983], p. 61). He argues that this constituted an attempt to resolve in occult myth conflicts that Yeats could not resolve in life (p. 71), and that it led to Yeats's endorsement of Patrick Pearse's ideology of blood sacrifice. Edward Said claims that Yeats's occult system symbolizes "his understandable attempts to lay hold of an extremely distant and extremely orderly reality felt as a refuge from the colonial turbulence before his eyes" ("Yeats and Decolonization," ed. Seamus Deane, *Nationalism, Colonialism and Literature* [Minneapolis: University of Minnesota Press, 1990], p. 93). Roy Foster has argued that Yeats's interest in the occult grew out of his identity as an Irish Protestant and that it places him in a tradition of Anglo-Irish writers like Robert Maturin, J. S. LeFanu,

Bram Stoker and Elizabeth Bowen, whose supernaturalism was in part a response to the rise of Catholic democracy and their own increasing marginalization ("Protestant Magic: W. B. Yeats and the Spell of Irish History," *Proceedings of the British Academy*, 75 [1989], 243–66). Despite this promising effort to historicize it, like Kearney and Said, Foster sees Protestant interest in the supernatural as "escapism" (p. 251).

58 Alex Owen's work on the gender politics of nineteenth-century spiritualism shows that spiritualism, as distinct from participation in the more elitist and occult societies, developed amidst an atmosphere of optimism, radical ideas and democratic principles. It appealed to women and the working classes and drew most of its prominent mediums from their ranks, and it had important alliances with feminism, dissenting religious philosophies and various reformist causes. Spiritualist doctrine was explicitly democratic, asserting that anyone and everyone could become a medium and gain access to the spirit world. (Alex Owen, *The Darkened Room: Women, Power and Spiritualism in Late Victorian England* [London: Virago, 1989]). Elizabeth Cullingford distinguishes between the politics of spiritualism, theosophy and the elitist Golden Dawn (*Gender and History in Yeats's Love Poetry* [Cambridge University Press, 1993], chapter 2). She argues that in the context of late nineteenth-century links among feminism, socialism, anti-imperialism and interest in the occult, we can read Yeats's occultism as "compatible with advanced socialist and feminist thought" (p. 42).

59 Benedict Anderson was the first to put this succinctly in *Imagined Communities: Reflections on the Origin and Spread of Nationalism* (London: Verso, 1983). More recently, Timothy Brennan has observed that "This background of spirituality and permanence is never lost, even in the historically specific cultural expressions of the national form" ("The National Longing for Form," *Nation and Narration*, ed. Homi Bhabha [London and New York: Routledge, 1990], p. 52).

60 For example, Terry Eagleton observes that "The metaphysics of nationalism speak of the entry into full self-realization of a unitary subject known as the people" ("Nationalism: Irony and Commitment," *Nationalism, Colonialism and Literature*, ed. Seamus Deane [Minneapolis: University of Minnesota Press, 1990], p. 28).

61 Seamus Deane, "Blueshirt," *London Review of Books* (June 4, 1981), p. 24.

62 Unpublished note of 1919, quoted in Flannery, *The Idea of a Theatre*, p. 55.

63 Quoted in George Mills Harper, *Yeats's Golden Dawn* (London: Macmillan, 1974), p. 83.

64 In his autobiography, Yeats wrote that "When two people, between whose minds there was even a casual sympathy, worked together under the same symbolic influence, the dream or reverie would divide itself between them, each half being the complement of the other" (*AY*, 173).

65 The most complete account of them appears in Harper's *Yeats's Golden Dawn*.

66 *Ibid.*, p. 88.

67 Quoted *ibid.*, p. 55.

68 Quoted *ibid.*, p. 77. Yeats repeated this claim later, arguing that the question facing the group was a choice of whether it was "to remain a Magical Order ... or to become wholly a mere society for experiment and research" (quoted *ibid.*, p. 80).

69 See also *AY*, 132: "Nations, races, and individual men are unified by an image, or bundle of related images, symbolical or evocative of the state of mind, which is of all states of mind not impossible, the most difficult to that men, race, or nation ..." and *AY*, 241.

70 Tom Gibbons, *Rooms in the Darwin Hotel: Studies in English Literary Criticism and Ideas 1880–1920* (Nedlands, W.A: University of Western Australia Press, 1973), chapter 1. The quote is from p. 11.

71 Allen Grossman argues that "the background of ceremonial magic always brings with it into Yeats's early poetry the problem of sexuality, as if sex were the hidden or occult subject" (*Poetic Knowledge*, p. 81).

72 See Alex Owen, *The Darkened Room*, chapter 2.

73 Harper, *Yeats's Golden Dawn*, p. 82.

74 Yeats himself downplayed the literary sources of his symbolism. In 1915 he wrote to Ernest Boyd: "My interest in mystic symbolism did not come from Arthur Symons or any other contemporary writer. I have been a student of the medieval mystics since 1887 and found in such authors as Valentin Andrea authority for my use of the rose. My chief mystical authorities have been Boehme, Blake and Swedenborg. Of the French symbolists I have never had any detailed or accurate knowledge" (*L*, 592).

75 As Allen Grossman observes, for the Yeats of this period, "The 'symbol' is a magical instrument the proper use of which reveals beneath the secondary world of appearances a primary world to the achievement of which the book, even 'the sacred book of the arts,' is purely instrumental. The symbol is a 'gate,' a tool of reverie" (*Poetic Knowledge*, p. 11). Elizabeth Bergman Loizeaux discusses the distinction between representative and evocative symbols, and Yeats's preference for the latter, in *Yeats and the Visual Arts* (New Brunswick and London: Rutgers University Press, 1986), pp. 43–8. In "Blake's Illustrations to Dante," Yeats described symbols as "blossoms, as it were, growing from invisible immortal roots, hands, as it were, pointing the way into some divine labyrinth" (*EI*, 117). Yeats's early works do contain other, more literary, theories of the symbol – he tended to emphasize these when he discussed the craft of writing, as opposed to symbolism's effect on the reader.

76 See also *EI*, 49.

77 Quoted in Harper, *Yeats's Golden Dawn*, p. 89.

78 Yeats retained this formulation as late as 1917, writing in *Per Amica Silentia Lunae*: "the passions, when we know that they cannot find fulfillment, become vision; and a vision, whether we wake or sleep, prolongs its power by rhythm and pattern, the wheel where the world is a butterfly" (*EX*, 341).

79 In "Magic" Yeats described an early experience in which an "evoker of spirits" induced visions in him, and he contrasted himself to an acquaintance who did not have as vivid a vision as Yeats by commenting "His imagination had no will of its own" (EI, 31).

80 See Moore, *The Unicorn*, pp. 218–20.

81 Helena P. Blavatsky, *Isis Unveiled* (Los Angeles: Theosophy Company, 1975 [1877]), p. 588.

82 See also *L*, 125.

83 Moore, *The Unicorn*, p. 220.

84 *Ibid.*

85 Harper, *Yeats's Golden Dawn*, p. 95.

86 See Owen, *The Darkened Room*, especially chapter 1.

87 *Ibid.*, p. 49.

88 *Ibid.*, p. 10.

89 Adrian Frazier, *Behind the Scenes: Yeats, Horniman, and the Struggle for the Abbey Theatre* (Berkeley: University of California Press, 1990), p. 51.

90 *Ibid.*

91 Frances Nesbitt Oppel points out that the pulpit and the press were among Nietzsche's targets. See *Mask and Tragedy: Yeats and Nietzsche, 1902–1910* (Charlottesville: University Press of Virginia, 1987), p. 85.

92 For example, in 1903 Yeats said that on the question of moral and immoral plays, "the pulpit and the newspaper are but voices of the mob" (*EX*, 112). On the press, see also *EX*, 167, *AY*, 313.

93 Loizeaux, *Yeats and the Visual Arts*, p. 137.

94 See Freyer, *W. B. Yeats and the Anti-Democratic Tradition*, p. 50.

95 Huyssen, *The Great Divide*, p. 52.

4   IN THE BEDROOM OF THE BIG HOUSE

1 "Protestant Ascendancy," in *The New Spirit of the Nation*, ed. Martin MacDermot (London: T. Fisher Unwin, 1894), p. 58.

2 Hostile readings generally extract Yeats's anti-Catholic and anti-democratic views from his poetry and prose as statements of political opinion, and have little to say about how such statements function in the texts in which they appear. Most sympathetic readings, on the other hand, have claimed that the politics of this aspect of Yeats's work is not a politics but an aesthetic, and/or have capitalized on the many levels of complexity and ambiguity in these poems. See, for example, Conor Cruise O'Brien, "Passion and Cunning: An Essay on the Politics of W. B. Yeats," *In Excited Reverie: A Centenary Tribute to W. B. Yeats*

1865–1939, ed. A. Norman Jeffares, (New York: St. Martin's Press, 1965), Donald Torchiana, *W. B. Yeats and Georgian Ireland* (Evanston IL: Northwestern University Press, 1966), Elizabeth Cullingford, *Yeats, Ireland and Fascism* (New York and London: New York University Press, 1981), Grattan Freyer, *W. B. Yeats and the Anti-Democratic Tradition* (Dublin: Gill and Macmillan, 1981), Bernard Krimm, *W. B. Yeats and the Emergence of the Irish Free State 1918–1939: Living in the Explosion* (Troy, NY: Whitson Publishing, 1981), Paul Scott Stanfield, *Yeats and Politics in the Nineteen-Thirties* (London: Macmillan, 1988), and Seamus Deane, *Celtic Revivals* (London: Faber and Faber, 1985).

3   For a brilliant formulation of how the middle Yeats imagines the foundation of the Irish State in terms that "subject all acts of founda- tion to the most rigorous examination within a set of aesthetic terms which are profoundly antithetical to any tradition of symbolism" (p. 60), see David Lloyd's "The Poetics of Politics: Yeats and the Founding of the State," *Anomalous States: Irish Writing and the Post-Colonial Moment* (Durham: Duke University Press, 1993).

4   Benedict Anderson, *Imagined Communities: Reflections on the Origin and Spread of Nationalism* (London: Verso, 1992), p. 16.

5   Richard Gill, *Happy Rural Seat: The English Country House and the Literary Imagination* (New Haven and London: Yale University Press, 1972), pp. 168, 170.

6   See, for example, *AY*, 165.

7   See Deane, "Arnold, Burke and the Celts," *Celtic Revivals*, especially pp. 23–4.

8   Maria Edgeworth, *The Absentee* (Oxford University Press, 1988 [1812]), p. 261.

9   Thomas Carlyle, *Reminiscences of My Irish Journey in 1849* (London: Sampson Low, Marston, Searle, and Rivington, 1882), p. 55.

10 See John S. Kelly, "The Fifth Bell: Race and Class in Yeats's Political Thought," *Irish Writers and Politics*, ed. Okifumi Komesu and Masaru Sekine (Gerrard's Cross: Colin Smythe, 1989).

11 Robert Lynd, *Home Life in Ireland* (London: Mills and Boon, 1909), p. 172.

12 Standish O'Grady, *Selected Essays and Passages*, ed. Ernest A. Boyd (Dublin: Talbot Press, n.d.), p. 180.

13 For example, in a response to Seamus Deane's characterization of Yeats, Augustine Martin claims current Yeats criticism is characterized by "a widespread misconception of what Yeats understood by words like 'aristocracy,' *sprezzatura* ... 'pride,' 'humility' and 'class'" ("What Stalked Through the Post Office?," *The Crane Bag*, 2:1 and 2:2, p. 313). Such an argument provides a valuable reminder that Yeats's construc- tions of such terms were often highly idiosyncratic, but it fails to acknowledge the interdependence of Yeats's ideal and material aristoc- racies. Torchiana makes similar claims in *Yeats and Georgian Ireland* (see,

for example, p. 89). Elizabeth Cullingford's *Yeats, Ireland and Fascism* contains one of the most compelling and balanced formulations of this argument.

14 W. J. McCormack traces the history of the term "Protestant Ascendancy," from its bourgeois and commercial origins in the late eighteenth century to its increasing identification with the landed gentry during the nineteenth century in his *Ascendancy and Tradition in Anglo-Irish Literary History From 1789–1939* (Oxford: Clarendon Press, 1985), especially chapter 2. He suggests that "This transference of the phrase from its commercial-bourgeois origins to a provenance of landed estate should be interpreted specifically in relation to the gradual erosion of landed estate as a political reality during the nineteenth century in Ireland; that is, it should be seen as the propagation of a false sociology" (p. 88). For my argument here, the important thing about Yeats's construction of such a false sociology is not its falseness but rather the fact that it was a response to the crisis and decline of the landed gentry. See also Seamus Deane, "The Literary Myths of the Revival," in *Celtic Revivals*. He argues that "[p]erhaps the most seductive of all Yeats's historical fictions is his gift of dignity and coherence to the Irish Protestant Ascendancy tradition" (p. 28). T. R. Henn also notes that in Ireland, "with every conceivable advantage, with wealth, leisure, security, the Big House contributed singularly little to the literary and the artistic production of the last hundred years ... the eminent names in literature came of humble or middle-class origins" (*Last Essays* [New York: Barnes and Noble, 1976], p. 218).

15 On Yeats and Balzac, see Stanfield, *Yeats and Politics*, and Warwick Gould, "A Crowded Theatre: Yeats and Balzac," *Yeats the European*, ed. A. Norman Jeffares (Gerrard's Cross: Colin Smythe, 1989).

16 A family which accommodated a vision of evil naturally lent itself to aristocratic politics. In "The Bounty of Sweden" he wrote "Nature, always extravagant, scattering much to find a little, has found no means but hereditary honour to sustain the courage of those who stand waiting for the signal, cowed by the honour and authority of those who lie wearily at the goal. Perhaps, indeed, she created the family with no other object, and may even now mock in her secret way our new ideals – the equality of man, equality of rights – meditating some wholly different end" (*AY*, 369).

17 Gonne's reply is instructive: "But the part of your letter where you attribute your change of thought to the study of Balzac is interesting. I have only read a little of Balzac. We both have come to the same philosophical conclusion – the all power of love & the sterility of hate; – the firm strong line, by different roads, you through Balzac, I through St. John. It leads you to vote for flogging bills & Treason Acts & Public Safety Acts. It leads me to found the Women's Prisoners' Defense League" (*GY*, 435).

18 See George Mills Harper, ed., *The Making of Yeats's 'A Vision': A Study of the Automatic Script*, vol. 1 (Carbondale and Edwardsville: Southern Illinois University Press, 1987), p. 53.

19 Terry Eagleton characterizes this tension in Yeats's aristocratic meditations this way: "Adherents of aristocratic ideology like Yeats are committed on the one hand to the values of order, ceremony, peace, stability and tradition – that's to say, to an impersonal organic hierarchy to which the individual subject is – precisely – subjected. All the values, in short, of the artistically admirable, politically revolting "Prayer for my Daughter." But this 'organicist' vein of aristocratism co-exists with its opposite: with a swaggering, anarchic, Byronic affirmation of the individual subject as autonomous and absolute, utterly self-grounded and self-generative, stooping (as Yeats writes) to no man's beck and call. Autarchy and authoritarianism, in short, are somehow sides of the same ideological coin" ("Politics and Sexuality in W. B. Yeats," *The Crane Bag*, 9:2 [1985], p. 139).

20 See, for example, Gill, *Happy Rural Seat*, and Daniel Harris, *Yeats, Coole Park and Ballylee* (Baltimore and London: Johns Hopkins University Press, 1974), chapter 3.

21 The drafts of the poem indicate that the roof-levelling wind embodies the forces of sterile Irish political opinion; the manuscripts refer to the storm as a "popular tempest," to the "bitterness" of political hatred, and to mob rule: "all must be with opinion driven wild." See Jon Stallworthy, *Between the Lines: Yeats's Poetry in the Making* (Oxford: Clarendon Press, 1971), pp. 29–30.

22 Elizabeth Cullingford's persuasive reading of the poem points out a similar conflict: "the poem indeed contains an unresolved tension between female autonomy and female subordination, between chastity and matrimony" ("Yeats and Women: *Michael Robartes and the Dancer*," *Yeats: An Annual of Critical and Textual Studies*, 4, p. 49), and Harris observes, "nowhere in his work are the opposing claims of individual aristocratic freedom and the historical coherence of the aristocratic order so unresolved as here" (*Yeats, Coole Park and Ballylee*, p. 146).

23 The drafts of the poem make it clearer that the speaker's knowledge of the evils of hatred comes out of his own experience; he says his mind "has grown half barren from much hate" (Stallworthy, *Between the Lines*, p. 35).

24 *Ibid.*, p. 43.

25 Daniel Harris claims that "the crucial poetic fact about 'Ancestral Houses' is that Yeats chose to avoid all references to the burnings" of Big Houses (*Yeats, Coole Park and Ballylee*, pp. 162–3).

26 The only other titles in the whole of his work in which "my" or "mine" appear are "To a Poet, who would have me Praise certain Bad Poets, Imitators of His and Mine," "A Prayer For My Daughter," and "A Prayer For My Son."

27 Denis Donoghue has observed that in "Ancestral Houses," "The beauty Yeats celebrates is bound up with that of women, the gardens where they walk, their patron Juno ..." ("The Political Turn in Criticism," *Irish Review*, 5 [Autumn 1988], p. 65).

28 Yeats used this image again in 1924 in "Compulsory Gaelic," in which Paul argues that for a nation "The greater part of its creative life – that of the woman of fashion, not less than that of the founder of a business or of a school of thought, should be the jet of a fountain that falls into the basin where it rose" (*UPII*, 442).

29 See also "The Phases of the Moon," in which Aherne says "the song will have it / That those that we have loved got their long fingers / From death, and wounds, or on Sinai's top, / Or from some bloody whip in their own hands" (*VP*, 375).

30 Ernest Renan, "What is a Nation?" *Nation and Narration*, ed. Homi Bhabha (London and New York: Routledge, 1990), p. 11.

31 See Harris, *Yeats, Coole Park and Ballylee*, chapter 3.

32 Michael North, *The Political Aesthetic of Yeats, Eliot and Pound* (Cambridge University Press, 1991), p. 40.

33 Harper, *The Making of Yeats's "A Vision,"* vol. I, p. 231.

5   DESIRING WOMEN

1 Georges Bataille, *Erotism: Death and Sensuality*, trans. Mary Dalwood (San Francisco: City Lights Books, 1986 [1957]), p. 121.

2 See, for example, John Unterecker, *A Reader's Guide to William Butler Yeats* (New York: Octagon Books, 1983 [1959]), p. 169.

3 See T. R. Henn, *The Lonely Tower: Studies in the Poetry of W. B. Yeats* (London: Methuen, 1950), p. 63, and Samuel Hynes, "All the Wild Witches: The Women in Yeats's Poems," *Sewanee Review*, 96 (1988), p. 571. Other critics claim that Yeats's female voices allowed him to treat sexual matters more objectively than the more obviously autobiographical male personae. See M. L. Rosenthal and Sally M. Gall, *The Modern Poetic Sequence: The Genius of Modern Poetry* (Oxford University Press, 1983), p. 116, and Curtis Bradford, *Yeats at Work* (Carbondale and Edwardsville: Southern Illinois University Press, 1965), p. 127.

4 See Elizabeth Cullingford, *Gender and History in Yeats's Love Poetry* (Cambridge University Press, 1993), chapter 11.

5 On the continuities between colonial Ireland and the Free State, and the new nation's resulting preoccupation with national self-definition, see Roy Foster, *Modern Ireland: 1600–1972* (Harmondsworth: Penguin, 1988), chapter 21, F. S. L. Lyons, *Ireland Since the Famine* (London: Fontana, 1986), pp. 471–550, and Terence Brown, *Ireland: A Social and Cultural History* (London: Fontana, 1981), chapters 1–3.

6 Clifford Geertz, *The Interpretation of Cultures* (New York: Basic Books, 1973), chapter 9.

7 For example, see Cheryl Herr, *Joyce's Anatomy of Culture* (Urbana and Chicago: University of Illinois Press, 1986), J. H. Whyte, *Church and State in Modern Ireland 1923–1970* (Dublin: Gill and Macmillan, 1971), and Dermot Keogh, *The Vatican, The Bishops and Irish Politics 1919–39* (Cambridge University Press, 1986).

8 See Patricia Twomey Ryan, "The Church, Education and Control of the State in Ireland," *Eire-Ireland*, 22:3 (Fall 1987), pp. 92–114, and Whyte, *Church and State*.

9 Margaret O'Callaghan, "Religion and Identity: The Church and Irish Independence," *The Crane Bag*, 7:2 (1983), p. 66.

10 *Ibid.*

11 *Ibid.*, p. 70.

12 Brown, *Ireland*, p. 43.

13 Michael Adams, *Censorship: The Irish Experience* (Dublin: Scepter Books, 1968), p. 15.

14 See O'Callaghan, "Religion and Identity," p. 74. The Lenten Pastorals of 1924 encouraged the Irish to condemn the "cross-channel unclean press" (Michael Adams, *Censorship*, p. 17). In 1927 the Bishop of Ardagh was reported as having said "In many respects the danger to our national characteristics was greater now than ever. The foreign press was more widely diffused amongst us; the cinema brought very vivid representations of foreign manners and customs; and the radio would bring foreign music and the propagation of foreign ideals" (quoted in Whyte, *Church and State*, p. 25). A joint pastoral of the same year warned "At the moment, [the devil's] traps for the innocent are chiefly the dance hall, the bad book, the indecent paper, the motion picture, the immodest fashion in female dress – all of which tend to destroy the virtues characteristic of our race" (quoted in Whyte, *Church and State*, p. 27).

15 For the latter argument, see Tom Inglis, *Moral Monopoly: The Catholic Church in Modern Irish Society* (Dublin: Gill and Macmillan, 1987), chapters 7–9.

16 *Ibid.*, especially p. 150. Inglis argues that, especially after the mid-century, controlling women was particularly important to the maintenance of Church power because Irish mothers provided the link between the Church and the individual, enforced Catholic morality in the home, and reared the next generation of Catholic subjects (see pp. 187–214).

17 See J. J. Lee, "Women and the Church Since the Famine," Margaret MacCurtain and Conncha O'Corrain, eds., *Women in Irish Society, The Historical Dimension* (Westport, CN: Greenwood Press, 1979).

18 While in 1851 there were 2500 priests and 1500 nuns, by 1901 Ireland's over 8000 nuns outnumbered priests by more than two to one. See Tony Fahey, "Nuns in the Catholic Church in Ireland in the Nineteenth Century," *Girls Don't Do Honors: Irish Women in Education in the*

Nineteenth and Twentieth Centuries, ed. Mary Cullen (Women's Educational Bureau, n.p., 1987). The figures cited appear on pp. 7–8.

19 Most revolutionary rhetoric was strongly anti-feminist. For example, Ellice Pilkington, the first organizer of the United Irishwomen, phrased the relationship between gender and Irish nationalism this way: "Back to the land is the cry to the men; Back to the home is the cry to the women" (Ellice Pilkington, *The United Irishwomen: Their Place, Work, and Ideals* [Dublin, 1911] repr. in Pat Bolger, ed., *And See Her Beauty Shining There: The Story of the Irish Countrywomen* [Dublin: Irish Academic Press, 1986], pp. 37–8. On the history of the relationship between women, feminism and Irish nationalism, see Rosemary Cullen Owens, *Smashing Times, A History of the Irish Women's Suffrage Movement 1889–1922* (Dublin: Attic Press, 1984), Margaret Ward, *Unmanageable Revolutionaries: Women and Irish Nationalism* (London: Pluto Press, 1983), and Cliona Murphy, *The Women's Suffrage Movement and Irish Society in the Early Twentieth Century* (New York: Harvester Wheatsheaf, 1989).

20 Peter Costello comments, "For a while, in the eagerness of a new world, an easiness emerged between the sexes in Ireland, a newer younger sense of spirit" (*The Heart Grown Brutal: The Irish Revolution in Literature, From Parnell to the Death of Yeats, 1891–1939* [Dublin: Gill and Macmillan, 1977], p. 180). But the provisional government disparaged women in politics and cracked down on prostitution (pp. 183–5). During the civil war, Cardinal Logue's pastoral letter condemning the republicans singled out republican women in particular for criticism (Ward, *Unmanageable Revolutionaries*, p. 192). The historian Catherine Rose claims that the 1920s and 1930s in Ireland saw "an almost maniacal hatred of women expressed by many Catholic bishops and priests" (Catherine Rose, *The Female Experience: The Story of the Woman Movement in Ireland* [Galway: Arlen House, 1975], p. 11). Some contemporary observers agreed. "It is high time," Oliver Gogarty told the Senate, that "the people of this country found some other way of loving God than by hating women" (quoted in Michael Sheehy, *Is Ireland Dying? Culture and the Church in Modern Ireland* [London: Hollis and Carter, 1968], p. 203).

21 The 1920s and early 1930s saw an increase in women's share of the industrial work force, mainly due to the establishment of new light and service industries (Ward, *Unmanageable Revolutionaries*, p. 234).

22 The clause recognized "the special position of the Holy Catholic Apostolic and Roman Church as the guardian of the faith professed by the great majority of the Citizens." It was deleted in a 1972 referendum (Inglis, *Moral Monopoly*, p. 77).

23 The new constitution enshrined the family as "the natural primary and foundational unit group of society, and as a moral institution possessing inalienable and imprescriptible rights" (quoted in Lyons, *Ireland*, p. 546). Of course, the "rights" of the family demanded that women

fulfill their duties. The constitution was explicit about the place of women in Irish society:

The State recognizes that by her life within the home, woman gives to the State a support without which the common good cannot be achieved. The State shall, therefore, endeavour to ensure that mothers shall not be obliged by economic necessity to engage in labour to the neglect of their duties in the home (Article 41.2, 2.1–2.2. Quoted in MacCurtain and O'Corrain, eds., *Women in Irish Society*, p. 60).

24 Whyte, *Church and State*, pp. 33–4.

25 See Conrad Arensberg, *The Irish Countryman: An Anthropological Study* (New York: Peter Smith, 1950 [1937]) and Conrad Arensberg and Solon T. Kimball, *Family and Community in Ireland* (Gloucester, MA: Peter Smith, 1961).

26 Brown, *Ireland*, pp. 19–20.

27 The classic case for a major change in marriage habits involving an increase in celibacy and a higher average age of marriage is made by K. H. Connell. See, for example, his "Catholicism and Marriage in the Century After the Famine," *Irish Peasant Society: Four Historical Essays* (Oxford: Clarendon Press, 1968). Other historians now qualify this by positing a post-famine rise in celibacy, but not in marriage age, or by pointing out the differences between the marriage practices of landless laborers, who tended to marry earlier, and land-owning farmers, who married much later due to considerations of property inheritance. See Art Cosgrave, ed., *Marriage in Ireland* (Dublin: College Press, 1985), especially chapters 4 and 5, and Inglis, pp. 175–9.

28 At the turn of the century, the proportion of people who never married in Ireland stood at 30 percent for men and 25 percent for women (Sean O'Faolain, "Love Among the Irish," John A. O'Brien, ed., *The Vanishing Irish: The Enigma of the Modern World* [London: W. H. Allen, 1954 (1953)], p. 57). The census of 1926 revealed that the Irish were still the most celibate nation on record. In 1926, 80 percent of all men aged twenty-five to thirty were unmarried, 62 percent of men aged thirty to thirty-five were unmarried, 50 percent of men aged thirty-five to forty were unmarried, and 26 percent of men aged fifty-five to sixty-five were unmarried. The figures for women were slightly lower: 62 percent of women aged twenty-five to thirty were unmarried, 42 percent of women aged thirty to thirty-five, 32 percent of women aged thirty-five to forty, and 24 percent of women aged fifty-five to sixty-five (Brown, *Ireland*, p. 19). In 1929 the Irish average age of marriage was still the highest in the world (Foster, *Modern Ireland*, p. 534). These trends were still in evidence as late as 1951 (Alexander J. Humphreys, *New Dubliners: Urbanization and the Irish Family* [New York: Fordham University Press, 1966], pp. 68–9).

29 Costello, *The Heart Grown Brutal*, p. 245, and Inglis, *Moral Monopoly*, p. 174.

30 See Janet A. Nolan, *Ourselves Alone: Women's Emigration From Ireland 1885–1920* (Lexington: The University Press of Kentucky, 1989). Nolan's figures (p. 50) apply to the period 1885–1920.

31 See Robert Kennedy, *The Irish: Emigration, Marriage, and Fertility* (Berkeley: University of California Press, 1973), especially chapter 7. Noting that in rural areas bachelors outnumbered marriageable women, Kennedy theorizes that "many Irish women preferred urban over rural life styles even if it meant the possibility of becoming a spinster" (p. 72).

32 David Cairns and Sean Richards comment: "paradoxically, constant exhortations to chastity multiplied immeasurably the extent to which sexuality was talked about in contemporary Ireland" (*Writing Ireland: Colonialism, Nationalism and Culture* [Manchester University Press, 1988], p. 116).

33 Yeats recorded this ambivalence in 1924 in a dialogue called "Compulsory Gaelic" (*UPII*, 439–49) and he criticized government compulsion in a senate speech (*SS*, 79).

34 See *SS*, 40, and Elizabeth Cullingford, *Yeats, Ireland and Fascism* (New York and London: New York University Press, 1981), p. 171.

35 J. H. Whyte cites Yeats as the "outstanding figure" of the group of literary men who represented the "one quarter from which systematic opposition came to the policy of giving Catholic moral standards the backing of the State" (Whyte, *Church and State*, p. 59).

36 Literature connected with birth control was a major target of people who objected to immoral publications. See Adams, *Censorship*, chapters 1 and 2 and Brown, *Ireland*, p. 69.

37 Twenty-three U.S. States made it a crime to publish or advertise contraceptive information (Adams, *Censorship*, p. 33), the same period saw a movement to control obscene publications in England and other countries (pp. 21–4), and in 1927 the League of Nations sponsored the International Convention For the Suppression of the Circulation of and Traffic in Obscene Publications (p. 24).

38 *Ibid.*, pp. 18–19, 27.

39 *Banned in Ireland: Censorship and the Irish Writer*, ed. for Article 19 by Julia Carlson (Athens: University of Georgia Press, 1990), p. 145.

40 Brown, *Ireland*, pp. 71–2. For Yeats's description of such attacks, see *L*, 705, 805).

41 For an account of Yeats's deliberately provocative intent and the controversy that ensued, see Cullingford, *Gender and History*, chapter 8.

42 See Robert Hogan and Richard Burnham, eds., *The Years of O'Casey, 1921–1926: A Documentary History* (Gerrards Cross: Colin Smythe, 1992), chapter 6. The majority of objections to the play were nationalist ones; detractors accused O'Casey of slandering the men of the Easter Rising, and were particularly offended by a scene in which an Irish flag is carried into a pub. Criticisms of Rosie Redmond, however, were also widespread and vehement.

43 Carlson, *Banned in Ireland*, p. 10.
44 Yeats wrote: "The basis of Irish nationalism has now shifted, and much that once helped us is now injurious, for we can no longer do anything by fighting, we must persuade, and to persuade we must become a modern, tolerant, liberal nation" (*UPII*, 452).
45 Brinsley Macnamara, *Look at the Heffernans!* (Dublin and Cork: Talbot Press, n.d.), p. 12.
46 Whyte, *Church and State*, pp. 20–1.
47 He also wrote to Olivia Shakespear: "My moods fill me with surprise and some alarm. The other day I found at Coole a reproduction of a drawing of two charming young persons in the full stream of their Saphoistic enthusiasm, and it got into my dreams at night and made a great racket there, and yet I feel spiritual things are very near me" (*L*, 715).
48 See, for example, his 1912 essay "Gitanjali" and the 1934 essay "The Holy Mountain," in which Yeats had praised a story about an eastern holy man for "symbolising an alliance between body and soul our theology rejects" (*EI*, 451). See also "The Mandukya Upanishad" (1935).
49 "Father and Child" was probably written in 1926 or 1927, "Before the World Was Made" was written in February 1928, "A First Confession" was written in June 1927, "Her Triumph" in November 1926, "Consolation" was probably written in June 1927, "Chosen" probably in early 1926, "Parting" and "Her Vision in the Wood" in August 1926, "A Last Confession" in the summer of 1926, "Meeting" was probably written sometime in 1926, and "From the 'Antigone'" was mostly finished by December 1927. Source: A. Norman Jeffares, *A New Commentary on the Poems of W. B. Yeats* (Stanford University Press, 1984), pp. 325–31.
50 George Mills Harper and Walter Kelly Hood report that Yeats must have begun revising almost immediately upon the publication of the first version (*A Critical Edition of Yeats's A Vision (1925)*, ed. George Mills Harper and Walter Kelly Hood [London: Macmillan, 1978], p. xlvii).
51 Jeffares, *A New Commentary*, p. 259.
52 Yeats wrote to Maurice Wollman in 1935 that "the poem means that the lover may, while loving, feel sympathy with his beloved's dread of captivity" (*L*, 840–1).
53 Michel Foucault, *The History of Sexuality, Volume 1: An Introduction* (New York: Vintage, 1980 [1976]), especially pp. 53–70.
54 See George Bataille, *Erotism*.
55 *Ibid.*, p. 36.
56 The quote is from p. 123. Bataille calls this process "Christianity's reduction of religion to its benign aspect: Christianity's projection of the darker side of religion into the profane world" (*Ibid.*, p. 120).
57 Michel Foucault, *Language, Counter-Memory, Practice*, ed. Donald F. Bouchard (Ithaca: Cornell University Press, 1977), pp. 29–30.

58 Patrick Keane has an excellent discussion of the poem's interaction with "The Collar" in *Yeats's Interactions With Tradition* (Columbia: University of Missouri Press, 1987), pp. 124–6.

59 For two influential conceptions of mimicry in contemporary theory, see Luce Irigarary, *This Sex Which is Not One* (Ithaca: Cornell University Press, 1985 [1977]), p. 76, and Homi Bhabha, *The Location of Culture* (New York and London: Routledge, 1994), chapter 4.

60 See Jeffares, *A New Commentary*, p. 326–8.

61 Elizabeth Cullingford, "Yeats and Women: *Michael Robartes and the Dancer*," *Yeats: An Annual of Critical and Textual Studies*, 4 (1986), p. 33.

62 See David R. Clark, "Yeats's Dragons: The Sources of 'Michael Robartes and the Dancer' and 'Her Triumph' as Shown in the Manuscripts," *Malahat Review*, 57 (January 1981), pp. 35–77.

63 George Bataille, *Visions of Excess: Selected Writings, 1927–1939*, ed. Allan Stoekl (Minneapolis: University of Minnesota Press, 1985), p. 119.

64 See Sir James George Frazer, *The Golden Bough: A Study in Magic and Religion*, abridged edn. (New York: Macmillan, 1966 [1922]), pp. 376–403. On Yeats and Frazer, see Warwick Gould, "Frazer, Yeats and the Reconsecration of Folklore," in *Sir James Frazer and the Literary Imagination*, ed. Robert Fraser (New York: St. Martin's Press, 1990), pp. 121–53.

65 Patrick Keane has argued convincingly that Yeats must be referring to "A Last Confession" here, rather than "The Friends of Youth" as Wade claimed (*Yeats's Interactions With Tradition*, p. 128).

66 Cullingford, *Gender and History*, pp. 224–6.

67 See Peter Stallybrass and Allon White, *The Politics and Poetics of Transgression* (Ithaca: Cornell University Press, 1986), especially the Conclusion.

6 THE RULE OF KINDRED

1 Elizabeth Cullingford offers overwhelming evidence to document her account of the significant divergences between Yeats's mature politics and continental fascism in *Yeats, Ireland and Fascism* (New York and London: New York University Press, 1981), especially chapters, 9–11.

2 See Paul Scott Stanfield, *Yeats and Politics in the Nineteen-Thirties* (London: Macmillan, 1988), chapter 5.

3 See Donald T. Torchiana, *W. B. Yeats and Georgian Ireland* (Evanston IL: Northwestern University Press, 1966), p. 341.

4 Quoted in A. Norman Jeffares, *W. B. Yeats: Man and Poet* (London: Routledge and Kegan Paul, 1949), p. 351–2.

5 *Ibid.*, p. 352.

6 A. Norman Jeffares, *W. B. Yeats: A New Biography* (New York: Farrar Straus Giroux, 1988), p. 269.

7 Michael North, *The Political Aesthetic of Yeats, Eliot, and Pound* (Cambridge University Press, 1990), p. 36.

8 Jeffares, *W. B. Yeats: Man and Poet*, p. 351.

9 For a clear example of this opposition, see "Genealogical Tree of Revolution" and "A Race Philosophy," reprinted in Jeffares, *W. B. Yeats: Man and Poet*, pp. 351–2. In *A Vision*, Yeats claimed "I had never put the conflict in logical form, never thought with Hegel that the two ends of the see-saw are one another's negation, nor that the spring vegetables were refuted when over" (*V*, 72–3). Yeats referred to the idea that "the spring vegetables were refuted when over" repeatedly when criticizing Hegel, but this particular criticism represents an obvious misreading of Hegel. In the passage to which Yeats refers, Hegel criticizes this way of thinking (see Frances Nesbitt Oppel, *Mask and Tragedy: Yeats and Nietzsche, 1902–10* [Charlottesville: University Press of Virginia, 1987], pp. 12–3).

10 Stanfield devotes a chapter of *Yeats and Politics* to Yeats's attitudes towards DeValera.

11 Yeats pointed to the historical importance of Mussolini being applauded for speaking of the "decomposing body of liberty" and commented "We may see the importance of that without admiring Mussolini or condemning him" (*UPII*, 434). He also claimed that one could admire the thoughts of a man like Peguy, Claudel or Murras "without admiring his practical politics" (*UPII*, 435).

12 If fascism was in many ways not what Yeats thought it was, the Blueshirts were not as fascist as Yeats thought they were. As Maurice Manning has argued, the blueshirts drew some of their inspiration from Continental fascism, but most of their political philosophies and alliances had more immediate determinants in the legacies of the Irish civil war. See Maurice Manning, *The Blueshirts* (Dublin: Gill and Macmillan, 1970). Manning argues that, while there were a number of similarities between the Blueshirts and European fascist movements, "It is probable that the majority of Blueshirts never saw their movement as a Fascist one" (p. 243), and the larger claim of his book is that "the whole Blueshirt phenomenon can be seen as a final instalment of the Civil War saga" (p. 248).

13 Aherne simply says "Even if the next divine influx be to kindreds why should war be necessary? Cannot they develop their characteristics in some other way?" (*V*, 53) and receives no reply.

14 "Dear predatory birds, prepare for war, prepare your children and all that you can reach … Test art, morality, custom, thought, by Thermopyle, make rich and poor act so to one another that they can stand together there. Love war because of its horror, that belief may be changed, civilisation renewed. We desire belief and lack it. Belief comes from shock and is not desired" (*EX*, 425–6).

15 Cullingford has acutely pointed out that "Yeats had once thought that fascism was turning away from final primary thought. He now realized that it was actually the epitome of that thought" (*Yeats, Ireland and*

Fascism, p. 218). Paul Stanfield makes a similar observation, remarking that Yeats "began by thinking [fascism] the stage succeeding communism in the breaking-up of democracy, and ended by thinking it the last, hysterical constriction of democracy, a finale rather than a prelude" (Stanfield, *Yeats and Politics*, p. 71).

16 For an excellent discussion of Yeats and the eugenic movement, see David Bradshaw, "The Eugenics Movement in the 1930s and the Emergence of *On the Boiler*," *Yeats Annual*, 9 (1992).

17 See Lyndsay Andrew Farrall, *The Origins and Growth of the English Eugenics Movement 1865–1925* (New York and London: Garland, 1985), chapter 3.

18 While American eugenists tended to emphasize race over nation, the movement in Britain was more preoccupied with the nation.

19 In some cases this distinction is a difficult one to make. For example, while Sir Francis Galton is generally seen as a major founder of the more scientific wing of the movement, Ruth Schwartz Cowan has argued that he "seems to have committed himself to the validity of mental heredity, not because he thought it was a solution to a great scientific problem, but because he was fascinated by the social programs that could be built around it" (*Sir Francis Galton and the Study of Heredity in the Nineteenth Century* [New York and London: Garland, 1985], p. 24).

20 "Struck by this in Swift's *Discourse of the Contests and Dissensions between the Nobles and the Commons in Athens and Rome*. 'I think that the saying "Vox populi vox Dei" ought to be understood of the universal bent and current of a people, not of the bare majority of a few representatives, which is often procured by little art, and great industry and application; wherein those who engage in the pursuits of malice and revenge, are much more sedulous than such as would prevent them' " (*EX*, 292).

21 Quoted in Torchiana, *Georgian Ireland*, p. 161.

22 In an early senate speech, Yeats told the senate, "We do not represent constituencies; we are drawn together to represent certain forms of special knowledge, certain special interests" (*SS*, 33). Paul Stanfield observes that "In his earliest Senate speeches he tended to emphasize that the Senate's authority rested not on its representing the people, but on the knowledge and ability of its members" (*Yeats and Politics*, p. 56) and that he became notorious for wanting to set up expert committees to study issues before the senate. Yeats held this view throughout his years in the senate. In his last senate speech he returned to this subject: "I think we should not lose sight of the simple fact that it is more desirable and more important to have able men in this House than to get representative men into this House" (*SS*, 151–2).

23 Raymond B. Cattell, *The Fight For Our National Intelligence* (London: P. S. King and Son, 1937).

24 For example, Yeats's library contained a pamphlet by Charles John

Bond, (Edward O'Shea, *A Descriptive Catalog of W. B. Yeats's Library* [New York and London: Garland, 1985], p. 39) which recommended the "arousal of a racial conscience" (Charles John Bond, "Some Causes of Racial Decay," *Essays and Addresses Sociological, Biological and Psychological By a Surgeon* [London: A. K. Lewis, 1930], p. 135).

25 See Bradshaw, "Eugenics Movement."

26 Cattell, *The Fight*, p. 61.

27 *Ibid.*, p. 135.

28 *Ibid.*, p. 59.

29 See G. R. Searle, *Eugenics and Politics in Britain 1900–1914* (Leyden: Noordhoff International Publishing, 1976), chapter 5.

30 See Farrall, *Origins and Growth*, chapter 6, and Searle, *Eugenics and Politics*, especially chapter 5 and the Conclusion.

31 Searle, *Eugenics and Politics*, pp. 56–59.

32 Quoted in Bradshaw, "Eugenics Movement," pp. 209 and 201.

33 *Ibid.*, p. 209.

34 See Farrall, *Origins and Growth*, chapter 2, and Searle, *Eugenics and Politics*, chapters 2 and 3.

35 See Searle, *Eugenics and Politics*, chapter 7.

36 See Cattell, *The Fight*, chapter 1.

37 Bradshaw, "Eugenics Movement," p. 191.

38 David Bradshaw gives a good account of the "polarisation" (*ibid.*, p. 190) of the British eugenics movement in the mid 1930s and remarks that Yeats's views, while not consonant with those of the London Eugenics Society, were "notable for their mainline orthodoxy" in relation to "the reactionary arm of British eugenics" (p. 211).

39 Sir Francis Galton, *Essays in Eugenics* (New York and London: Garland, 1985 [1909]), p. 42.

40 Paul Stanfield observes that Yeats's ideas "combine a radically geneticist approach with a radically environmentalist approach" (*Yeats and Politics*, p. 151).

41 In a discussion of the family background of his friends Edward Martyn and George Moore, Yeats wrote "I have been told that the crudity common to all the Moores came from the mother's family, Mayo squireens, probably half-peasants in education and occupation, for his father was a man of education and power and old descent. His mother's blood seems to have affected him and his brother as the peasant strain has affected Edward Martyn. There has been a union of incompatibles and consequent sterility ... Both men are examples of the way Irish civilization is held back by the lack of education of Irish Catholic women. An Irish Catholic will not marry a Protestant, and hitherto the women have checked again and again the rise, into some world of refinement, of Catholic households. The whole system of Irish Catholicism pulls down the able and well-born if it pulls up the peasant, as I think it does. A long continuity of culture like that at Coole could not

have arisen, and never has arisen, in a single Catholic family in Ireland since the Middle Ages" (*Mem*, 270–1).

42　Seanchan the poet tells two young girls: "The mothers that have borne you mated rightly / They'd little ears as thirsty as your ears / For many love songs."

43　Quoted in Stanfield, *Yeats and Politics*, p. 214.

44　Galton, *Essays in Eugenics*, p. 26.

45　Roswell H. Johnson, "Mate Selection," *Eugenics, Genetics and the Family*, Second International Congress of Eugenics, 1921, vol. I (New York and London: Garland, 1985), p. 422.

46　Cattell, *The Fight*, p. 156.

47　*Ibid.*, p. xiv.

48　Louis I. Dublin, "The Higher Education of Women and Race Betterment," *Eugenics in Race and State*, Second International Congress of Eugenics, 1921, vol. II (New York and London: Garland, 1985), pp. 377–8.

49　*Ibid.*, p. 384.

50　*Ibid.*, p. 385.

51　While he left open the possibility that "the Minister may in many cases be right," and that the bill was a desirable one, Yeats argued that "there is the danger of making it difficult for women to marry and discouraging marriage if there is any undue discrimination against women on the ground that they will withdraw from the Service on marriage" (*SS*, 104) and he requested more information about the bill.

52　See, for example, Bradshaw, "Eugenics Movement," p. 189.

53　Also in *L*, p. 910. He told Dorothy Wellesley, "for the first time in my life I am saying what are my political beliefs" (*L*, 902).

54　These are the men who Yeats described in "A Packet to Ezra Pound": "My Dear Ezra, Do not be elected to the Senate of your country. I think myself, after six years, well out of that of mine. Neither you nor I, nor any other of our excitable profession, can match those old lawyers, old bankers, old business men, who, because all habit and memory, have begun to govern the world" (*V*, 26). Yeats claims that these men retain their "moral ascendancy" and contrasts them to politicians (*V*, 26).

55　In 1930 he wrote, "We have not an Irish Nation until all classes grant its right to take life according to the law and until it is certain that the threat of invasion, made by no matter who, would rouse all classes to arms" (*EX*, 338).

56　Quoted in Torchiana, *Georgian Ireland*, p. 357.

57　Sandra F. Siegel, ed., *Purgatory: Manuscript Materials Including the Author's Final Text*, by W. B. Yeats (Ithaca and London: Cornell University Press, 1986), p. 43.

58　See W. J. McCormack, *Ascendancy and Tradition in Anglo-Irish Literary History From 1789–1939* (Oxford: Clarendon Press, 1985), chapter 10.

59 In "Commentary on 'A Parnellite at Parnell's Funeral'" (1935), Yeats described the Anglo-Irish degeneration of the nineteenth century this way:

The influence of the French Revolution woke the peasantry from the medieval sleep, gave them ideas of social justice and equality, but prepared for a century disastrous to the national intellect. Instead of the Protestant Ascendancy with its sense of responsibility, we had the Garrison, a political party of Protestant and Catholic landowners, merchants and officials. They loved the soil of Ireland; the returned Colonial Governor crossed the Channel to see the May flowers in his park; the merchant loved with an ardour, I have not met elsewhere, some sea-board town where he had made his money, or spent his youth, but they could give to a people they thought unfit for self-government, nothing but a condescending affection. (*VP*, 833–4)

McCormack discusses this source and one in Lady Gregory's journals as indications that the text renders the old man's elegy suspect on pp. 378–84 of *Ascendancy and Tradition*.

60 *A Decade of Progress in Eugenics*, Third International Congress of Eugenics, 1932 (New York and London: Garland, 1984), p. 511 (plate 1).

61 The poem's last line reads "Man has created death" (*VP*, 476).

62 Torchiana identifies these men all as statesmen whom Yeats felt had abdicated their responsibilities in some way: George II, King of Greece, Lord Nuffield, who endowed an Oxford college in the name of applied science, Sir Hubert Gough, accused of dividing Ireland during the Curragh Incident, and Frederick Edwin Earl of Birkenhead, credited with helping introduce the oath into the treaty of 1922 (Torchiana, *Georgian Ireland*, pp. 355–6).

63 Sandra F. Siegel gives this account of Yeats's revisions: "The fictional Old Man became increasingly complex as Yeats continued to revise the version. In the earliest versions the Old Man is shrewdly accurate about himself. As the Boy's provocative behavior and the Old Man's sense of himself as evil are gradually pruned away, the revisions served to emphasize the confusion within the Old Man. As a result, the motives that prompt him to act appear to be at odds with his verbal account of his behavior" (*Purgatory*, p. 6).

64 See, for example, "Beggar to Beggar Cried," and "The Three Beggars."

65 See Torchiana, *Georgian Ireland*, pp. 350–65.

66 Near the end of the play, as Cuchulain is about to be murdered, Cuchulain claims to see the shape his soul will take next and asserts its creative power: "I say it is about to sing" (*VPl*, 1061).

67 For an excellent discussion of Yeats's critique of Marxism, see Cullingford, *Yeats, Ireland and Fascism*, chapter 8. Cullingford observes that Yeats saw his own philosophy of history as "more pessimistic but less bloodthirsty than Hegel's or Marx's" (p. 123).

Bibliography

Adams, Michael, *Censorship: The Irish Experience*, Dublin: Scepter, 1968.
Adorno, Theodor, *Minima Moralia: Reflections From Damaged Life*, trans. E. F. N. Jephcott, London: Verso, 1974 (1951).
Ahmad, Aijaz, *In Theory: Classes, Nations, Literatures*, New York and London: Verso, 1992.
Anderson, Benedict, *Imagined Communities: Reflections on the Origin and Spread of Nationalism*, London: Verso, 1983.
Arensberg, Conrad, *The Irish Countryman: An Anthropological Study*, New York: Peter Smith, 1950 (1937).
    and Solon T. Kimball, *Family and Community in Ireland*, Gloucester, MA: Peter Smith, 1961.
Arnold, Matthew, *The Complete Prose Works of Matthew Arnold*, 11 vols., ed. R. H. Super, Ann Arbor: University of Michigan Press, 1960–77.
    On the Study of Celtic Literatures, ed. Alfred Nutt, Phoenix, Long Acre: David Nutt, 1910.
Ashcroft, Bill, Gareth Griffiths and Helen Tiffin, eds., *The Empire Writes Back*, London and New York: Routledge, 1989.
Bataille, Georges, *Erotism: Death and Sensuality*, trans. Mary Dalwood, San Francisco: City Lights, 1986 (1957).
    Visions of Excess: Selected Writings, 1927–1939, ed. Allan Stoekl, Minneapolis: University of Minnesota Press, 1985.
Beizer, Janet, *Ventriloquized Bodies: Narratives of Hysteria in Nineteenth-Century France*, Ithaca: Cornell University Press, 1994.
Benjamin, Walter, *Illuminations*, ed. Hannah Arendt, New York: Schocken, 1968.
Benson, Eugene, "De-Mythologizing Cathleen ni Houlihan: Synge and His Sources," *Irish Writers and the Theatre*, ed. Masaru Sekine, Irish Literary Studies 23, Gerrards Cross: Colin Smythe, 1986.
Berlant, Lauren, *The Anatomy of National Fantasy: Hawthorne, Utopia, and Everyday Life*, University of Chicago Press, 1991.
Bessai, Diane E., "'Dark Rosaleen' as Image of Ireland," *Eire-Ireland* 10:4 (Winter 1975).
Bhabha, Homi, "Introduction: Narrating the Nation," *Nation and Narration*, ed. Homi Bhabha, New York: Routledge, 1990.

The Location of Culture, New York and London: Routledge, 1994.

Blavatsky, Helena P., *Isis Unveiled*, Los Angeles: Theosophy Company, 1975 (1877).

Bloom, Harold, *Yeats*, New York: Oxford University Press, 1970.

Bond, Charles John, "Some Causes of Racial Decay," *Essays and Addresses Sociological, Biological and Psychological By a Surgeon*, London: H. K. Lewis, 1930.

Bolger, Pat, ed., *And See Her Beauty Shining There: The Story of the Irish Country Women*, Dublin: Irish Academic Press, 1986.

Boyce, George, *Nationalism in Ireland*, London, Croom Helm and Dublin: Gill and Macmillan, 1982.

Bradford, Curtis, "Yeats and Maud Gonne," *Texas Studies in Literature and Language*, 3:4 (Winter 1962), pp. 452–74.

Yeats at Work, Carbondale and Edwardsville: Southern Illinois University Press, 1965.

Bradshaw, David, "The Eugenics Movement in the 1930s and the Emergence of *On the Boiler*," *Yeats Annual*, 9 (1992).

Brantlinger, Patrick, *Rule of Darkness: British Literature and Imperialism, 1830–1914*, Ithaca: Cornell University Press, 1988.

Brennan, Timothy, "The National Longing for Form," *Nation and Narration*, ed. Homi Bhabha, London and New York: Routledge, 1990.

Bromwich, Rachael, *Matthew Arnold and Celtic Literature*, Oxford: Clarendon Press, 1965.

Brown, Terence, *Ireland: A Social and Cultural History 1922–1985*, London: Fontana, 1981.

Ireland's Literature: Selected Essays, Mullingar: The Liliput Press and Totowa, NJ: Barnes and Noble, 1988.

"Saxon and Celt: The Stereotypes," *Literary Interrelations: Ireland, England and the World; Volume III: National Images and Stereotypes*, ed. Wolfgang Zach and Heinz Kosok, Tubingen: Gunter Narr Verlag, 1987.

Bryant, Sophie, "The Celtic Mind," *Contemporary Review*, 72 (July–December 1897), London: Isbister, 1897.

The Genius of the Gael: A Study in Celtic Psychology and Its Manifestations, London: T. Fisher Unwin, 1913.

Burke, Edmund, *Reflections on the Revolution in France*, ed. Thomas Mahoney, Indianapolis and New York: Bobbs-Merrill, 1955.

Butler, Judith, *Gender Trouble: Feminism and the Subversion of Identity*, New York: Routledge, 1990.

Cairns, David, and Shaun Richards, " 'Woman' in the Discourse of Celticism: A Reading of *In the Shadow of the Glen*," *Canadian Journal of Irish Studies*, 13:1 (June 1987).

Writing Ireland: Colonialism, Nationalism and Culture, Manchester University Press, 1988.

Canetti, Elias, *Crowds and Power*, trans. Carol Stewart, New York: Farrar Straus Giroux, 1962 (1960).

Cardullo, Bert, "Notes Toward a Production of W. B. Yeats's *The Countess Cathleen*," *Canadian Journal of Irish Studies*, 11:2 (December 1985).

Carlson, Julia, ed., *Banned in Ireland: Censorship and the Irish Writer*, Athens: University of Georgia Press, 1990.

Carlyle, Thomas, *Reminiscences of My Irish Journey in 1849*, London: Sampson Low, Marston, Searle, and Rivington, 1882.

Cattell, Raymond B., *The Fight For Our National Intelligence*, London: P. S. King and Son, 1937.

Clark, David R., "Vision and Revision: Yeats's *The Countess Cathleen*," *The World of W. B. Yeats*, ed. Robin Skelton and Ann Saddlemyer, Seattle: University of Washington Press, 1967 (1965).

"Yeats's Dragons: The Sources of 'Michael Robartes and the Dancer' and 'Her Triumph' as Shown in the Manuscripts," *Malahat Review*, 57 (January 1981).

Clark, Samuel, and James S. Donnelly, Jr., eds., *Irish Peasants: Violence and Political Unrest, 1780–1914*, Manchester University Press, 1983.

Clarke, Brenna, *The Emergence of the Irish Peasant Play at the Abbey Theatre*, Ann Arbor: University Microfilms International Research Press, 1975.

Comerford, R. V., *The Fenians in Context: Irish Politics and Society 1848–82*, Dublin: Wolfhound Press, 1985.

Connell, K. H., *Irish Peasant Society: Four Historical Essays*, Oxford: Clarendon Press, 1968.

Connolly, James, *The Reconquest of Ireland*, Dublin: At Liberty Hall, 1915.

Corkery, Daniel, *Synge and Anglo-Irish Literature*, Cork University Press, 1955.

Cosgrave, Art, ed., *Marriage in Ireland*, Dublin: College Press, 1985.

Costello, Peter, *The Heart Grown Brutal: The Irish Revolution in Literature, From Parnell to the Death of Yeats, 1891–1939*, Dublin: Gill and Macmillan, 1977.

Cowan, Ruth Schwartz, *Sir Francis Galton and the Study of Heredity in the Nineteenth Century*, New York and London: Garland, 1985.

Cribb, J. J. L., "Yeats, Blake and *The Countess Kathleen*," *Irish University Review*, 11:2 (Fall 1981).

Cullingford, Elizabeth, *Gender and History in Yeats's Love Poetry*, Cambridge University Press, 1993.

"'Thinking of Her ... as ... Ireland': Yeats, Pearse and Heaney," *Textual Practice*, 4:1 (1990).

"Yeats and Women: *Michael Robartes and the Dancer*," *Yeats: An Annual of Critical and Textual Studies*, 4 (1985).

Yeats, Ireland and Fascism, New York and London: New York University Press, 1981.

Curtis, Lewis Perry, Jr., *Anglo-Saxons and Celts: A Study of Anti-Irish Prejudice in Victorian England*, Bridgeport, CT: Conference on British Studies at the University of Bridgeport, 1968.

Apes and Angels: The Irishman in Victorian Caricature, Newton Abbot, Devon: David Charles, 1971.

Deane, Seamus, "Blueshirt," *London Review of Books* (June 4, 1981).

Celtic Revivals: Essays in Modern Irish Literature, 1880–1980, London and Boston: Faber and Faber, 1985.

"Heroic Styles: The Tradition of an Idea," *Ireland's Field Day*, IN: University of Notre Dame Press, 1986 (1984).

A Decade of Progress in Eugenics, Third International Congress of Eugenics, 1932, New York and London: Garland, 1984.

Dijkstra, Bram, *Idols of Perversity: Fantasies of Feminine Evil in Fin-de-Siecle Culture*, Oxford and New York: Oxford University Press, 1986.

Dineen, Reverend P. S., *Lectures on the Irish Language Movement*, Dublin: M. H. Gill and Son, for the Gaelic League, 1904.

Donoghue, Denis, *William Butler Yeats*, New York: Viking, 1971.

"The Political Turn in Criticism," *Irish Review*, 5 (Autumn 1988).

Dowling, Linda, "The Decadent and the New Woman in the 1890s," *Nineteenth Century Fiction*, 33:4 (March 1979).

Dublin, Louis I., "The Higher Education of Women and Race Betterment," *Eugenics in Race and State*, Second International Congress of Eugenics, 1921, vol. II, New York and London: Garland, 1985.

Eagleton, Terry, "Nationalism: Irony and Commitment," *Nationalism, Colonialism, and Literature*, ed. Seamus Deane, Minneapolis: University of Minnesota Press, 1990.

"Politics and Sexuality in W. B. Yeats," *The Crane Bag*, 9:2 (1985).

Edgeworth, Maria, *The Absentee*, Oxford University Press, 1988 (1812).

Ellis, Henry Havelock, *A Study of British Genius*, London: Constable, 1927 (new edn., rev. and enlarged).

Ellmann, Richard, *Four Dubliners*, New York: George Braziller, 1988.

The Identity of Yeats, London: Macmillan, 1954.

Fahey, Tony, "Nuns in the Catholic Church in Ireland in the Nineteenth Century," *Girls Don't Do Honours: Irish Women in Education in the Nineteenth and Twentieth Centuries*, ed. Mary Cullen, n.p.: Women's Educational Bureau, 1987.

Fanon, Franz, *Black Skin, White Masks*, New York: Grove Weidenfeld, 1967.

The Wretched of the Earth, trans. Constance Farrington, New York: Grove Weidenfeld, 1963.

Farrall, Lyndsay Andrew, *The Origins and Growth of the English Eugenics Movement 1865–1925*, New York and London: Garland, 1985.

Faverty, Frederick, *Mathew Arnold the Ethnologist* (Evanston: Northwestern University Press, 1951).

Finneran, Richard, George Mills Harper, and William M. Murphy, eds., *Letters to Yeats*, volume I, London and Basingstoke: Macmillan, 1977.

Fitzgerald, William G., ed., *The Voice of Ireland, A Survey of the Race and Nation From All Angles By the Foremost Leaders at Home and Abroad*, Dublin and London: Virtue and Company, n.d.

Flannery, James, *W. B. Yeats and the Idea of a Theatre*, New Haven and London: Yale University Press, 1976.

Foster, Roy, *Modern Ireland: 1600–1972*, Harmondsworth: Penguin, 1988.

"Protestant Magic: W. B. Yeats and the Spell of Irish History," *Proceedings of the British Academy*, 75 (1989).

Foucault, Michel, *The History of Sexuality, Volume 1: An Introduction*, New York: Vintage, 1980 (1976).

Language, Counter-Memory, Practice, ed. Donald Bouchard, Ithaca: Cornell University Press, 1977.

Robert Fraser, ed., *Sir James Frazer and the Literary Imagination*, New York: St. Martin's Press, 1990.

Frazer, Sir James George, *The Golden Bough: A Study in Magic and Religion*, abridged edn., New York: Macmillan, 1966 (1922).

Frazier, Adrian, *Behind the Scenes: Yeats, Horniman, and the Struggle for the Abbey Theatre*, Berkeley: University of California Press, 1990.

Freud, Sigmund, *Group Psychology and the Analysis of the Ego*, New York and London: Norton, 1989 (1959).

and Josef Breuer, *Studies on Hysteria*, trans. and ed. James Strachey, New York: Basic Books, 1955 (1895).

Freyer, Grattan, *W. B. Yeats and the Anti-Democratic Tradition*, Dublin: Gill and Macmillan, 1981.

Galton, Sir Francis, *Essays in Eugenics*, New York and London: Garland, 1985.

Garvin, Tom, "Priests and Patriots: Irish Separatism and Fear of the Modern, 1890–1914," *Irish Historical Studies*, 25:97 (May 1986).

Geertz, Clifford, *The Interpretation of Cultures*, New York: Basic Books, 1973.

"Primordial and Civic Ties," *Nationalism*, ed. John Hutchinson and Anthony D. Smith, Oxford University Press, 1994.

Gibbons, Luke, "Constructing the Canon: Versions of National Identity," *The Field Day Anthology of Irish Writing*, vol. II, New York: Norton, 1991.

"Race Against Time: Racial Discourse and Irish History," *Oxford Literary Review*, 13 (Spring 1991).

Gibbons, Tom, *Rooms in the Darwin Hotel: Studies in English Literary Criticism and Ideas 1880–1920*, Nedlands: University of Western Australia Press, 1973.

Gill, Richard, *Happy Rural Seat: The English Country House and the Literary Imagination*, New Haven and London: Yale University Press, 1972.

Gilman, Sander L., *Difference and Pathology: Stereotypes of Sexuality, Race, and Madness*, Ithaca and London: Cornell University Press, 1985.

Gonne, Maud, *Dawn, Lost Plays of the Irish Renaissance*, ed. Robert Hogan and James Kilroy, Proscenium Press, 1970.

A Servant of the Queen, London: Victor Gollancz, 1938.

"Yeats and Ireland," *Scattering Branches*, ed. Stephen Gwynn, London: 1940.

Gould, Warwick, "A Crowded Theatre: Yeats and Balzac," *Yeats the European*, ed. A. Norman Jeffares, Gerrards Cross: Colin Smythe, 1989.

Greene, David H., and Edward M. Stephens, *J. M. Synge, 1871–1909*, New York: Macmillan, 1959.

Gregory, Lady Augusta, *Our Irish Theatre*, London and New York: G. P. Putman's Sons, 1913.

Grossman, Alan, *Poetic Knowledge in the Early Yeats: A Study of The Wind Among the Reeds*, Charlottesville: University Press of Virginia, 1969.

Haraway, Donna, *Simians, Cyborgs and Women: The Reinvention of Nature*, New York: Routledge, 1991.

Harper, George Mills, ed., *The Making of Yeats's 'A Vision': A Study of the Automatic Script*, two vols., Carbondale and Edwardsville: Southern Illinois University Press, 1987.

Yeats's Golden Dawn, London: Macmillan, 1974.

Harper, George Mills, and Walter Kelly Hood, eds., *A Critical Edition of Yeats's A Vision (1925)*, London: Macmillan, 1978.

Harris, Daniel, *Yeats, Coole Park and Ballylee*, Baltimore and London: Johns Hopkins University Press, 1974.

Harwood, John, "Olivia Shakespear and W. B. Yeats," *Yeats Annual*, 4 (1986), pp. 75–98.

Henn, T. R., *Last Essays*, New York: Barnes and Noble, 1976.

The Lonely Tower: Studies in the Poetry of W. B. Yeats, London: Methuen, 1950.

Herr, Cheryl, "The Erotics of Irishness," *Critical Inquiry*, 17:1 (Autumn 1990).

Joyce's Anatomy of Culture, Urbana and Chicago: University of Illinois Press, 1986.

Hirsch, Edward, "The Imaginary Irish Peasant," *PMLA*, 106:5 (October 1991).

Hobsbawm, Eric, *The Age of Empire 1875–1914*, New York: Vintage Books, 1989.

"Mass-Producing Traditions: Europe, 1870–1914," *The Invention of Tradition*, ed. Eric Hobsbawm and Terence Ranger, Cambridge University Press, 1983.

Nations and Nationalism Since 1780: Programme, Myth, Reality, Cambridge University Press, 1990.

Hogan, Robert, and Richard Burnham, eds., *The Years of O'Casey, 1921–1926: A Documentary History*, Gerrards Cross: Colin Smythe, 1992.

and James Kilroy, eds., *The Irish Literary Theater 1899–1901*, Dublin: Dolmen Press, 1975.

Laying the Foundations 1902–1904, Dublin: Dolmen Press, 1976.

and Liam Miller, eds., *The Playboy Riots*, Dublin: Dolmen Press, 1971.

Holdsworth, Carolyn, "Shelley Plain: Yeats and Katharine Tynan, *Yeats: An Annual of Critical and Textual Studies*, 2 (1983), pp. 59–92.

Humphreys, Alexander J., *New Dubliners: Urbanization and the Irish Family*, New York: Fordham University Press, 1966.

Hutchinson, John, *The Dynamics of Cultural Nationalism: The Gaelic Revival and the Creation of the Irish Nation State*, London: Allen and Unwin, 1987.

Huyssen, Andreas, *After the Great Divide: Modernism, Mass Culture, Post-*

modernism, Bloomington and Indianapolis: Indiana University Press, 1986.

Hynes, Samuel, "All the Wild Witches: The Women in Yeats's Poems," *Sewanee Review*, 96 (1988).

Ap Hywel, Elin, "Elise and the Great Queens of Ireland: 'Femininity' as Constructed by Sinn Fein and the Abbey Theatre, 1901–1907," *Gender in Irish Writing*, ed. Toni O'Brien Johnson and David Cairns, Milton Keynes and Philadelphia: Open University Press, 1991.

Inglis, Tom, *Moral Monopoly: The Catholic Church in Modern Irish Society*, Dublin: Gill and Macmillan, 1987.

Irigary, Luce, *This Sex Which is Not One*, Ithaca: Cornell University Press, 1985 (1977).

Jameson, Fredric, "Third-World Literature in the Era of Multinational Capitalism," *Social Text*, 15 (Fall 1986).

Jeffares, A. Norman, *A Commentary on the Collected Poems of W. B. Yeats*, Stanford University Press, 1968.

A New Commentary on the Poems of W. B. Yeats, Stanford University Press, 1984.

W. B. Yeats: A New Biography, New York: Farrar Straus Giroux, 1988.

W. B. Yeats, Man and Poet, London: Routledge and Kegan Paul, 1949.

and A. S. Knowland, *A Commentary on the Collected Plays of W. B. Yeats*, Stanford University Press, 1975.

Johnson, Roswell H., "Mate Selection," In *Eugenics, Genetics and the Family*, Second International Congress of Eugenics, 1921, vol. 1, New York and London: Garland, 1985.

Joyce, James, *The Critical Writings of James Joyce*, ed. Ellsworth Mason and Richard Ellmann, London: Faber and Faber, 1959.

Ulysses, ed. Hans Walter Gabler, New York: Random House, 1986.

Keane, Patrick J., *Terrible Beauty: Yeats, Joyce, Ireland, and the Myth of the Devouring Female*, Columbia: University of Missouri Press, 1988.

Yeats's Interactions With Tradition, Columbia: University of Missouri Press, 1987.

Kearney, Richard, "Myth and Motherland," *Ireland's Field Day*, IN: University of Notre Dame Press, 1985.

Transitions: Narratives in Modern Irish Culture, Manchester University Press, 1988.

Kelleher, John V., "Matthew Arnold and the Celtic Revival," *Perspectives in Criticism*, ed. Harry Levin, Harvard Studies in Comparative Literature, 11:20, Cambridge: Harvard University Press, 1950.

Kelly, John, "The Fifth Bell: Race and Class in Yeats's Political Thought," *Irish Writers and Politics*, ed. Okifumi Komesu and Masaru Sekine, Gerrards Cross: Colin Smythe, 1989.

Kennedy, Robert, *The Irish: Emigration, Marriage, and Fertility*, Berkeley: University of California Press, 1973.

Keogh, Dermot, *The Vatican, the Bishops and Irish Politics 1919–39*, Cambridge University Press, 1986.

Kline, Gloria C., *The Last Courtly Lover: Yeats and the Idea of Woman*, Ann Arbor: University Microfilms International Research Press, 1983.

Knowland, A. S., *W. B. Yeats: Dramatist of Vision*, Totowa, NJ: Barnes and Noble, 1983.

Krans, Horatio Sheafe, *William Butler Yeats and the Irish Literary Revival*, London and New York: McClure, Phillips and Co., 1904.

Krimm, Bernard, *W. B. Yeats and the Emergence of the Irish Free State 1918–1939: Living in the Explosion*, Troy, NY: Whitston Publishing, 1981.

Laity, Cassandra, "Yeats's Changing Images of Maud Gonne," *Eire-Ireland*, 22:2 (Summer 1987).

"W. B. Yeats and Florence Farr: The Influence of the 'New Woman' Actress on W. B. Yeats's Changing Images of Women," *Modern Drama*, 28:4 (December 1985).

Lang, Andrew, "The Celtic Renascence," *Blackwood's Magazine*, 975 (Februrary 1897).

Le Bon, Gustave, *The Crowd: A Study of the Popular Mind*, Dunwoody, GA: Norman S. Berg, 1895.

The Psychology of Peoples, New York: Macmillan, 1898.

Lebow, Richard Ned, *White Britain and Black Ireland: The Influence of Stereotypes on Colonial Policy*, Institute for the Study of Human Issues, 1976.

Levinson, Leah, and Jerry H. Natterstad, *Hanna Sheehy-Skeffington: Irish Feminist*, Syracuse University Press, 1986.

Lloyd, David, *Anomalous States: Irish Writing and the Post-Colonial Moment*, Durham: Duke University Press, 1993.

"Arnold, Ferguson, Schiller: Aesthetic Culture and the Politics of Aesthetics," *Cultural Critique*, 2 (Winter 1985–6).

Nationalism and Minor Literature: James Clarence Mangan and the Emergence of Irish Cultural Nationalism, Berkeley: University of California Press, 1987.

"The Poetics of Politics: Yeats and the Founding of the State," *Anomalous States: Irish Writing and the Post-Colonial Moment*, Durham: Duke University Press, 1993.

Loizeaux, Elizabeth Bergman, *Yeats and the Visual Arts*, New Brunswick and London: Rutgers University Press, 1986.

Longenbach, James, *Stone Cottage: Pound, Yeats and Modernism*, New York and Oxford: Oxford University Press, 1988.

Lynd, Robert, *Home Life in Ireland*, London: Mills and Boon, 1909.

Lyons, F. S. L., *Culture and Anarchy in Ireland*, Oxford: Clarendon Press, 1979.

Ireland Since the Famine, London: Fontana, 1986 (1971).

"Yeats and the Anglo-Irish Twilight," *Irish Culture and Nationalism 1750–1950*, ed. Oliver MacDonagh, W. F. Mandle and Pauric Travers, London and Basingstoke: Macmillan, 1983.

MacCurtain, Margaret, and Conncha O'Corrain, eds., *Women in Irish Society, The Historical Dimension*, Westport, CT: Greenwood Press, 1979.

Macnamara, Brinsley, *Look at the Heffernans!* Dublin and Cork: Talbot Press, n.d.

Mangan, James Clarence, *Irish and Other Poems*, Dublin: M. H. Gill and Son, 1904.

The Prose Writings of James Clarence Mangan, ed. D. J. O'Donoghue, London: A. H. Bullen, 1904.

Manning, Maurice, *The Blueshirts*, Dublin: Gill and Macmillan, 1970.

Martin, Augustine, "What Stalked Through the Post Office?" *The Crane Bag*, 2:1 (1977).

Martyn, Edward, *The Heather Field and Maeve*, London: Duckworth, 1899.

Marx, Karl, and Frederick Engels, *Ireland and the Irish Question*, ed. R. Dixon, London: Lawrence and Wishart, n.d.

Selected Works, New York: International Publishers, 1968.

Maxwell, D. E. S., and S. B. Bushrui, eds., *W. B. Yeats, 1865–1965: Centenary Essays of the Art of W. B. Yeats*, Nigeria: Ibadan University Press, 1965.

McClelland, J. S., *The Crowd and the Mob: From Plato to Canetti*, London: Unwin Hyman, 1989.

McCormack, W. J., *Ascendancy and Tradition in Anglo-Irish Literary History from 1789–1939*, Oxford: Clarendon Press, 1985.

McKeon, Michael, "Historicizing Patriarchy: The Emergence of Gender Difference in England, 1660–1760," *Eighteenth-Century Studies*, 28:3 (1995).

Mercier, Vivian, "Victorian Evangelicalism and the Anglo-Irish Literary Revival," *Literature and the Changing Ireland*, ed. Peter Connolly, Irish Literary Studies, 9, Totawa, NJ: Barnes and Noble, 1982.

Moore, Marianne, *The Complete Poems of Marianne Moore*, Harmondsworth: Penguin, 1981.

Moore, Virginia, *The Unicorn: William Butler Yeats' Search for Reality*, New York: Macmillan, 1954.

Moran. D. P., *The Philosophy of Irish Ireland*, Dublin: James Duffy and Co., 1905.

More, Paul Elmer, *The Drift of Romanticism*, Shelburne Essays, Eighth Series, Boston and New York: Houghton Mifflin, 1913.

Shelburne Essays, First Series, New York and London: G. P. Putman's Sons, 1904.

Moscovici, Serge, *The Age of the Crowd: A Historical Treatise on Mass Psychology*, Cambridge University Press, 1985 (1981).

Mosse, George L., *Nationalism and Sexuality: Respectability and Abnormal Sexuality in Modern Europe*, New York: Howard Fertig, 1985.

The Nationalization of the Masses: Political Symbolism and Mass Movements in Germany From the Napoleonic Wars Through the Third Reich, New York: Howard Fertig, 1975.

Moynahan, Julian, "Lawrence, Woman and the Celtic Fringe," *Lawrence and Women*, ed. Ann Smith, London: Vision, 1978.

Murphy, Cliona, *The Women's Suffrage Movement and Irish Society in the Early Twentieth Century*, New York: Harvester Wheatsheaf, 1989.

Nandy, Ashis, *The Intimate Enemy: Loss and Recovery of Self Under Colonialism*, Oxford University Press, 1983.

The New Spirit of the Nation, London: T. Fisher Unwin, 1894.

Nolan, Janet A., *Ourselves Alone: Women's Emigration From Ireland 1885–1920*, Lexington: The University Press of Kentucky, 1989.

Nordau, Max, *Degeneration*, London: William Heineman, 1913.

North, Michael, *The Political Aesthetic of Yeats, Eliot, and Pound*, Cambridge University Press, 1990.

Nye, Robert A., *The Origins of Crowd Psychology: Gustave Le Bon and the Crisis of Mass Democracy in the Third Republic*, London and Beverly Hills: SAGE Publications, 1975.

O'Brien, Conor Cruise, "Passion and Cunning: An Essay on the Politics of W. B. Yeats," *In Excited Reverie: A Centenary Tribute to W. B. Yeats, 1865–1939*, ed. A. Norman Jeffares and K. G. W. Cross, New York: St. Martin's Press, 1965.

O'Brien, John A., ed., *The Vanishing Irish: The Enigma of the Modern World*, London: Allen, 1954 (1953).

O'Callaghan, Margaret, "Religion and Identity: The Church and Irish Independence," *The Crane Bag*, 7:2 (1983).

O'Donnell, F. Hugh, *Souls For Gold: Pseudo-Celtic Drama in Dublin*, London: Nassau Press, 1899.

O'Grady, Standish, *The Crisis in Ireland*, Dublin: E. Ponsonby, 1882.

Selected Essays and Passages, ed. Ernest A. Boyd, Dublin: Talbot Press, n.d.

Oppel, Frances Nesbitt, *Mask and Tragedy: Yeats and Nietzsche 1902–10*, Charlottesville: University Press of Virginia, 1987.

O'Rourke, Lorenzo, ed. and trans., *Victor Hugo's Intellectual Autobiography*, London, 1907.

O'Shea, Edward, *A Descriptive Catalog of W. B. Yeats's Library*, New York and London: Garland, 1985.

Owen, Alex, *The Darkened Room: Women, Power and Spiritualism in Late Victorian England*, London: Virago, 1989.

Owens, Rosemary Cullen, *Smashing Times, A History of the Irish Women's Suffrage Movement 1889–1922*, Dublin: Attic Press, 1984.

Park, Robert E., *The Crowd and the Public and Other Essays*, Chicago and London: University of Chicago Press, 1972 (1904).

Parker, Andrew, Mary Russo, Doris Sommer, and Patricia Yaeger, *Nationalisms and Sexualities*, New York: Routledge, 1992.

Parkin, Andrew, "Women in the Plays of W. B. Yeats," *Woman in Irish Legend, Life and Literature*, ed. S. F. Gallagher, Gerrards Cross: Colin Smythe, 1983.

Parkinson, Thomas, *W. B. Yeats: Self-Critic*, Berkeley: University of California Press, 1951.

Parry, Benita, "Signs of Our Times: Discussion of Homi Bhabha's *The Location of Culture*," *Third Text*, 28/29 (Autumn/Winter 1994).

Pick, Daniel, *Faces of Degeneration: A European Disorder, c.1848–c.1918*, Cambridge University Press, 1989.

Pilkington, Ellice, *The United Irishwomen: Their Place, Work and Ideals*, Dublin, 1911.

Plunkett, Sir Horace, *The United Irishwomen: Their Place, Work, and Ideals*, Dublin, 1911, repr. in *And See Her Beauty Shining There: The Story of the Irish Countrywomen*, ed. Pat Bolger, Dublin: Irish Academic Press, 1986.

Praz, Mario, *The Romantic Agony*, Oxford University Press, 1970 (1933).

Putzel, Steven, *Reconstructing Yeats: The Secret Rose and the Wind Among the Reeds*, Dublin: Gill and Macmillan; Totowa, NJ: Barnes and Noble, 1986.

Rafroidi, Patrick, *Irish Literature in English: The Romantic Period 1789–1850*, 2 vols., Gerrards Cross: Colin Smythe, 1980.

Renan, Ernest, *The Poetry of Celtic Races and Other Studies*, trans. and ed. William G. Hutchison, London: Walter Scott, 1896.

"What is a Nation?" *Nation and Narration*, ed. Homi Bhabha, London and New York: Routledge, 1990.

Revard, Stella, "Yeats, Mallarme and the Archetypal Feminine," *Papers on Language and Literature* (supplement, Fall 1972).

Riley, Denise, *Am I That Name? Feminism and the Category of "Woman" in History*, Minneapolis: University of Minnesota Press, 1988.

Riordan, Maurice, "Matthew Arnold and the Irish Revival," *Literary Interrelations: Ireland, England, and the World; Volume III: National Images and Stereotypes*, ed. Wolfgang Zach and Heinz Kosok, Tubingen: Gunter Narr Verlag, 1987.

Rose, Catherine, *The Female Experience: The Story of the Woman Movement in Ireland*, Galway: Arlen House, 1975.

Rosenthal, M. L., and Sally M. Gall, *The Modern Poetic Sequence: The Genius of Modern Poetry*, Oxford University Press, 1983.

Rubin, Gayle, "Thinking Sex: Notes For a Radical Theory of the Politics of Sexuality," *The Lesbian and Gay Studies Reader*, ed. Henry Abelove, Michele Barale and David Halperin, New York and London: Routledge, 1993.

"The Traffic in Women: Notes on the 'Political Economy' of Sex," *Women, Class and the Feminist Imagination. A Socialist-Feminist Reader*, ed. Karen V. Hansen and Ilene J. Philipson, Philadelphia: Temple University Press, 1990.

Russell, George (AE), "Nationality and Imperialism," *Ideals in Ireland*, ed. Lady Augusta Gregory, London: Unicorn, 1901.

Ryan, Patricia Twomey, "The Church, Education and Control of the State in Ireland," *Eire-Ireland*, 22:3 (Fall, 1987).

Saddlemyer, Ann, and Robin Skelton, eds., *The World of W. B. Yeats*, Seattle: University of Washington Press, 1967 (1965).

Said, Edward W., *Culture and Imperialism*, New York: Alfred Knopf, 1993.

"Yeats and Decolonization," *Nationalism, Colonialism and Literature*, ed. Seamus Deane, Minneapolis: University of Minnesota Press, 1990.

Orientalism, New York: Vintage, 1979.

Searle, G. R., *Eugenics and Politics in Britain 1900–1914*, Leyden: Noordhoff International Publishing, 1976.

Sedgwick, Eve Kosofsky, "Nationalisms and Sexualities in the Age of Wilde," *Nationalisms and Sexualities*, ed. Andrew Parker, Mary Russo, Doris Sommer, and Patricia Yaeger, New York: Routledge, 1992.

Sheehy, Michael, *Is Ireland Dying? Culture and the Church in Modern Ireland*, London: Hollis and Carter, 1968.

Showalter, Elaine, *The Female Malady: Women, Madness, and English Culture 1830–1980*, New York: Pantheon, 1985.

Sexual Anarchy: Gender and Culture at the Fin de Siecle, New York: Penguin, 1990.

Sidnell, M. J., "Yeats's First Work For the Stage," *W. B. Yeats 1865–1965: Centenary Essays on the Art of W. B. Yeats*, ed. D. E. S. Maxwell and S. Bushrui, Nigeria: Ibadan University Press, 1965.

Siegel, Sandra F., ed., *Purgatory: Manuscript Materials Including the Author's Final Text*, by W. B. Yeats, Ithaca and London: Cornell University Press, 1986.

Smith, Peter Alderson, *W. B. Yeats and the Tribes of Danu*, Gerrards Cross: Colin Smythe, 1987.

The Spirit of the Nation, second edn., revised, Dublin: James Duffy, 1844.

Spurr, David, *The Rhetoric of Empire: Colonial Discourse in Journalism, Travel Writing and Imperial Administration*, Durham and London: Duke University Press, 1993.

Stallworthy, Jon, *Between the Lines: Yeats's Poetry in the Making*, Oxford: Clarendon Press, 1971.

Stallybrass, Peter, and Allon White, *The Politics and Poetics of Transgression*, Ithaca: Cornell University Press, 1986.

Stanfield, Paul Scott, *Yeats and Politics in the Nineteen-Thirties*, London: Macmillan, 1988.

Stepan, Nancy, *The Idea of Race in Science: Great Britain 1800–1960*, Hamden, CT: Archon, 1982.

Synge, John Millington, *Collected Works*, 4 vols., ed. Alan Price, London: Oxford University Press, 1966.

Taylor, Richard, *A Reader's Guide to the Plays of W. B. Yeats*, New York: St. Martin's Press, 1984.

Theweleit, Klaus, *Male Fantasies, Volume 1: Floods, Bodies, History*, Minneapolis: University of Minnesota Press, 1987.

Torchiana, Donald T., *W. B. Yeats and Georgian Ireland*, Evanston, IL: Northwestern University Press, 1966.

Townshend, Charles, *The British Campaign in Ireland 1919–1921*, London: Oxford University Press, 1975.

Unterecker, John, *A Reader's Guide to William Butler Yeats*, New York: Octagon, 1983 (1959).

Ure, Peter, *Yeats the Playwright*, London: Routledge and Kegan Paul, 1963.

van Ginneken, Jaap, *Crowds, Psychology, and Politics 1871–1899*, Cambridge University Press, 1992.

Vlaspolos, Anca, "Gender-Political Aesthetics and the Early and Later Yeats," *Yeats: An Annual of Critical and Textual Studies*, 8 (1990).

Ward, Margaret, *Unmanageable Revolutionaries: Women and Irish Nationalism*, London: Pluto Press, 1983.

Weeks, Jeffrey, *Sex, Politics and Society: The Regulation of Sexuality Since 1800*, London and New York: Longman, 1981.

Weininger, Otto, *Sex and Character*, trans. from sixth German edn., London: William Heineman, 1906.

White, Anna MacBride and A. Norman Jeffares, eds., *Always Your Friend: The Gonne-Yeats Letters 1893–1938*, New York and London: Norton, 1992.

Whyte, J. H., *Church and State in Modern Ireland 1923–1970*, Dublin: Gill and Macmillan, 1971.

Williamson, Judith, "Woman is an Island: Femininity and Colonization," *Studies in Entertainment: Critical Approaches to Mass Culture*, ed. Tania Modleski, Bloomington: University of Indiana Press, 1986.

Wittig, Monique, *The Straight Mind and Other Essays*, Boston: Beacon Press, 1992.

Yeats, William Butler, *The Autobiography of William Butler Yeats*, New York: Macmillan, 1965.

The Celtic Twilight, London: Lawrence and Bullen, 1893.

The Collected Letters of W. B. Yeats, Volume I, 1865–1895, ed. John Kelly, Oxford: Clarendon Press, 1986.

Essays and Introductions, New York: Macmillan, 1961.

Explorations, New York: Macmillan, 1962.

The Letters of W. B. Yeats, ed. Alan Wade, New York: Macmillan, 1955.

Letters to the New Island, ed. George Bornstein and Hugh Witemeyer, New York: Macmillan, 1989.

Memoirs, transcribed and ed. Denis Donoghue, London: Macmillan, 1972.

"Postscript," *Ideals in Ireland*, ed. Lady Augusta Gregory, London: Unicorn, 1901.

Prefaces and Introductions, ed. William H. O'Donnell, London: Macmillan, 1988.

The Senate Speeches of W. B. Yeats, ed. Donald R. Pearce, Bloomington: Indiana University Press, 1960.

Uncollected Prose, Vol. I, collected and ed. John P. Frayne, London: Macmillan, 1970.

Uncollected Prose, Vol. II, collected and ed. John P. Frayne and Colton Johnson, New York: Macmillan, 1975.

The Variorum Edition of the Plays of W. B. Yeats, ed. Russell K. Alspach, London: Macmillan, 1966.

The Variorum Edition of the Poems of W. B. Yeats, ed. Peter Allt and Russell K. Alspach, New York: Macmillan, 1957.

A Vision, New York: Macmillan, 1937.

A Critical Edition of Yeats's "A Vision" (1925), ed. George Mills Harper, London: Macmillan, 1978.

ed., *Beltaine*, London: At the Sign of the Unicorn and Dublin: At the "Daily Express" Office, 1 (1899–1900).

ed., *Fairy and Folk Tales of the Irish Peasantry*, London: Walter Scott, 1888.

ed., *The Oxford Book of Modern Verse, 1892–1935*, New York: Oxford University Press, 1936.

Young, Robert, *Colonial Desire: Hybridity in Theory, Culture and Race*, New York: Routledge, 1995.

Index